The Digital City

Also by Michel S. Laguerre

AFRO-CARIBBEAN FOLK MEDICINE: The Reproduction and Practice of Healing

AMERICAN ODYSSEY: Haitians in New York City

THE COMPLETE HAITIANA: A Bibliographic Guide to the Scholarly Literature, 1900–1980 (2 vols)

DIASPORIC CITIZENSHIP

ETUDES SUR LE VODOU HAITIEN

THE INFORMAL CITY

THE GLOBAL ETHNOPOLIS: Chinatown, Japantown and Manilatown in American Society

THE MILITARY AND SOCIETY IN HAITI

MINORITIZED SPACE: An Inquiry into the Spatial Order of Things

URBAN LIFE IN THE CARIBBEAN

URBAN MULTICULTURALISM AND GLOBALIZATION IN NEW YORK CITY

URBAN POVERTY IN THE CARIBBEAN: French Martinique as a Social Laboratory

VOODOO HERITAGE

VOODOO AND POLITICS

The Digital City

The American Metropolis and Information Technology

Michel S. Laguerre

University of California, Berkeley

⚡ 603/2016   12-6-07

HN
80
S4 L33
2005

c. 1

First published 2005 by
PALGRAVE MACMILLAN
Houndmills, Basingstoke, Hampshire RG21 6XS and
175 Fifth Avenue, New York, N.Y. 10010
Companies and representatives throughout the world

PALGRAVE MACMILLAN is the global academic imprint of the Palgrave Macmillan division of St. Martin's Press, LLC and of Palgrave Macmillan Ltd. Macmillan® is a registered trademark in the United States, United Kingdom and other countries. Palgrave is a registered trademark in the European Union and other countries.

ISBN-13: 978–1–4039–9710–4 hardback
ISBN-10: 1–4039–9710–1 hardback

This book is printed on paper suitable for recycling and made from fully managed and sustained forest sources.

A catalogue record for this book is available from the British Library.

Library of Congress Cataloging-in-Publication Data
Laguerre, Michel S.
   The Digital city : the American metropolis and information technology / Michel S. Laguerre.
      p.   cm.
   Includes bibliographical references and index.
   ISBN 1–4039–9710–1 (cloth)
   1. San Francisco Bay Area (Calif.)—Social conditions.   2. Sociology, Urban—California—San Francisco Bay Area.   3. Telecommuting—California—San Francisco Bay Area.   4. High technology industries—California—San Francisco Bay Area.   5. Cyberspace—California—San Francisco Bay Area.   6. Information technology—Social aspects—California—San Francisco Bay Area.   7. Internet—Social aspects—California—San Francisco Bay Area.   I. Title.
   HN80.S4L33 2005
   303.48′33′097946—dc22   2005047526

10   9   8   7   6   5   4   3   2   1
14   13   12   11   10   09   08   07   06   05

Printed and bound in Great Britain by
Antony Rowe Ltd, Chippenham and Eastbourne

To the memory of my mother Anilia Roseau Laguerre and my sister Solange Pardovany

Contents

Acknowledgments

Undertaken under the auspices of the Berkeley Center for Globalization and Information Technology, the field research for this book was financed by a small grant from the University of California's Institute for Labor and Employment; secretarial assistance was provided by the Institute of Governmental Studies, and the project benefited from two small grants from the *Committee on Research* for travel and the transcriptions of interviews. During the research and writing of this book, I became deeply indebted to various people and institutions that helped me along the way. My gratitude is given first and foremost to the cyber workers in the local and state governments and the IT industry that made the outcome of this book possible. While too numerous to mention here, I have selected a few among them for special recognition and beg the indulgence of others for my oversight: Farimah Koleini at Marin County Assessor's Office, Farshad Ghaffari at Sun Microsystems, Bob Joseph at Quantum, Barbara Korta at Verio, Joshua Vermette at Yahoo, Amanda Lau at Sibel e-business, David Gibbs at Planet.out.com, Chris Atkins at Mindspring Earthlink, Charles Peza at Weinberg Group (a scientific consulting firm), and Vivian Towe at Siliconspot. I very much appreciate the help of the following collaborators from San Francisco's City Hall who showed me the way early on: Cynthia Clark, Rion Dugan, Stuart Baker, Sean Elsbernd, Tony Hall, Lilian Hare, Richard Isen, Rod Loucks, Jennifer Schuler, Moe Vasquez, Naomi Weinstein, Mark Westlund, Susan Kelley, Jill Lerner, Jay Banfield, Jeremy Epstein, and Jamil Niazi. I am thankful to Robin Stein and Ryan Centner, two wonderful research assistants and graduate students in Political Science and Sociology, who each conducted a pilot study for this project by interviewing a set of informants on the virtual office and digital government. In addition, Robin arranged for me to meet with informants and accompanied me in the performance of some formal interviews at City Hall. The transcription of these taped interviews was undertaken by a cohort of undergraduate students enrolled in the *Undergraduate Research Apprenticeship Program*: Brian Wei, Carol Chu, Mikalyn Roberts, Stephanie Diane Ko, Ann Pu, Jennifer Yee, Rokne Jazayeri, Prateek Sureka, John C Tsai, Sara Pickett, Raymond Pascual, Jodie Atkinson, Bethany Burns, Sridhar Seralathan, and Debbie Yeh.

The first draft of this book was written during a sabbatical leave I took in 2001–2002 to be a visiting scholar in the *Program in Science, Technology and Society* (STS) at MIT. I want to thank Roe Smith for arranging my year-long stay at MIT, and Nazli Choucri and Sharon Eisner Gillett for inviting me to present my work-in-progress to the campus community. I delivered a series of five lectures on IT, based on chapters in this book, at MIT and Harvard University. These lectures were delivered at faculty seminars at STS, Internet and Telecom Convergence, Comparative Media Studies, and the Center for International Studies at MIT and in the e-Development Seminar Series at the Kennedy School of Government at Harvard University.

Chapters of this book were also previously delivered or discussed at other venues, including the University of Paris-Pantheon (January 2004), the American Sociological Association meetings in San Francisco (August 2004), the Center for Science, Technology and Society at the University of Santa Clara (April 2003), the University of Parma, Italy (March 1999), and the IBM Center for the Business of Government in Washington, DC (October 2004). I sincerely thank the members of the audiences who attended these sessions for their questions and comments. Chapter 6, "Virtual Time: The Processuality of the Cyberweek," was previously published in *Information, Communication and Society*, Volume 7, Number 2, pp. 223–247, 2004.

I owe personal debts of gratitude to Bruce Cain and Marc Levin who have been very supportive of my efforts at the Berkeley Center for Globalization and Information Technology; to my research assistants Jill Greenlee, Jennifer Yee, Ann Pu, Lauren Kaplan, and Debbie Yeh who all contributed to various aspects of the research; to Bud Bynack who copyedited the manuscript with great care and professionalism and in the process has immensely improved its readability; to Jennifer Nelson, my wonderful editor at Palgrave Macmillan, for her support, advice, and genuine collegiality; to Ellinchen who prepared the index and to Reena Godi who diligently oversaw the production of the book.

California, Berkeley
January 2005

Preface

The digital transformation of society on a global scale, brought about by the use of information technology (IT), is symptomatic of the new virtual arena that is embedded in, and added to, the existing formal and informal public spheres. A paramount site that has become the battleground of this digital transformation, expansion, and absorption is the metropolis because of the agents, institutions, and infrastructure in its midst that feed and enable such virtual practices. Therefore, this book focuses on the ways in which the city has expanded and transformed as a result of digitization. What interests us here is not simply the innovative digital practices that are now in place in industry, government, educational settings, and the city at large, but also the understanding and explaining of how these practices are essential or emblematic in the definition of the hybrid identity of the metropolis.

The "digital city" concept encompasses the virtual domain into which the city has expanded, including the embeddedness of the virtual in the real and the real in the virtual; the infrastructure that makes possible and sustains cyberspatial connectivity; and the hybrid social entities the new global identity of the metropolis has generated that have recently become intrinsic in its functioning. In other words, I see urban residents, and the institutions they maintain, engaging in digital practices that have become inherent to the operation of everyday life in the city, and using virtual connectivity as a substitute for offline activities to enhance their performance, or as a component in their quotidian interaction to either reinforce or undermine formal practices of society. Therefore, digitization has imploded in various aspects of the deployment of the urban system. In this light, virtuality, like formality, is understood as one aspect of reality. Like informality, it is a pole of the modern city, and as such, it has become intrinsic to the operation of various urban institutions. To be brief, I use the "digital city approach" to explain the behavior of the metropolis, just as earlier I used the "informal city approach," before virtuality became a central feature of the city, to explain the functioning of urban institutions of society.

Digitization—meaning here both the cyberspatial expansion and virtual embodiment of the city—is seen as comprising five main domains: the social network matrix through which virtual interaction occurs; the virtual communication paths that have been established; the physical infrastructure that makes virtual interconnectivity possible; social activities and institutions of society that have become digitized; and the mobility of this reengineered digitized social system. The infrastructure that sustains the operation of computers and allows them to communicate with each other is a driving force in the social fragmentation of the metropolis. Such a social fragmentation may remain even after the rules that created the infrastructure are withdrawn. Therefore, the unmaking of rules now requires the remaking of the digital infrastructure as well.

The picture of the digitized city that has emerged from empirical research conducted in the Silicon Valley/San Francisco Metropolitan Area is characterized by *unevenness*, where digital practices in some institutions are not standardized because of the diversity of software in existence; where high level digitization and low level digitization co-exist in the same ecosystem; where some institutions are beginning to slowly digitize their daily practices while others are already in a fully digital speed and mood; where the digital infrastructure in some neighborhoods is efficient and in others not yet up to standards; where public access to the Internet is available in some neighborhoods and not in others; where immigrant communities are off-line, physically living in the same contiguous space, but on-line, are transnationally connected to their various countries of origin; and where *digital marginality* comes about as a result of the divide between the connected and the unconnected, which is not the same thing as the divide between the rich and the poor.

An essential feature of the digitized city is the globalization practices in which it is involved. It is a globally connected city through its individual residents and institutions, and also through being an interconnected node in an interactive global ecosystem of local nodes. This localized global node uses various forms of cyberspatial connectivity, such as e-commerce, the virtual interactive banking system, digital diasporas, telecommuting, and other similar digital practices. The local articulation of these two trends—virtualization and globalization—in the production of the digital city is a cornerstone of what this book analyzes, conceptualizes, and explains. Of course, unveiling the logic of the digitized city, which sets it apart from previous urban forms, allows us an opportunity to shed light on the parameters of this multi-nodal matrix.

The digital city is a social formation that has yet to reach its full capacity and deployment because most of the entities that comprise it are not yet fully digitized; the infrastructure is not fully deployed everywhere in the city; and access to computers and other electronic gadgets, where one can use the Internet, is limited in terms of availability. The digitized city has become a local node of global interactivity in three discernible ways:

by the global interactions it generates through its various components, by being the corridor through which global communication is rerouted to its final extraterritorial destination, and by being at the receiving end of extraterritorially initiated communication. The digitized city is affected differently in each of these roles, a process which accounts for its repositioning as one node in transnational networks of global nodes.

Introduction

This book evolves out of a research project on information technology and society that seeks to understand some aspects of the digitization of the American city. The transformation of various sectors of society brought about by the advent of information technology (IT) and the virtual mode of communication that the Internet makes possible led me to study the nature of these changes and their implications for daily life in the contemporary American metropolis. The book focuses on actual IT practices in the Silicon Valley/San Francisco Metropolitan Area, documenting and explaining how those practices are remolding social relations, global interaction, and workplace environments.

The digital city

The term "digital city" as I use it here refers to a set of virtual practices or repertoires of practices that are undertaken in a sustainable manner by the individual residents and groups of a particular city for the purpose of interacting, simulating, explaining, reinforcing, monitoring, neutralizing, criminalizing, expanding (locally or globally), processing, transacting, or undermining any political, social, economic, religious, or communicational aspect of the daily activities of the urban community.[1] The digital city thus is an embodied site—the virtual façade of the modern city—where some aspects of social interaction and traditional daily activities are carried out and thereby transformed. It is a space into which the city has expanded, a space that can be made and unmade and that also can materialize unexpectedly in the flexible physical space of the city. The digital city thus is not a separate, parallel, interstitial, marginal, or enclave reality, but a new, almost unstudied component of

1

the city itself. What follows maps some of the dimensions of the digital city and analyzes the ways in which it operates.

The digital city both influences and is shaped by formal and informal urban practices. The digital city globalizes, pluralizes, and rehierarchizes aspects of urban social action. In particular, as we will see, virtual communities and virtual diasporas both integrate and divide the city in distinct interacting units, generating new transnational logics that guide their action and incorporating into the city's social landscape a new dimension of practice. Globalization thus becomes an intrinsic mechanism in the functioning and governance of the city because of the virtual sphere in which it is embedded. At the same time, the façade of the virtual city reflects the peculiarities of the physical city, which, despite the globality of its mode of expression, accounts for the distinctness of each digitized city. Each city has the potential to develop its virtual alter ego, as all of the cities in the Bay Area, for example, already have done with some modicum of success.

Research setting

The Bay Area's efficient IT infrastructure, the level of education of its residents, the research institutions that it houses, the not-for-profit agencies that it nurtures, and the numerous diasporic communities that contribute to its cultural diversity have made the greater Silicon Valley/ San Francisco Metropolitan Area the epitome of the digital city. It serves as a hub of IT firms, from informatics, bioengineering, and nanotechnology to venture capital firms, Web design management services, and e-commerce operations. Not only has it served as the birthplace of the IT industry—as a vibrant technopolis, and as a rich milieu of entrepreneurial innovation—but its success has attracted some of the best minds in the world—computer engineers, entrepreneurs, corporate lawyers, business people, project managers, and consultants. It has become an important power center in the nation because of its contribution to the national economy, and it retains that status despite the economic downturn experienced by the technology sector in the early years of the millennium. It has attracted both poor and rich immigrants and has transformed the local political, social, and economic climate because of the pressure the industry brings to bear on traffic, housing, water supply, schools, hospitals, and electricity.

The rise of IT in the Silicon Valley/San Francisco Metropolitan Area has resulted in the reconfiguration of the urban environment in a number of ways. One effect has been the social integration of the whole area. Because of the high cost of housing, its labor force has been increasingly forced to move to neighboring communities. People who live in the outer zones thus commute to Silicon Valley or San Francisco for work, school, entertainment, or church. The resulting traffic problems have promoted telecommuting, which permits people in firms that allow such a nomadic practice to participate in the workplace without always being physically present in it. While the outlying local municipalities continue to maintain their autonomy and their identity, they have been incorporated into the larger metropolis. A major factor in this process has been the rise of the digital city.

Another effect of the rise of the digital city, however, has been the displacement of neighborhood populations. As a result of the boom in the e-commerce industry, for example, poor Filipino families who had been living in the South Park area of San Francisco were forced to move out because gentrification by dot-commers resulted in high rents. The same phenomenon resulted in the flight of poor residents from the Mission district to other marginal quarters of the city. San Francisco was not the only city that experienced such population and neighborhood changes. The city of Fremont saw the rise of the Indian immigrant population transform whole neighborhoods into a South Asian diasporic technopolis.

Such displacements are symptomatic of the growing gap between the wealthy, who benefit from the economic successes of the IT revolution, and the poor, who do not. Social problems plague the digitized city on both sides of that gap. Stories abound in the *New York Times* about workers who are forced to sleep in their cars because they are unable to find appropriate housing, on the one hand, and about children of the *nouveaux riches* who cannot cope with their families' new-found wealth, on the other. So do stories about those who lost their jobs, houses, cars, and their investments in high-tech stocks when the high-tech bubble burst.

Finally, however, the digital city has also resulted in the globalization of the local. Residents of the area are involved in various forms of border-crossing practices that link the Bay Area to the rest of the world. Firms exploit such links for obvious reasons of production and to extend their transactions. Immigrants do so to relate to their homelands, while activists network with overseas Non-Governmental Organisations (NGOs), and academics use the networks that link the digital city to the rest of the world for research and educational purposes.

The Bay Area milieu thus is made up of various IT niches. While some people use IT intensively because of the kind of work they do, others use it more sporadically for personal needs, browsing the Web or exchanging electronic correspondence. These differences are amplified by the global networks of users, who at times influence local practices.

The research for this study was carried out in the San Francisco/Silicon Valley Metropolitan Area between July 2000 and August 2001 and between October 2002 and January 2003 through fieldwork and participant observation.[2] Throughout the period, I traveled to San Francisco and Silicon Valley to meet and interview key players—managers, programmers, staff engineers, computer technicians, office workers, telecommuters, and employees of two government agencies (municipal and state)—in various info-tech industries. The interviews were open-ended and informal, allowing collaborators to comment on specific aspects of their work and to register their observations on the digital work process. The compilation of these interviews provided the raw data upon which the analysis in this book is based.

Outline of the chapters

Chapter 1 begins with an analysis of the various ways in which the relations of the city to information technology and information technology to globalization have been studied. This strategy allows me to explain the overall nature of the IT infrastructure and the relationship of the global to the local as materialized in the digital city. Explaining globalization in the context of the process of digitization as it infiltrates the variety of sites in the metropolis unveils the unevenness and complexity of the digitization process, as it transforms the existing spaces, practices, and institutions of the city.

Chapter 2 examines various types of telecommuting practices in Silicon Valley in order to understand more concretely the diffusion and reconfiguration of work in the digitized city in terms of the relations between the central office and the home or other sites of work as it is disseminated and fragmented both physically and temporally by IT. It examines the ways in which telecommuting affects both the relations among coworkers and between workers and managers because of the choice it affords to work either inside or outside the central office. Finally, it focuses on the phenomenon of the partial decentralization and partial centralization of the digitized office under the regime of telecommuting in its local and globalized dimensions.

Chapter 3 explores the digitizing of work from the point of view of the digitizing office, rather from that of the telecommuter. It describes the practices that characterize the digitizing office and the ways in which IT installs a digital component in the traditional office, transforming it in ways that generate new conditions and new problems for managers and workers alike, creating a nomadic corporate culture with strong globalizing tendencies.

Chapter 4 examines the making of a digital city hall, an expansion of city hall that brings government into the virtual realm. In that process, the IT team and its Webmasters have assumed an important new role in the administrative politics of the city, presenting the virtual façade of city hall and its policies to citizens and the city employees and departments alike. This chapter analyzes the content and structure of the digital city hall, the transformation of communications between the digital city hall and the urban citizenry, the limitations of the Web for the implementation of democratic politics, and the globalization of city hall and explains how virtualization is a central factor in that process.

The malleable space of the virtual realm is an important component of the infrastructure of the digital city. One sociological dimension of that space is inhabited by virtual diasporas, communities of immigrants who live in dispersed physical locations and who use cyberspace to communicate among themselves and with the homeland.

Chapter 5 analyzes the cyberexpansion of traditional diasporas. It examines transnational connections of the diasporans and how virtual diasporas globalize and extraterritorialize the internal politics of nation-states, focusing on the activities of two virtual diasporas—Chinese at the time of the prodemocracy demonstrations in Tiananmen Square, and Haitians during the second election of Jean Bertrand Aristide.

Like space, time takes on different characteristics in the digitized city. The Internet has contributed to a new way of problematizing time as embodied in human agency and social institutions, a time that is produced on a global scale, irrespective of time zones.

Chapter 6 examines the contours, content, and deployment of virtual time and of the cyberweek that it makes possible. It contrasts real time with virtual time to show the malleability of the latter, examine the ways in which the collapse of temporal boundaries and the compression of time-distance have manifested themselves in the cybertiming and flextiming of the civil week, explore the global and local aspects of the cyberweek, and analyze the practical ramifications of virtual time in the daily life of the digital city.

The concluding chapter positions the digitized city vis-à-vis the forces of globalization, focusing on the way in which the global implodes into the local and the local explodes into the global. It examines the variety of global digital practices that characterize the digital city, the fragmentation of local digital space by globalization, and the network of globally connected digital nodes in which digital city participates. The analysis shows how digitization is an uneven process because it affects various places differently and how some institutions in the city are more digitized than others, which can be explained not simply because of local conditions, but also because of global interaction. This chapter concludes by summing up the salient features and parameters of the digital city as the virtual façade of the physical city.

1
IT as Process and Globalization as Outcome

On a sunny midday spring Sunday in 2000, accompanied by a research assistant who spent five years working for a dot-com firm while still attending college in Southern California, I met at a restaurant in downtown Berkeley with a postgraduate engineer and computer programmer who works for a major Silicon Valley telecommunications company. I asked him to tell us what the concept of the digital city evokes for him before we began a focused conversation on his expertise and work practices that would allow me to understand an aspect of the digital infrastructure and transformation of the American metropolis.

So, you ask me what I would expect when I hear the title *Digital City*. I would expect two things immediately. I would expect it to cover the virtual city aspect of things, the virtual community, sort of thing where it is not a physical thing. You are not talking about any real community, but about the digital city. If you can imagine all of these people that are on chat, e-mail, and all these things. For instance, at Yahoo, we are trying to make it a community. You sign up for Yahoo and you get your e-mail, chat, and you can use these games, and calendar. You have this community of people on-line that spans someone in China, the United States, another person in Egypt, or whatever, brought together into this community. That's one aspect I would think of...sort of this aspect of bringing people together into this digital community as opposed to a real community with neighbors. Another thing that comes to mind is the city type of San Francisco. As San Francisco becomes digital, as things become more and more computerized, what does that do to the city, what does that make it become, what does that do to people in real communities? How do they live and how they deal with life, neighbors, and maybe the interaction of the two? Does having the digital city in the sense of the digital community, does that change people's expectations of a real city and does that change the way they deal with the real city, their real neighbors, and their real life? For the past three years, it has been the only time where it has been possible to have a lot of friends on-line and never meet them in person. They might not even know where they live or even their real name. It could be Jon@Yahoo. They won't even know if the real name is Jonathan or if that is just an alias. How do they see their friendships? Do they consider their friends on-line as good as friends as other people? Are their friendships different? I know a lot of people that do chat. They can say things on-line and be a different person off-line. Even down to the fact that you can be three different people with three different names and no one could know that all those aliases are all you. Do people have different friendships on-line, or are they the same? Are they just extending the same sort of things to other places? That's what comes to mind. That's kind of a city making things easier to do. You do not have to stand in line at the DMV [Department of Motor Vehicles]. You might go into the ability to do things like that on-line and how it makes things easier. (Male engineer working at Yahoo)

It is important to first explain what we mean by "the digital city" and how such a concept reflects the contemporary American city. The concept of the digital city poses an epistemological problem concerning its definition and relations to the physical city of urban government, urban planning, and urban geography. The metaphor used to define it may change the parameters of analysis, may influence negatively or positively urban policies, and may enhance or impair our ability to understand in its just measure the phenomenon of digitization. Thinking of the digital city as a parallel city in the making, different from the physical space of the city, or as an enclave housed by the physical city, or as the transformation of the physical city as a result of the virtualization of some of its practices each leads to different emphases and results.

The third of these approaches is the most comprehensive, as we will see in a variety of ways in what follows. The process of digitization transforms aspects of the physical city, adding a new dimension to the city as a whole, one that connects the practices carried out in the real and virtual worlds along a continuum between those two poles.

The digital identity of the city

One can study the American metropolis from the perspective of formal, digital, and informal systems. In this book, I study the city in terms of digital systems to understand the operation of the digital world, the relations between the digital and the formal city, the relations between the digital and the informal city, and the operation of the formal city as a result of that digital relationship and embeddedness. Globalization, in turn, embeds all of these relations because the local sites of interaction are nodes in transnational networks and are not immune from being influenced by such extraterritorial social connections.

Three features of the relations between the informal and the formal have been identified in the scholarly literature: that human agency is the initiator of both, and they are complementary factors from the standpoint of the actor; that they are related to one another as poles of a continuum; and that each pole maintains its identity, despite being on a continuum, and as a consequence each develops its own internal logic.[1] Hence, one speaks of the informal city in relation to the visible city with its physical boundaries and formal modes of operation. They are at the same time the same and different.

We may ask: is the relation between the digital city and the real city the same as the relation between the informal city and the formal city? Or rather, is the relation between the digital city and the real city the same as the relation between the informal and the formal cities and the relations between the informal city and the digital city, if any? The theory expounded here is congruent with the explanation of the relations between the formal city and the informal city: human agency is the initiating mechanism that activates both the formal city and the digital city, and the digital cannot be understood outside its relations to the formal that gives it birth. It also explains that the digital city is a pole on a continuum with the formal city and with the informal city, and as such has a distinct identity and follows a different logic. In addition, however, with IT, the relations between the digital and the real, both formal and informal, are globalized because they encompass actors in different national settings. The relations between the digital and the real must therefore be studied within the context of local–global relations.

The informal and the digital are distinct from each other in terms of their identity and operate under different logics. Neither of them can function without the intervention of human agency. The computer can relate two or more actors to each other only after it has been programmed by human agency to do so. Furthermore, while some teleactivities are done in an informal way, others are formal activities. So the digital city has both informal and formal features while remaining distinct from both the formal city and the informal city. As a pole of a continuum with the real, it, too, is both the same and different.

The digital city thus is theorized here not only as a pole different from, but connected to the real, but also as an extension of the real city. It is an extension because of the identity between the digital and the real as a continuum, and a pole because of the difference between it and the real as poles of that continuum. This is so because "new social and economic relationships are being forged within the virtual spaces of the Internet,"[2] which contribute to urban residents' expansion of their sphere of interaction. These interactions have become part of daily life because of the blurring of the two spheres, the digital and the real, through the mediation of human agency.

The IT revolution is transforming the social life of the city in a number of ways: as it provides a physical infrastructure that digitizes routine daily activities of society; as it induces a new pattern of mobility, that is, the movement of work and information instead of people, thereby collapsing space with time, as happens in telecommuting; and as it feeds the globalization process by making possible real-time interaction with people beyond national boundaries. My goal is to explore the nature of this transformation, using the city as a point of anchorage and theater of action.

Conceptualizing the digital city as a pole along a continuum with the physical city directs our attention to the transformation of the city on three levels: the virtual expansion of the physical city as it materializes, for example, in the use of the Internet to attract tourists; the creation of a cyberdomain of interaction where the city functions under a different logic because interaction is not face-to-face, is telemediated, and operates in a more fluid spatial sphere; and the reconstitution of the city in its formal, informal, and digital dimensions, which become intertwined with each other, so that their respective spheres of interaction are transformed into an integrated whole.

IT and the city: Approaches and interpretations

Several authors have attempted to frame the problem of the relations between the city and IT in order to highlight the presumed or observed transformational changes that will concern us. Their approaches have helped us to avoid pitfalls inherent in addressing the phenomenon of the digital city and at the same time have afforded ways in which to strengthen our argument.

Approaching the digital city from the point of view of political economy, Castells[3] sees the "informational city" as "the fundamental matrix of institutional and economic organization" of a society that has resulted from the restructuring of the US capitalist economy in "the informational mode" of development. He contrasts the informational mode with the preindustrial and industrial modes, proposing that,

while in the pre-industrial modes of development knowledge is used to organize the mobilization of greater quantities of labor and means of production, and in the industrial mode of development knowledge is called upon to provide new sources of energy and to reorganize production accordingly, in the informational mode of development knowledge mobilizes the generation of new knowledge as the key source of productivity.[4]

He further argues that informationalism has led to the transformation of the global city into a "dual city," comprising both the informal and formal economies, "a shared space within which the contradictory spheres of the local society are constantly trying to differentiate their territories."[5] This duality manifests itself not only in the reshaping of the physical territory of the city by concentrating formal economic activities in central sites and informal ones in satellite sites, but also in the economy (formal versus informal), global connections (cosmopolitanism versus localism), and in the urban form (shaped by the dominant elite knowledge workers versus informal entrepreneurs). As we have begun by suggesting, however, this formulation leaves open the question of the relations between the real and the virtual city.

In *The Rise of the Network Society*,[6] however, Castells introduces the concept of "real virtuality" to suggest the entanglement of the real with the virtual. He also introduces the concept of "the space of flows," which is a characteristic of the network society made possible by IT which engenders globalization, and which is the space where this entanglement occurs. Although he sees the physical city developing in new forms, such as the edge city or the megacity that comes about because of its technology-intensive infrastructure, he tends to downplay place in favor of the space of flows. As he quips, "the global city is not a place, but a process."[7] He further notes that in this digital environment, "the network of communication is the fundamental spatial configuration: places do not disappear, but their logic and their meaning become absorbed in the network."[8] In this top-down approach, he sees urban actors being divided by tele-mediated interactions into two population segments "the interacting and the interacted, meaning those who are able to select their multidirectional circuits of communication, and those who are provided with a restricted number of prepackaged choices."[9] In his view, IT thus not only provides an infrastructure for the deployment of globalization, but also contributes to shaping the internal architecture of the urban social system.

In a somewhat similar vein, Fathy[10] approaches the digital city via the interplay between socioeconomic activities and the shape of city forms as enhanced by the use and application of IT. He refers to this emerging city as a "telecity" and conceives of it as based on "the superimposition of virtual networks of activities, made possible by the application of new information technologies and the shift toward information-based activities; and the existing physical form of the city."[11] He further identifies two major characteristics of the telecity. The first, requisite to its formation, is "that a critical mass of inhabitants in a geographical landscape are engaged in interactive communication networks where remote services, facilities, and work dominate city life." The second is a criterion of its functioning:

> The telecity demands a multinodal, nonhierarchical structure to accommodate layers of "teleactivities," which are socioeconomic activities based on interactive, individualized, and asynchronous communication systems to connect persons, tasks, and information regardless of their actual locations.[12]

While Castells's model has a global outlook because of the invocation of transnational networks, Fathy's work is more focused on the local city scene as a platform for urban planning. Like Castells, Boyer sees what she calls "the cybercity"[13] as enmeshed in global flows that restructure its identity, and she conceives of the inhabitants as living in "a space of flows defined by global networks of computers— a free-floating membrane of connectivity and control encircling the globe in ultra-rapid fashion and enabling a new economic order of multinational corporations to arise" thanks to the shift from "disciplinary" to "modulating control facilitated by computer technology."[14] Seen in this light, cybercity residents seem to be "continuously in motion—be it driving the freeways, shopping at the mall, or pushing carts through supermarket aisles." In her postmodern interpretation, however, she sees a gap "between the city that we can visualize and the invisible city that is constituted in and through its fields of information circulation.

Furthermore, the radically decentered non-place of the metroscape defies existence as an imageable form because of its very dispersal."[15] She thus finds a progressive invasion of the physical city by the virtual city, instead of the other way around. One may speak of a colonization of the real by the virtual. As she puts it, "in consequence, the city and its public sphere become increasingly virtual as we move toward interpersonal systems of communication and the 'netropolis' at the expense of face-to-face communication in physical and public space."[16] In this way, she contrasts the netropolis of cyberspace with the metropolis of the postindustrial city as two opposite, but complementary poles of urban social life.

The concept of the "virtual city" is sometimes used to refer to the construction of the city on the World Wide Web as a set of icons that represent various elements of the city and city life. It is constructed to facilitate citizens' use of city services, to allow greater participation of the citizenry in city affairs, to effect publicity for the city, and to expand the arena of operation of the city, and thus, again, can be seen as a component of the real city and on a continuum with it.[17] As McGuigan[18] puts it, "Amsterdam's Digitale Stad is an outstanding instance of how the city is reimagined in cyberspace and in a manner which relates to life in an actual city." In this view, the virtual city is a representation in cyberspace of the postindustrial city.

Complementary in this regard is the "technocity" approach, an agenda-setting project concerning the need for the use of technology in enhancing urban life. It calls for a "mature social control of technology."[19] According to this vision, "the real learning within the technocity would be seen as having reached maturity if it were seen to be the responsibility of the users of the city, the citizens of this new space, to take a proactive hand in ensuring that the technocities are places designed for as well as by society."[20]

For Batty,[21] city structure has evolved into a new IT infrastructure made up of computer networks that dominate and transform the architecture of power in the city. The new power structure is telemediated, with the logic of computer networks serving as the engine of the process. In this view, the "computable city"—because of the power mustered by the computers, the lattices of relations that the network of computers generate and sustain, and the virtual dynamics that the network brings to bear on the local urban environment—is the new identity that the modern city has acquired.

What is envisioned for the future, from this point of view, is the further integration of these digital and real poles through, for example, the virtualization of the home, as the suburban digital home showcased by Bell Atlantic indicates:

> In the kitchen, a person can point a clicker at a television screen to browse the specials at a local grocery store, order the week's food and specify a delivery time. In the family room, the television is wired to instantly retrieve movies from a remote electronic library. Upstairs, children can order video games or study topics like the Civil War by calling up documentaries.[22]

The virtualization of a building into a smart or intelligent building is another manifestation of this transformation. The concept of a smart building refers to "an integrated management system for elevators, energy, security and other building services; an integrated telecommunications network for local, long-distance and enhanced services; or a building that provides integrated telecommunications and building management services."[23]

This view of the virtual city must be contrasted with the perspective of Martin, who sees these entities as "communities, campuses, laboratories, or corporate offices, scattered across the earth but connected electronically. Virtual cities will not make real cities obsolete. They will be different."[24] In the same vein, an earlier version of the digital city, proposed under the concept of "wired city"[25] and later overshadowed by the all-inclusive notion of information society, refers to "experiments and projects involving the use of advanced information and communication technologies for the provision of services to households and businesses."[26] In contrast to the previous paradigms, which mark an all-encompassing shift in urban living, the wired city approach is presented as "one element, one dimension of this kind of electronic networking that flourishes organically in the urban environment. In turn, this electronic networking operates alongside a range of other kinds of networking, both mediated and interpersonal." What the concept of the "wired city" promises is not a complete overhaul of the city form, but rather a multiplicity of teleactivities. As Howkins[27] puts it, "Instead of a new built environment involving a physical reconfiguration of facilities, we are promised an electronic environment of teleshopping, teleeducation, telecommuting and so on, in which these activities are reconfigured electronically." Once the electronic infrastructure is in place, Wiggins[28] projects the "information city" as one that "is electronically wired, reducing if not removing the need for face-to-face contact between people."

The problem with conceptualizing the digital city as a parallel or enclaved phenomenon alongside of or within the physical city is that these two models do not adequately represent the relations of the real to the virtual. They assume that the virtual is separate from the real, as in the case of the parallel model, or that the virtual is a subaltern sector domesticated within the real, as in the case of the enclave analogy. These assumptions do not accord with the empirical evidence because they ascribe to the virtual an autonomous status. In contrast, the continuum approach reveals the proper relations of the virtual to the real. These entities are coproduced by human actors who participate in both, one is the extension of the other, and both are in constant interaction with each other, or better still, each one permeates the life of the other.

Information technology, globalization, and the city

The relation between technology and society has often been treated in terms of the effect of one on the other and vice versa. This formulation vacillates between technological determinism and social determinism.[29] For example, comparing the effect of earlier technologies with the effect of new technologies on society, McDowell and Simon[30] note that the former is "like equipping a home with indoor plumbing: it saved time and made the experience more pleasant," while the latter has become "a catalyst" for change. However, comparing similar claims of technological effects on protoindustrial, industrial and postindustrial organizations, Winter and Taylor[31] advocate enlarging the frame of reference so as to encompass "the roots and enablers of the changes, those social, political, legal, economic, and cultural factors" that must be taken into consideration to provide a better interpretation of the phenomenon. In this light, Jackson and van der Wielen[32] see the adoption of IT "as a social and political process, in which actors do not passively 'adapt to' new technologies but actively shape them to their own ends, transforming them as they conceive of new configurations."

We believe that the way to avoid this privileging of the technological on the one hand or the social on the other when discussing the relationship of the two is to approach the issue from the angle of human agency. In this perspective, technology is viewed as both "unpredictable and intractable"[33] because people may use it for applications for which it was not designed, even though the technology itself channels use into determined applications. In other words, a device used for one purpose may be manipulated to undermine that same purpose or for a totally different purpose. The Internet was developed for military and commercial purposes to enhance the welfare of society, but it did not take that long for people to use it for criminal undertakings. IT viewed in this way is a flexible vessel, channel, or a conduit through which human agents generate and maintain synchronous and asynchronous local and extra-territorial relations.

Problems similar to those encountered in the framing of the relations between technology and society are also found in explaining the relations between IT and globalization. One or the other is said to be determinative in their relationship. Some argue that IT determines the path of some aspects of globalization. James believes that IT and globalization can be considered as two separate entities. He bases his argument on the claim that there are "numerous respects in which these two important phenomena are unrelated to one another."[34] He then sees a one-way effect of IT on globalization. As he puts it, "since there are various mechanisms through which information technology exerts a powerful influence over globalization, those same mechanisms must also tend to shape the patterns of gains and losses that globalization itself induces."[35]

For Pronk, too, IT must be seen as a "driving force behind globalization." Its role here, however, is not determinative, but rather is of an enabling nature.[36] He writes that "technological progress enables us to process, store, retrieve and communicate information in whatever form, unrestrained by distance, time and volume. It is communications and information technology that intensify economic interdependence on a world scale."[37]

On the other hand, those who view the relationship from the point of view of public policy see globalization as determining the use of IT as one of its instruments. Masuda[38] sees their relationship in terms of a global rhetoric whereby Western values can be imposed on Third World countries in order to further the American and Western European capitalist penetration of these markets. An interesting variant of this policy approach is the view that a combination of social policies and technological policies affect globalization. In this light, Ducatel *et al.*[39] argue that "given that private and public sector organizations alike are under pressure to reduce their costs by restructuring their activities and the goods and services that they offer, the ways that ICTs [information and communications technologies] are deployed tend to reflect these objectives and do not necessarily cause them."

In fact, there is no single, one-way determinative relationship between IT and globalization. We begin to understand this when we recognize that cities do not develop their IT infrastructure in an homogeneous fashion, but in a way that reflects different needs (business areas versus residential areas), inequalities of residential status (some neighborhoods fare better in terms of city services than others, such as the poor neighborhoods), and national security concerns (government, military, and defense facilities). As a result, IT is not implemented identically everywhere within the traditional city limits. There is, first, an institutional industrial reason for this. For example, some institutions have been implementing this technology for some time and are still experimenting; some others are doing it step by step, expanding and improving the process as they go along; some others are still in the beginning of the process; and still others are yet to become an active participant in the process. Second, there is a policy reason for this unevenness, because the city may favor the commercial and financial districts for IT wiring at higher speed over the districts of the poor. And third, there are the different roles users play in accessing the Internet, whether they own a computer or not. Lack of access may depend on their motivations, literacy, computing skills, or poverty. For these reasons, there is a necessary unevenness in the shape of the digital city (and hence in the description of it undertaken here) that reflects the unevenness of the adoption and implementation process across the board. The digital city is always an unfinished project still in the making.

By fragmenting and recomposing social relations in this varied setting, IT makes and unmakes new units in the complex social matrix of cities. Morley and Robins[40] speak of the outcome as generating "new dynamics of re-localization," as leading to the formation of a new "global–local nexus," and as repositioning the relations between "global space and local space."

The effect of IT on globalization in the digital city thus is varied, multiplex, and fragmented. IT thus must be seen as a complex process, not a univocal cause, and globality as one of its outcomes. Globalization emerges from a variety of local practices and processes carried out in local places, and connecting people in global networks of interaction meets local resistances, as well as local support. A fundamental characteristic of a network is that it divides because it unites, it segments because it is intrinsic to group formation, and it produces heterogeneity because it homogenizes. This occurs regardless if it is a local, regional, transnational, or global network. The local continues to maintain its identity and may resist the network logic and carve its own path of resistance despite being one of its nodes. In this sense, globality does not eliminate the performativity of identity in local places.

We therefore conceive of the processes of IT and their globalizing outcomes as producing heterogeneity and diversity instead of homogeneity because of the recognition that locality adapts to the new digital reality without disappearing as a distinct entity. So globality does not collapse locality and manifests itself through different transnational circuits comprising different global publics (religious, political, economic, diasporic, etc.). The local node becomes a context for the distillation and arrangement of diverse publics and for feeding the heterogeneity of globality. Therefore, IT enhances the ability of the node to fulfill these functions.

The globalizing tendencies of the IT infrastructure of globalization thus implode in a variety of ways into the structure of the local in the digital city. In the global architecture of the IT infrastructure, IT is a process that is materialized as globalization via locality. As process and outcome, IT and globalization are not related as simple cause and effect, but appear within the local in a variety of "unpredictable and intractable" forms.

In this global frame, one does not speak of a "wired city" as a project, but rather of the advent of a "wired global society,"[41] the "wired nation,"[42] the "wired society,"[43] the "network nation,"[44] or even the "network society."[45] The IT revolution is supposed to lead to "universal connectivity," that is, to "the capacity of any computer-based system to talk to any other."[46]

The IT network infrastructure of globalization

The global architecture of the IT infrastructure is thus anchored in a variety of local possibilities, resistances, institutions, and practices. If the effect of IT on globalization in the digital city is varied, multiplex, and fragmented, it is because, the global architecture of the IT infrastructure is structured in that way.

As applied to IT, "infrastructure" takes a much larger meaning than it does in other uses. To explain this difference, I rely on the account by Bainbridge[47] for the conceptual clarity that his definition brings to bear on the concept.

> Traditionally, the word infrastructure has been defined in two ways. In both civil engineering and the military, infrastructure referred to the permanent physical installations required for major activities.... In the social sciences, infrastructure referred more generally to the underlying framework or fundamental resources shared by a community or organization, including non-physical as well as physical public goods.... When applied to information technology ... one must consider infrastructure as broadly defined, notably including hardware, software, multi-use and multi-user databases, and the social organizations that create and apply them.

Here, by "infrastructure," I refer to a set of variables: first, the mechanical system, which is what makes communication possible (satellites, cable networks, computer equipment), and the geographical dispersion of these tools; second, the policy environment, which sets limits on what can be done and on the diversity of arrangements provided by these tools; third, the level of development, which differs from one country to another and which limits the boundaries of the possible; fourth, social structure, which includes the stratification of existing social networks and which affects the different ways in which activities such as storage and processing can be undertaken; and finally, power relations, which feed the structure of inequality and the opportunities that the tools afforded by the mechanical system provide in terms of connectivity and networking. The following issues frame the narrative developed below that describes the globalization process: What is the IT infrastructure? What is the architecture of the IT infrastructure? What is the shape of the global outcome in terms of the architecture of its vertical and horizontal connectivity? And how does digital globality constitute itself in terms of logic, social relations, dynamics, circularity or mobility, and locality?

By "IT infrastructure," I refer to its organizational apparatus and the various mechanical devices that make it operative in its various manifestations.[48] This study is limited in the technological scope it embraces and concerns itself with the use of the microcomputer and those things that provide a technological platform for its deployment, including "computers, video games, fax machines, zip drives, high-speed printers, copiers, voice mail, modems, cell phones, CAD/CAM equipment, satellite dishes, and digital recordings."[49] One should also add routers and switches, because of their importance in the smooth operation of electronic networks. As Schiller[50] notes, "routers are the specialized machines that direct and manage network traffic, while switches encode signals and establish connections between network locations." In this light, Mitchell[51] speaks of a "worldwide digital information infrastructure," while Harasim[52] refers to the process as the "internationalization of electronic network infrastructure."

I propose that this architecture is engineered by a series of processes, such as anchorage, connectivity, the decomposition and recomposition of social networks, and a multiplex hierarchy that both causes and reflects fragmentation. Anchorage implies that the hardware that is necessary so that IT-related activities can be processed is in place across territorial boundaries. The materiality of infrastructure in distinct places is emphasized here. If the globalization of the infrastructure is to occur, the existence of these tools, their access, and the computing skills of the actors are paramount to make the process a reality.

Anchorage in and by itself is not enough. Connectivity is essential, irrespective of bandwidth or speed. Interaction on a global scale occurs when human agents cause two or more computers to communicate with each other across the boundaries of nation-states through the use of compatible software. So connectivity is what expands the domain of global social interaction and transactions. Global networks are mediated by IT, and connectivity helps us to understand the specificity or distinctness of their parameters. The example below provided by one of the managers of a multinational IT firm shows how one such network is constituted:

We do use emerging technologies extensively to do teamwork. For instance, at my work, there are tools that you use that enable you, let's say that you are in New Jersey or New York, and I happen to be in California, I can collaborate with you using certain tools where we share documents, where we share presentations, we share Excel spreadsheets, or anything that you can think of. All that is done in a collaborating fashion using emerging technologies. We do use those things extensively. We have something that's built into Microsoft called "NetMeetings." It is a tool where you could collaborate in such a way where you can share project plans and people can modify what's been done and post that. For instance, I will share with you a couple of collaboration tools that we use. It may not make any sense to you, but I think that it will be worthwhile to mention some of them. The concept of public folder, which is a way to have a folder, it is called public, but it is not really public; it is really secure in the context of your team or team members that you identify. You can use that public folder to do a lot of things. Not only can you post documents within folders, but you can also use the team folder to schedule your work, vacation, major milestones, or anything that you can think of. You can use public folder to brainstorm between teams. (Male computer technician working at Quantum)

Global networks are constantly in the making and remaking because of different interests of actors over time. As a result, different cyberspatial configurations are involved, some intersecting with others, some existing in parallel spaces, and still others inside existing networks carving niches with people of same interests. We call these networks "infrastructure" because they sustain the architecture of the process of the globalization of the digital city.

The diversity of global circuits and networks brought about by the diversity of virtual ecologies or virtual ecological zones feeds the multiplex nature of the architecture of the IT infrastructure. This architecture is fragmented by community of interests, temporality, inequality, and power. Sassen[53] distinguishes three types of cybersegmentation. "One is the commercializing of access. . . . A second is the emergence of intermediaries to sort, choose, and evaluate information for paying customers. A third is the formation of privatized 'firewalled' corporate networks on the web."

Massey provides another perspective on the fragmentation of the social system by focusing on the extraordinary diversity of practices that one finds in any network of telemediated relationships, a diversity that reflects the segmentation of society. "Different social groups have distinct relationships to this anyway-differentiated mobility: some are more in charge of it than others; some initiate flows and movement, and others don't; some are more on the receiving end of it than others; some are effectively imprisoned by it."[54]

Temporal fragmentation is another factor that feeds the diversity of the process. It occurs not simply because of the differences between time zones, but also because of one's inability to remain in front of the computer all day long and the technical problems of connectivity one may encounter. The following example summarizes well the causes of the problem:

The time shift is a big consideration. Often, if you are as far away as Asia or Europe, a lot of times you will send an e-mail, and they will be asleep. They respond at the beginning of their workday, when I get off of work. So it is a kind of difficult to communicate with people across the sea. For instance, in Europe, I think there are a certain amount of strategically placed offices. In Spain, there is a two-hour buffer at the beginning and ending of the workday where the Spanish and U.S. overlap and there is open communication. That's basically why I think that most of the work is done out of Santa Clara and why they don't distribute around the world, because it is difficult to communicate.

It is a very staggered conversation. Even a lot of stuff that goes on in Santa Clara is also staggered like that. There is always stuff going on, that's the nature of computing and programming. You can take on many different projects and run into one glitch that will take a week to resolve. So there is a lot of that and you have to wait for responses. (Male computer technician working at Quantum)

Globalization does not eliminate locality, because it comprises a transnational network of local nodes. In fact, locality as a site of globalization has its distinct ecology, not only because of the particular configuration of hardware and software that it houses, but also because it is a node in a transnational network of nodes. These diverse ecological peculiarities of the system form the infrastructure of the global identity of the network.

The globalization of the digital city

To speak of the digital city as a globalized entity, then, one must address technology as process. In this vein, Garcia[55] identifies two key meanings of globalization in relation to digital communication: one refers to the "distribution of communication networks and information flows on a worldwide, equally accessible basis" and the other to "social interactions and transactions that transcend territorial, state boundaries, and thereby supersede both national and intergovernmental decision-making processes." Since the prophetic words of Marshall McLuhan on the transformation of the world into a "global village," diverse views have been presented on the ways in which telecommunications have contributed to the globalization of the contemporary city. Graham[56] sees urban areas across the globe becoming "combined into a single, globally interconnected, planetary metropolitan system." In contrast, Noam provides an alternative way of understanding the process. As he puts it, "communications media will not create a global village, but instead help organize the world as a series of electronic neighborhoods transcending national frontiers."[57]

The global is understood here as the linking of place-based entities (people, institutions, goods) through border-crossing spatial and temporal interactions. This process-oriented definition begins and ends with human agency in local settings as the embodied site that governs the itinerary or trajectory of these transnational interactions. Here, IT in its various manifestations is produced, used, and manipulated to achieve human and institutional goals. Globalization embedded in, imploded, or influenced by IT is understood in terms of interactional, institutional or organizational, and infrastructural border-crossing and crisscrossing networks of connectivity. These three corridors of action are means through which the globalization of the digital city is explored. "Interactional globalization" refers to mechanisms whereby human agency becomes the hub of transnational networks of relations. This is globalization seen at the local and individual level. "Organizational globalization" refers to the situation whereby border-crossing practices are the mechanisms developed for the functioning of institutions tied to extralocal institutions. Headquarters and subsidiary institutions that are located in diverse countries are in synergy with each other as part of their modus operandi. And "infrastructural globalization" refers not only to organizational matrices, but also to the tools and devices that serve as channels through which these interactions take place. Dodge and Kitchin[58] explain the various paths of this global infrastructure when they argue that

> The Internet consists of a global network of computers that are linked together by "wires"—telecommunications technologies (cables of copper, coaxial, glass, as well as radio and microwaves). Each linked computer resides within a nested hierarchy of networks, from its local area, to its service provider, to regional, national and international telecommunication networks. The various links have different speeds/capacities.... Although some networks are relatively autonomous... almost all allow connections to other networks by employing common communication protocols... to form a global system.

In short, the technology that effectuates the digital city in its local specificity is globalizing, the processes that anchor themselves in the local are globalizing, the actors that participate in those processes and manage their deployment are part of a global network, and the outcomes of these border-crossing activities are global because they integrate individuals inside and outside the boundaries of the state.

Conclusion

In its broadest sense, the book addresses the issue of how the city is being remade in the digital environment. In this light, I argue that the digital does not refer simply to what happens in the virtual, but to the amalgamated IT process that embeds the city in the processing of its virtual dimension. What we are witnessing is not "change en masse at the same time"[59] because IT does not permeate every aspect of the city. The metropolitan area studied here is a segmented city because of the unevenness of the process. Some institutions are using IT and in the process are changing their identities; some others target units for IT experimentation; some are moving slowly, others with all deliberate speed in the adoption of IT.

The city exhibits a variable architecture of IT-use with at least three distinct niches that reflect its technology-based segmentation. From this standpoint, one may speak of a "predigital city," areas that are not yet connected to the Net, including most particularly residential homes in poor neighborhoods; a "hybrid digital city," areas where digitization is not dominant, but coexists with pockets of people who are still in the predigitization era; and the "digitized city," areas where digitization is the main mode of operation and older forms are subservient to it.[60] Because the city is made up of such a diverse ecology of IT practices, one must pay attention to this unevenness in order to understand the digitization and globalization process of the city.

2
Teleworkers and Telemanagers: IT and Telecommuting in the Digital City

The revolution in IT has transformed the nature of work in the digital city, altering the location of the work site, reshaping the space of the workplace, changing the nature of work time, reconfiguring work practices and office interactions, and complicating the relations between management and workers. It has also globalized work practices. However, only a handful of studies have examined these transformations.[1]

This chapter shows how digital work has fractured the workplace and dispersed the workforce, necessitating the invention of strategies by which both workers and managers have tried to cope with the changes wrought by the rise of digital work in an economic and social regime heretofore characterized by the practices of the Industrial Revolution. "Digital work" is a generic concept that covers a number of disparate working activities that have different orientations and that affect labor conditions differently. The chapter analyzes the organization of digital work, its multiple ecologies, and the ways in which workers experience digital globalization. There are a number of such digital niches in every American metropolis, workplaces at various stages of IT development and implementation, and inside any industry there may be disparate or uneven modes of digitization. As a result, there is a multiplicity of digital work practices. What follows does not aim at providing an exhaustive typology of IT worker types in Silicon Valley, but rather at analyzing a representative sample of these practices to show how IT is reshaping the face of labor in general and the workplace in particular. To do so, the chapter focuses on telecommuting as one of the mechanisms that feeds the existence of the digital city because of the virtual channel through which it operates.

Telecommuting

The multiplicity of digital-work practices is evident within the overall category of telecommuting itself. In its basic form, telecommuting allows the geographical and temporal dispersion of workers and work. The reflections of a computer programmer who works for a major telecommunications firm in Silicon Valley show the basic parameters—and the appeal—of the practice.

"I started working at home less than a year ago. Before that, I was driving to Santa Clara every day, and I experienced that the best times to commute down there was if I left Oakland at 10:00 A.M., getting down to Santa Clara at 11:00, and leaving at 7:00 P.M., and that caused me to organize my day in such a way so that I would often go out and do things before I went to work. I would wake up usually around 8:00 A.M. and would either sit and read a book, have coffee, or go out and do some rock climbing, or something like that, and often I would hang out with people in the Berkeley area with friends in school before going to work. I found that to be a very different feeling than just going straight to work, by starting my day differently. Coming home, I would leave the office at 7:00 P.M., which will put me home at 8:00. Basically that means I would just go home and go to sleep. There was not much time to have an evening. I kind of liked that, except for the driving part, of course.

"Recently, I shifted to working at home, which is a lot freer than me having to go into the office because I can basically do whatever I want. My feeling on my job, I am a programmer, is that they are paying me to do a job and not how long it takes to do that job. They are just paying me to get the work done, and as long as I am doing that, I can feel free to take some leeway. For instance, when I work at home, I spend a lot of time gardening, working in the yard, taking walks, often with friends or by myself. It is a much freer feeling than having to be in the office eight hours a day. I think I actually get a lot done when I am at home. So that causes me to organize my day around work. I spend most of the day thinking about work, and if there is anything to do or if there is a problem to solve, I will be thinking about it, but I will only be working if there is stuff to be done immediately. Otherwise, I will be thinking about it and taking some time for myself. I still get all the work done, eight hours a day usually. That causes me to have mornings and evenings free, usually.

"And there is the third option, which is I take the train down when going to work once a week. That's about the same commute, except that it allows me to go to work earlier, which is kind of nice. The train leaves around 7:30 A.M. and it drops me back off at around the same time in Oakland, around 7:30 P.M. Even though that's a twelve-hour day, technically, I still like it a lot better because it allows me to sit on the train, and I see a lot of people with laptops on the train and will watch movies or DVDs on the train or they will have the wireless modem connections."

Although telecommuting thus allows work to be dispersed,[2] this in itself is not a new phenomenon, as the dispersion of work between headquarters and subsidiaries prior to the advent of telecommuting shows. What distinguishes telecommuting is communication via computer to another, distant place for work purposes and the freedom to work at a convenient place and time. Telecommuting thus involves both fixed and mobile places of work,[3] work sent from one place to another through the use of IT, the ability to work away from the central office, and management at distance. As the reflections of an appraiser who works for a state government agency in the San Francisco Metropolitan Area illustrate, there are reasons for both workers and those for whom they work to appreciate telecommuting as an innovation that combines self-determination and increased satisfaction for the worker with increased work output.

I can do the same amount of work as many other people in less time because of the way I have set up my code, my own project, and stuff like that. The only way I can describe it is that I have gotten a sense of how much can be done in a day, what needs to be done. For instance, if people need me, or if I feel that something needs to be done very soon, I will work more. I will work late in the evening. I will work more frantically. If there is nothing really going on, then I often judge that I am done sooner. Really, it is a balance between what I just mentioned and what people expect, because there are still expectations.

Obviously, my working experience has been more pleasant. I am not as tired as before when I got home at five o'clock. If my son had soccer, I had to go pick him up at 6:00, by 6:30, I was exhausted. I had to cook dinner. Then I would be dead by 9:00 P.M. Now I have energy. I may take a nap for twenty minutes during the day, but that just boosts me up for the rest of the night. That wasted time at work is replaced by fixing dinner. After dinner, my husband and daughter go back to their work and I have time to be online or do more work.

In its elementary form, "telecommuting" thus refers to waged or salaried labor enabled by IT and undertaken outside the central office where such work is usually carried out. It implies the *decoupling* of the workplace from the central office, followed by either the *recoupling* of the home with waged labor or the *decoupling* of that labor from any particular site, since work can now be carried out anywhere the telecommuter can find a plug to receive or process input and transfer output.[4]

Once we begin to survey the ways in which this seemingly simple practice has been characterized, however, the multiplicity of the ways that it has been inflected in the work environment begins to become clear. While some useful concepts such as "flexible work,"[5] "outwork,"[6] and "location-independent"[7] work have been proposed to identify the essential nature of telework, Steinle[8] argues that no one criterion should be selected to define it, rather a constellation of parameters is necessary. He mentions "work organization," "location of work," and "contractual arrangements" as relevant parameters. For Beer and Blanc,[9] however, three different central concepts are at the basis of all the definitions of telework, namely, "organization," "location," and "technology." Bussing[10] identifies four variables that define strategic aspects of telecommuting: "location, time, technical devices, and contract." For Kugelmass,[11] though, telecommuting occurs when three basic criteria—flexiplace, flextime, and electronic communication—are met in the deployment of one's work.[12]

The difficulty of defining telework is dictated by the flexibility of its forms. Here we have a concrete example of the way in which the processes by which the overall IT infrastructure is materialized produce outcomes that, although globalized, are also varied, multiplex, and fragmented. Most of the research on telecommuting, however, seems to agree that the best ways to begin to understand the phenomenon involve the variety of locations where the practice is carried out, when it is done and with what frequency, and who is allowed to do it. According to the information supplied by my informants, telecommuting practices exemplify the tendency of IT in the digital city to fragment and diffuse the sites where work is carried out, dividing and in many cases isolating workers while enabling new forms of association not permitted in the workplace. Telecommuting practices likewise shatter and recombine the traditional structures of work time and restructure the work force in ways that require new attitudes from workers and management alike.

Ultimately, the new arrangement of work inside and outside the traditional workplace thus requires a new understanding of space, of time, and of social identity and hierarchy, since these concepts are central to that process. IT decouples work from place and recouples it with space in flexible nodes of a local or transnational global spatial circuit. It also collapses the distinction between work time and other times, producing new temporal structures that are flexible, not rigid. Telecommuting permits work to occur at any time, escaping the temporal discipline imposed by management. Telecommuting thus is also used to perform individuality. Digital work is no longer group work done together at the same time, but desynchronized group work. IT thus brings a new notion of social interaction, as well.

The physical and social fragmentation of the workplace

One way to identify different forms of telecommuting is to analyze them in terms of the locations in which the practice is carried out. Thus, Stanworth and Stanworth distinguish between telecommuters who are attached to a specific workplace, those who spend time at a workplace and also work elsewhere, and those who do not have a fixed workplace.[13] Daniels, Lamond, and Standen[14] find teleworking occurring in three basic forms: "home-based telework," "teleworking from a remote office," and "mobile telework." Remote offices consist of satellite facilities, telecenters, and telecottages. Nilles[15] identifies two basic types of telecommuting from which other forms emerge, the home and the telework center, and sees everything else as variant of these two types. Korte and Wynne[16] distinguish four types of telework: home-based telework, alternating telework, mobile telework and the telework center, which itself comprises satellite offices, neighborhood offices, telecottages, and offshore offices. On the basis of location, Di Martino and Wirth[17] distinguish four types of telework: "electronic homework," "satellite centers," "neighborhood centers," and "mobile work." Huws[18] distinguishes between "multi-site teleworking," "telehomeworking," "freelance teleworking," "mobile teleworking," and "relocated back office teleworking." Typologies based on location are important because they reveal different ecologies of digital work in their specificity. However, a typology can also be made on the basis of connectivity, that is, networked relation to a central node. Here again, however, we get a similar set of categories: the central head-quarters and the home workplace, satellite offices, drop-in centers, and mobile workplaces.

A basic assumption common to all of these typologies is that there is a difference between telecommuting and simply working on a home computer or e-mailing files home to be worked on there. Kugelmass thus distinguishes official from unofficial telecommuting.[19] It is official when it is recognized as such and compensated. It is unofficial when it is an unpaid activity that is not a separate work option endorsed by an employer. The individual who from time to time takes work home to continue working there thus is unofficially telecommuting, and this has been done by managers and workers for years. In the same vein, Olson[20] makes a distinction between the bona fide teleworker, who does it on the basis of contractual arrangement with management, and someone who does it on his or her own and receives no compensation for it. Again, the latter is the old practice of working full time in the office and occasionally bringing unfinished work home to be completed in the evening or on weekends.

Official telecommuting results in the physical dispersion of the work-place in a way that the well-known practice of "bringing work home" does not. As one informant put it,

> If I wanted to go to a different state for two weeks, I could take a laptop with me and I would have the freedom to do that. If I needed to stay home like some of the engineers who have newborn babies, I could stay home. It does not impact their work at all. It is still very simple and easy to get it done. There is almost no difference with me sitting at home behind my computer and sitting at work behind my computer as far as the work I need to do behind the computer. The only difference is talking to people in person.

For some teleworkers, cell phones, cell phones with e-mail capabilities, and, in the days before these became available, pagers have added to the flexibility of telecommuting, and thus to the fragmentation of the workplace, enabling them to send and receive short text messages and to communicate verbally with the central office from wherever they may be. "I have a pager which I can get e-mails on. I have a two-way pager," one informant whose boss travels a lot told me. "She can e-mail me, and I can get it on my pager and see what exactly she wants. If she needs me to come into work on a Saturday or Sunday, I can get her page, and e-mail her back from my pager." Such practices make the digital office "trans-parent," as one informant noted in discussing the benefits of working from no fixed site: "I don't have a cell phone. If I had a cell phone, it would be even more transparent. I could answer the calls anywhere and would have it. Sometimes the voice mail piles up here before I come back."

Whether the official or bona fide telecommuter carries out the work on a routine basis in a specific place or in different places, the dispersion of work sites used by telecommuters adds a new dimension to the labor process. While the duplication of sites meets specific management goals, it also provides an infrastructure for work-related activities. The infrastructure both provides flexibility and sets limits or constraints on the ways in which telecommuting can be done.

Management and telecommuters alike have commented on the fact that productivity is higher among telecommuters than among the other workers. The explanation often given by telecommuters is that, since they are not at the workplace, they want to convince management that they are working hard at home. They also think that since they can work at home, they access the computer whenever they have free time and that they produce work for the firm at night and on weekends, something that regular commuters usually do not do. So high productivity is correlated with the extra amount of work they produce on behalf of the firm using their own free time.

> Once we started telecommuting, our production was higher than the people who were in the office. Right now it is not because the way the computer is set up—we don't have DSL. Lots of the time I use my own phone or cell phone. I don't mind, because I want the work to get done. In general, the production is higher provided the computer is working fine and that we are connected via a line to the server. Sometimes it is slower because of the modem. Once that's fixed, we will go back to producing more through telecommuting. (Female telecommuter, Marin County Assessor's Office)

However, the idea that the computer increases the workload while increasing productivity is a view shared by many. Of course, this comparison can be made only by those who have worked under the traditional regime. "I think that it has made it easier, but it has increased the workload," one informant said. "It's made it faster for us to get through a workload, but it has increased it. The workload we have to get through is enormous."

Flexibility in the choice of work sites also can make workers feel more productive. The telecommuter may access or use the central office, the satellite office, the drop-in center, and the home office at different times and for different reasons. The home may be the principal place of work, but the teleworker may sporadically commute to use the facilities of a drop-in center, may commute regularly to a satellite office, or simply may commute once a week to the central office to meet the supervisor or collaborate with coworkers.[21] As one programmer put it,

I like the one or two days that I go into the office because of the politics.... Occasionally, I have to meet with people, and that cannot be effectively done at home. As for inspiration, I think I get better work done at home aside from the fact that the development tools I have in the office are slightly better than the ones I have at home. That's really negligible, I think. I do my best thinking when I have the freedom to take my mind off what I am doing. For instance, when I have a really hard problem that I have to think about and solve, I cannot just code. A lot of the time I think while I code, and that's the best way to do it. For example, the other day, I ran into a very hard problem that I actually had to take off and think about, and I went into my garden, worked in my yard, shoveled some dirt. While I was doing that, I was pondering the problem, and it's a widely and old well-known fact that when you're trying to think of something, the best way to do it is to take your mind off of it. And for me, being in the office, I am kind of stuck in my little cube.

The term "hoteling" has been used to characterize forms of telecommuting such as this, forms that go beyond simply working from home.[22] Hoteling is not exclusive to places outside the central office. It can be done inside that office by employees who are not assigned a permanent desk there, as Shaw[23] found in the case of Midwest IBM employees who must call ahead of time to reserve a desk if they want to use the office facilities. The same phenomenon is known in the IT literature as "hot desking," "the strategy of abandoning fixed desks and providing laptops, cell phones and Internet connections so employees can work where they choose."[24] As the example of the IBM employees shows, however, the flexibility of work sites that telecommuting makes possible may not always be under workers' control. They, in fact, may have no choice in what site, if any, serves as their principal place of work, since power and management remain centralized, even though work sites are dispersed.

The physical dispersion of the workplace fragments it socially. Telecommuting considerably reduces face-to-face interaction. Working in a central office, workers can chat almost about everything, and such interactions can happen on the spur of the moment. For telecommuters, this face-to-face contact occurs perhaps once a week, and certainly not on a daily basis. Much of the communication between teleworkers and the rest of the firm is telemediated. The result is a certain amount of isolation from the social bonds of the office, from management, and from the office grapevine through which workers may collect valuable information about the current state of the business, promotion opportunities, and myriad other things.

> I know a lot of people and I myself work at home. I actually go into the office once a week and the rest of the time I log into the network from home. A lot of the times when I work at home I find that I will wake up at 9:00 A.M., log into my computer, and work an entire day without speaking to a single human being. It is very different from going into the office and running into people in the hallways. (Male engineer at Yahoo)

Some workers see both advantages and disadvantages in this.

> I think that the person is actually at a convenience because they don't have to deal with all of the he-said she-said stuff. Gossip, you know, there is more than enough. She might be at an inconvenience because she might be isolated. She does not get to come into the office and hear everything. . . . She comes in the office about once a week, but it is not a specific time. She comes in when we have a new workload for her and it is at her convenience. (Male manager at Assessor's Office)

As one informant put it, echoing comments by others, "I go to the office once a week because I feel the need to remind people that I still work there."

Telemediated isolation can have paradoxical effects. It can stimulate a sense of autonomy and self-reliance. Some teleworkers emphasize the freedom, the capacity for self-management, and the sense of efficacy that telecommuting affords them.

> It's a lot of freedom. A lot of politics in the office, if we get there two minutes late or more, the bosses would always comment about it. Now we don't have to worry about the time we show up. They were always strict about it. During the day there was a lot of wasted time in the office by people talking to each other. At home I don't have to waste time talking to different people. Now that I go to the office every once in a while to take stuff, to return or to get records, people just talk and talk; it's a lot of wasted time to me. I communicate with everyone by e-mail just as efficiently or more efficiently by e-mail than I would verbally because writing an e-mail has the advantage of allowing me to think about what I'm saying more thoroughly, I can

edit things, and really pass on what I am trying to get across as opposed to a brainstorming session. I think that my relationship with my coworkers is rather unique because over the years of working at Yahoo (I am in my fourth year), I have written a lot of software that I only know about, so that puts me in the position of being my own boss. (Male computer programmer at Yahoo)

However, such feelings of efficacy and autonomy can undercut or complicate the hierarchical relations of the more traditional workplace, producing a situation in which official organization charts and the actual structure of the workplace lack congruence. This, again paradoxically, can result in a sense of confusion on the part of the teleworker. As the same informant noted,

> Technically I have a supervisor just because of the politics of organization. You have to have someone to report to who reports to someone else about you, and so forth. But I can hardly get his attention. If I need something, he's there, but usually his only purpose is as a coworker and that reports to me basically, so I am sort of a pawn. I am sort of an island of myself and to the company because I work on the software all by myself and I help other people out when they need it and require other people's help when I need it because we are all working on the same product overall. My relationships with my coworkers are fuzzy, at best. I don't really work with anyone.

The social fragmentation of the workplace among people who are working on the same project can thus hamper productivity. I spoke to another telecommuting engineer who works for Yahoo and asked him why he feels he has to go to the San Francisco office once or twice a week. His answer was that staying at home does not provide a creative environment for him. If he were trying to figure out some problem, it would take him hours at home. At the office, he can talk to other engineers and other people who could help him, so going back to the office seems important for him in order to do his work. "It's a change of scenery. I think that's important, at least for me, a change of scenery. Doing anything all the time will wear on you in many different ways."

In addition to fragmenting the face-to-face social contacts that help enable collaborative work, telecommuting fragments the informal social contacts that are important for both enterprise solidarity and personal advancement. Office parties are one example. Management takes these parties very seriously because they socialize workers in the common corporate culture. As one manager said: "If you are having a barbecue for everyone, I would say . . . almost everyone would want to be there because those are almost crucial social opportunities that have a price that is limitless. If you are a smart employee and if you telecommute, you better be there. We won't tell you to be there, but I think any mature employee would understand that."

Another manager added,

Those are those untold little things. We won't tell you that you have to be there, but at least at my work, it is not an issue. People are there because they understand how valuable that is, the mingling of people, the listening of what are going on, and the showing of teamwork. If everyone's having good time and you are not there, that means that you do not care, that means that you are so involved that everything's secondary. It creates so many potential headaches that you would probably want to be there all the time.

There is thus strong institutional pressure on the telecommuter to resist the fragmentation that telecommuting encourages. Not all telecommuters respond to these prescriptions, however. Their physical isolation from the central workplace and the focus on productivity interfere with participation. As one informant put it,

If there is an office party, sometimes I will go, but not all the time. The telecommuters don't participate in a lot of this stuff. We are e-mailed and told, but we don't go. It means that there is an hour or two taken off of our time. It is a distraction. If we are not on production, we won't be able to work our load. It has to show that you are working.

The result is a basic disconnect between the expectations of some managers located in central offices and the practices of their telecommuting workers.

Management sees the fragmentation of the workplace produced by telecommuting as an impediment to the integration of the workers and reproduction of corporate culture. It thus could serve as a real impediment to advancement. One manager stated, "I was concerned that isolating people in their homes and not getting back in the office too often was going to be a hindrance to their development."

While attending office parties is not mandatory, for example, official meetings of the firm are. These are scheduled to impart new information to workers, to maintain the cohesiveness of the organization, and to allow for networking and the sharing of ideas. Just as the parties socialize workers into the culture of the firm, the official meetings allow workers and management to identify with the firm. Here, management insists that fragmentation be replaced by solidarity.

If there is a major teleconferencing or videoconferencing, we would express very clearly in a message, we would e-mail or voice mail everyone, that regardless of what is happening, we would like for you to be there, unless you are sick. We won't say that in so many words, but the message will be so clear that you will do that. The reason for that is very simple. We want to make sure that the concept of team stays pretty much intact even while you are telecommuting. We don't want to hurt you or have you get hurt inadvertently by not participating in those things.

Management is also concerned about its ability to exert surveillance and control to ensure that the work of the firm get done.

I think that one of the things that is downside for the telecommuters is that they have to show their face once in awhile to show management that they were still employed.... We were also concerned that some people were evidently working very late hours, maybe in favor of doing something else during the day. Some people were doing other kinds of jobs, part-time sort of things, and trying to do our work secondarily. Maybe it was not their highest priority.

For their part, digital workers deal differently with their physical isolation from the central office. Some make short trips to the office, others talk to their friends on the phone.

I know that from my perspective that my tendency was to be on my own and to focus on my work, and I have to make more of an effort now to connect. There are times when I feel isolated or that something is passing me by and that I am not connected. When I feel that, I go to the office, show my face, say hi, and do things on a personal basis. I observe some of my colleagues; they are a lot chattier on the phone. They would call me much more readily to say hi and ask how things were. I guess it is a different experience for them than me because it is more of a conscientious effort. I have to get someone to tell me what's going on. I just had this conversion with this lady who works for me, a young woman about 27 or 28 who just started working from home, and it was funny. She said that she could not go to the computer without putting her makeup on in the morning. She would get up, get dressed, put her makeup on, and go to work. I long ago stopped doing this, but it is amazing that my routine has settled into the point that I am not going to the office, my office is at home, so I am ready for work here. (Female consultant at Verio)

For psychological reasons, some teleworkers prefer to dress formally at home, again to give themselves the impression that they are at work. As one informant said, "Being in pajamas is fun at first." However, "Psychologically, things don't work. It just helps me if I change and then I can do my work during the day."

Relations are fragmented not just between telecommuters and other workers and between telecommuters and managers, but also among telecommuters themselves. To compensate, some meet regularly to sort out their feelings and relations to the workplace, management, and coworkers. As one manager noted,

In addition to office parties they are invited to attend, the telecommuters have banded together and have had breakfast meetings so they can kick around ideas periodically. It used to be fairly routine, and I think that it's kind of ad hoc at this point. It is just so they can get together once in a while and discuss their unique issues as telecommuters. I thought that was an interesting development, that they did that on their own.

The compensatory bonds between telecommuters, however, are based on their differences from both ordinary workers and from centralized managers, another way in which telecommuting fragments the workplace.

The connection between telecommuters and the workers and managers at central offices is problematic in another, purely technical sense, but one that further separates telecommuters from others in the digital workplace. The IT equipment and thus the technical basis for connecting the home office with the central workplace is likely to be lacking in speed and bandwidth.

It is a major problem for some individuals. There is a level of frustration and they become a little bit scared because what they agreed upon with their managers they are unable to do. . . . That's not that big of a problem in California, but we do encounter it. There are people that live in Tracy and Santa Cruz, which is a little bit remote, and they encounter the problem. I try to bring those things on the table and see what can be done to address it. To a certain extent, sometimes if it is not something that can be addressed technically, you just have to reset expectations for those folks. Management is fully aware of the fact that there will be somewhat less productivity than what was originally expected of that person. (Male manager at Quantum)

One reason why some firms establish satellite offices is to provide tele-commuters a technologically efficient place to work, with all the necessary equipment, that makes difficult physical commuting unnecessary.

They work within those places, like Dublin and Pleasanton, because 680 traffic is so bad. . . . We do have satellite offices in Dublin, Pleasanton, and I think we are currently trying to open one in Santa Cruz, for the reasons I just mentioned. Really what we do is rent a place. We go to firms that have good network connectivity. We go to an ISP sometimes, an Internet Service Provider. Then we put an office over there, a virtual office. We put x numbers of terminals that all link up to the office and then we identify the employees. They work as if they are at the main office. (Male manager at Quantum)

The actual ability of telecommuters to connect efficiently with the central office over the Internet is a major problem that cannot be easily solved. Management sees it as having three prongs: the problem that the equipment in the home of the telecommuter may not have the capacity of those at the central office, the speed problem posed by modems and other connectivity devices, and the technical problem of keeping home computers serviced and running, often requiring the visit of a technician to these dispersed sites.

We have some challenges that we are dealing with right now with in relation to the telecommuters. They are technical challenges, which have been impacting our production in the last year. The speed of the network has slowed down. They use dial-up modems and it has been a real problem because of the speed. We are now looking into providing DSL for those who have that available to them. Unfortu-nately, not everyone does. We are also probably going to be scrapping our workflow system that we have been trying to work with in favor of another one, because we are trying to speed things up. Right now we are having a lot of difficulty with our network and the speed of our server. (Male manager at Quantum)

Finally, the relocation of work to home, or to any site the worker chooses, has had costs—financial, social, and psychic—that complicate the relationship between a worker and his or her employer in new and sometimes unforeseen ways. The movement of paid labor from the workplace to the home is accompanied by shifting household dynamics on a number of levels. Working at home is not simply one more activity added to household activities, but rather affects many aspects of household life.[25]

Telecommuting redistributes expenses between worker and employer and within the worker's household. So far, the literature on telecommuting has paid a good deal of attention to how it may reduce traffic jams, air pollution, and commuting time, how it brings the disabled to the industrial mainstream, how it formalizes the isolation of the telecommuter, and how it may enhance personal freedom and happiness by giving women an opportunity to care for small children at home. However, little attention has been paid to the extra expenses incurred by the telecommuter.

Telecommuting entails a diverse set of direct expenses: the purchase of a car, its maintenance, repair and gas, including insurance, for trips to the central office or for telecommuting outside the home; the purchase of computer equipment and its upkeep, if this is not furnished by the firm; home expenses related to the maintenance of an office, such as electricity and gas (some of it tax deductible); and expenses related to the use of a home office, such as the extra telephone line that may be needed for transfer of files and central office communications by e-mail.

> Staying at home involves costs. I have to turn on the heater all day. I have to run electricity. Incidentally, running a computer is about the same as leaving a light bulb on. The electricity is not that much used, but there is the expense of leaving the computer on, the lights, heat, but that is offset by the gas. I used to have to refill my tank every two days. That's an hour of driving twice each way. That's far and expensive. Nowadays, I cannot even remember the last day I got gas. I desperately need it right now, but it's very infrequent that I fill up my tank. (Male computer programmer at Yahoo)

Management is well aware of the transfer of costs from the firm to the worker. In some cases, the firm provides free equipment and technical assistance to the telecommuter. This practice is often used to ensure the compatibility of software, the appropriateness of the hardware, and the adequate speed for telecommunication with the central office.

The computer belongs to the corporation. In case of a technical problem, the corporation sends a technician, or the employee brings it back. What we do to minimize that problem is to provide a laptop to the employees. They use that laptop at home and at the office, so it is the same system. If you are unable to do your work at the office or at home, you won't be able to do in the other place also. We did that purposely as a way to minimize the hardware problem that could eventually surface, and we addressed it very nicely and proactively. (Male manager at Quantum)

Not every firm in Silicon Valley furnishes the teleworker the equipment to do the work at home, however. Some informants complain about the costs they have had to bear and their inability to force management to address this issue.

I have a modem connection at home that work gave me. I don't have my own telephone line. I am not going to get a telephone just for that. They aren't going to pay for that themselves. I'm trying to get a DSL line from work, and that's been a hassle because they have been very careful with spending, even before the economy went down. They are expecting you to pay for your own DSL or high-speed connection to do work helping them. I actually have communicated several times with management. If I wanted to check on something... it is very beneficial for them that I am able to log in fast and take care of that. That means that they are expecting you to pay. The talk is about improving that, but I haven't seen that yet. (Female employee, state government office)

Between these extreme positions, one finds firms that share the costs with the employees. A manager provides the following rationale for this practice:

We pay for the second line, we provide the computer now, and all the supplies that you need. With the cost of electricity these days and the fact that the telecommuters are at home and need to keep the heat and the lights on, that could turn out to be a fairly significant cost. Our thought on that is that we want to meet them part way. Whether it is halfway or not, I don't know. They are certainly getting a huge benefit from this, and they need to absorb some of the costs from it, as well.

Moss and Carey[26] present some quantitative evidence in their cost and benefit analysis of a sample of telecommuters in New York. This close look at telecommuting in reference to household budget processes sheds light on this aspect of household life as it is being transformed by the introduction of IT.

> Telecommuters saved an average of $11.92 per day or $44.10 per month (based upon an average of 3.7 telecommuting days per month) due to lower costs for food, gasoline, subway fares, dry cleaning, and other daily costs associated with work. However, these savings were offset to some degree by increased costs for energy. Telecommuters in the study indicated that, on average, the cost of air conditioning and lighting in summer months raised their electric bills by $11.00 per month; the cost of daytime heating and lighting in winter months raised their utility bills by $7.95; and their extra use of the telephone on telecommuting days raised their phone bills by $9.35 per month. (Moss and Carey 1994: 21)

Teleworkers have become aware of these extra costs and have developed strategies to reduce them because of the effect they may have on household budgets. The same austerity measures they use in daily household activities to reduce costs are applied to work done on behalf of the firm in their households. They figure out that they may end up paying for these expenses, either because the firm may not cover these costs or because of the extra hassle involved in asking for reimbursement. "If I am at the hotel, I will upload my mail, work on it, disconnect, work on it, and then connect again and download. I am conscious of trying to minimize my time on-line."

Telecommuting thus is not simply a matter of social relations between the worker and the firm. It also involves infrastructural change in the home, as well. In terms of both expense and the disruption of the household, something like wiring the household to make it IT-friendly and remodeling an office for telecommuting work can be significant. The costs are solely the responsibility of the worker, although they may be exploited for tax purposes.

More significantly, the movement from the central office to the home changes the dynamics of the household.[27] One issue that came up quite often in my discussions with telecommuters is that in this new type of labor, it becomes very difficult to separate leisure from work. Telework can become so integrated in the digital worker's daily life that it becomes more difficult to distinguish formal work from domestic work. The firm or workplace now shares the space of the household and competes with the household for time and activities. In the traditional era, there was a clear separation between the work week, which ended on Friday, and the leisure time that would start on Saturday. Now, since people can work or take time off anytime, it is no longer possible to establish clear temporal distinctions between labor time and domestic time.

> People tend to work a lot more when they telecommute or when they have a work environment compared to how they used to work in the old days. The reason for that is that because of the human factor being what it is. If you are at home and have a provided system with you, then you have network connectivity with work, and tend to do as much work as you can any time. When an idea comes to mind, you jump to the computer and try to catch it. What really ends up happening is, and that is definitely my case, I definitely work a lot more hours than I used to in the conventional way of doing things. (Male engineer at Yahoo)

People say that they cannot break away from the connectivity that the computer offers. Some speak about their addiction to the computer. Easy access seduces them and makes them available to others, and that induces them to work when they are not supposed to.

> I am always connected. Every day, even if it is Saturday or Sunday, I will check my e-mail and I will always respond to it, too. I would say that seven days a week, I am connected. By being connected all the time, and being able to answer stuff late at night, it is much easier to go and do it and get it out of the way. It takes a little bit of stress off the workweek, but the workweek is sort of stretched. It is not like I can walk way from my job and not think about it. It is always there. (Male engineer at Yahoo)

The interference of IT work with household life is a major factor in the restructuring of the dynamics of the household. Digital workers report that telecommuting has created problems because of the temptation to be in front of the computer instead of being with the rest of the family.

> I don't have a timeframe; I can work very early, or I'll work very late. I definitely work on Saturday and Sunday or even on vacation. I carry something called a Blackberry, which is a small little box, which provides me with my e-mail. What I will end up doing, in my case, is

using the Blackberry and my laptop, and stop to do work. It's kind of overwhelming, to a certain extent. No one is forcing you to do it, which's the interesting aspect of it. No one is forcing you, but you are so engaged in that so-called virtual way of working, before you know it, it becomes second nature to you in a sense. Sometimes my wife gets after me, but if I am not careful, even when I am off, the box provides me with my messages, and I can always reply to my messages. I am always working, really, twenty-four hours a day, seven days a week. For all practical purposes, it could be that way. I guess the challenge for everyone, including myself, is learning how to balance the whole thing, because otherwise you could end up working nonstop. That's not good, you could end up getting burned, also. (Male employee at Quantum)

The destructuring and dissemination of work time

As this informant suggests, the diffusion of the sites from which tele-commuting is carried and the consequent fragmentation of the workplace profoundly affect the nature of work time, undermining the distinctions between work time and family time, work time and leisure time, or indeed between work time and any other category of time, thus disseminating work time across the temporal spectrum. Sometimes this reordering is solely in the province of the worker, if the employer allows the worker to control the distribution of his or her time. In other cases, management wants to ensure the availability of the workers at certain hours. In many cases, however, the working hours of the firm do not necessarily correspond to the working hours of the workers. The flexibility that allows the teleworker to work at any time at the worker's convenience (flextime) combines with the flexibility to work at any place (flexiplace) to remap the organizational matrix of work. The flexibility that allows the tele-worker to work anywhere entails the flexibility to work anytime, and vice versa.

A few people have laptops where they can come to work and plug it into a bay, but they have a bigger monitor, keyboard, mouse. When they want to go home, they snap the laptop out and use it as a regular laptop. They use it at home. The company provides Internet connections. I had a good computer at home with Internet connections already set up. What the employee wants, the employee gets. One guy in particular, a pretty good employee, personally likes to go to Tahoe a lot. He had a big commute, woke up really late, was taking a couple of classes. He just wanted to... maybe the forty hours a week thing did not work out too well for him, so he requested a laptop. He will take off Thursday or Friday morning for Tahoe, take his laptop, and work out there when he has time and at nights after classes, in the mornings, it is very accommodating to him. (Male employee at Yahoo)

Labor is further fragmented by the practices of firms that allow flextime and flexiplace, flextime but not flexiplace, or flexiplace but not flextime. These arrangements have different consequences and affect working conditions differently. They require a different regime of surveillance, provide different incentives to workers, and project different images of the workplace.

Just as we need to distinguish official from unofficial telecommuting, however, we need to distinguish permanent from transitory telecommuting, because each affects the firm and the worker's life differently. Kraut (1989: 21) thus distinguishes between home workers who routinely work at home from those who do it only sporadically. Telecommuting is transitory when it is carried out in an ad hoc fashion. The firm allows it for specific circumstances and for a short period of time, sometimes to carry out a specific project. It is permanent when it is part of the work arrangement of the worker or simply because it is a formal policy of the firm. The distribution of official telecommuting into permanent and transitional forms is another aspect of the fragmentation of the virtual office.

Transitory telecommuting often is done because of circumstances beyond one's control, such as illness. Indeed, that circumstance provides one of the most striking examples of the dissemination of work time and the collapse of distinctions between work time and rest time. In the traditional office, illness confers official permission to stop work. In the virtual office, however, it is not always considered an obstacle to working on-line. The destructuring of work time thus changes the meaning and expectations of obligations undertaken under traditional contractual arrangements. As one informant put it, "I mean, any work that I am doing from home is extra work unless I ask if I can work from home, but I only do that if I am sick or really need to for some reason."

Transitory telecommuting often provides a way to accommodate persons with family responsibilities:

They could either lose us as employees or let us work from home. One of the core values is to respect the employees, so they do. We have people who work home at all times for medical reasons or because they have children. They are very accommodating as long as you do your job. (Female telecommuter in Silicon Valley)

Transitory telecommuting is also sometimes literally transitory. It is used as a way to smooth the transition when workers are identified for layoff. Since they are already working at home, it is believed that it will become less painful for both parties when such individuals are formally dismissed from the firm. "In a way, the ones working from home are sort of working on discrete projects that will end, and they will no longer be working for the company," said one manager.

In permanent telecommuting, the collapse of all distinctions that separate work time from other times becomes a central aspect of the digital worker's life. Both forms of telecommuting, however, have profound effects on the organization of time in the home, which is now part of a network of real and virtual offices. Telecommuting changes the traditional temporal boundaries in the household, mixes them, and recombines them to produce a new temporal frame that itself is always subject to change.

I sometimes shift some of that work on the weekends. A lot of the time on Sunday afternoons I start after my daughter goes back to Berkeley. When I first started, it was fun to do my work at night. During the day, I could do a lot of other stuff. After a while, I found that I was working at nights, and I did not want that because I am tired and want to sit and watch TV or be with my husband and kids. I try to discipline myself. (Female employee, Marin County Assessor's Office)

Actually, the breakdown of the distinction between work time and other times that digital work makes possible affects official and unofficial telecommuters, as well as temporary and permanent telecommuters, and even those who just bring work home from time to time. In effect, IT makes many workers telecommuters, regardless of whether they are recognized as such or describe themselves in that way.

Among programmers interviewed in Silicon Valley, I found that even those who work in the central office so as to interact with coworkers also do extra work at home. This extra labor is not paid for by the firm and falls outside the usual categories of workplace compensation because these individuals are not registered as telecommuters or as hourly workers entitled to overtime. They feel the need to go back to the computer in the evening and on weekends to solve problems they could not solve in the office, to retrieve e-mails they had no time to read in the office, or simply to complete work initiated in the office. These individuals, in effect, work a second shift for which they are not paid. Sometimes management becomes aware of this practice. When it does, it routinely advises such workers to spend time with their families or to relax their minds, since they are not compensated for this extra labor. The motivation for this kind of behavior may be explained in terms of workplace competition, the subjective criteria for performance evaluation, and the personal drive for success.

What this amounts to is the disappearance of the distinction between work time and overtime. Under the old temporal regime, overtime was work performed outside the allotted time and sometimes outside the allocated place. Overtime was better compensated than regular work because it was supposed to be a burden—a burden not because of the workload itself, but because of the time at which it had to be done, in time allotted to other pursuits, such as rest and family matters. These elements that define overtime in the central workplace context cannot be easily transferred to telecommuting. Under the regime of IT, the distinction between work time and time for rest or family is blurred, and the worker may not be in any position to identify what constitutes overtime. Overtime, to the extent that it exists, becomes a matter of negotiation between management and employees.

Management takes different positions vis-à-vis overtime, depending on circumstances. A common practice by management is reported by a telecommuter working for a multinational electronic firm headquartered in Silicon Valley.

> Sometimes after a project is done, they may give you a week off for the time you spent working until midnight, what is called the "crunch time". That's after a year, you might get a week off as comp time. They do that once in awhile. At what times does overtime come in? No one thinks of overtime. Overtime is nonexistent. It's your salary, and that's it. What matters is what you produce.

DiMartino and Wirth[28] see this as the trend of the future when they argue that "overtime, perhaps without compensation, may become habitual, and may take the form of additional, quite substantial work just to complete the 'extra bit' which is required."

Some firms experience crunch time during production cycles, when deadlines have to be met. Others experience a similar need for overtime during peak seasons, periods of work more intense and more protracted than ordinary weekly work. Di Martino and Wirth[29] note that a company may use teleworking as a "work peak buffer" in order to allow it to meet the demands of this intense period. As one informant noted,

This time of the year is very crucial. By June eighth, we have to finish all of the permits and all of the work. . . . We have to finish whatever we have on our list. I am working more than I am supposed to. For example, if I am supposed to do four a day, now I am doing six a day. I usually wake around 8:00. Usually my son and husband leave at 7:30, so I am pretty much awake at that time. I worked yesterday until 10:00 at night. There were intervals from going to pick up my son and all that and making dinner. I worked all day yesterday. I have to work this way for the next couple of weeks so I am able to finish everything that I have just to make myself happy.

Telecommuting thus allows work time to be expanded, contracted, and divided in new ways. Because of the effects of telework on work time, however, existing legislation governing the operation of labor markets increasingly lacks congruence with actual work practices. There consequently is a clear need for new legislation in this area. The distribution of working hours has changed, even though the hours of the working day may remain the same. The nature of overtime has changed, and its very definition has become ambiguous. Workers face new expenses incurred at home, have new and previously unanticipated needs, and new relations with management.[30]

What is new here is not the fact one may work in different shifts at home, but the capability—or rather, the necessity—of mixing work time with other activities at home and at the central office that have different time frames. Digitization affects time in at least three temporal domains: the home, a hybridized household with two temporalities, one of which provides a temporal enclave so that the worker may achieve some kind of distance from household activities to concentrate on paid work; the workplace, which also becomes temporally hybridized because of the different time frames it intersects (commuters with fixed time and telecommuters with flexible time); and the workers themselves, who must negotiate the differences between several time frames—between the temporal structure of their work day when they work at home and the temporal structure of the work day at the central office, between the temporal structure of their work day when they work at home and the temporal structure of their work day when they commute to the office, and between the temporal structure of their work day when they work at home and the temporal structure of daily home life.

As the necessity of negotiating the differences between the temporal structures of the home and the central office shows, the computer simultaneously allows the dissemination of work time and subjects the telecommuter to new forms of interaction with the temporal regimes required by management. It allows people to work at different times, as well as in different locations, and thereby expands the time and space of work, but only via connection with the firm's mainframe or with the central office's network. The mainframe or network thus becomes the eye in the Panopticon that regulates digital workers. The relations between teleworkers and their managers thus also are restructured by the revolution in IT.

Teleworkers and telemanagers: Reconfiguring labor relations

Not all workers are capable of negotiating between the multiple temporalities that telecommuting entails, not all are willing to do so, and not all managers are convinced that their workers are capable of doing so and still remain productive. Thus, who can successfully telecommute, who should be allowed to telecommute, and why they should be allowed to do so become major issues for digital workers and for their relations with management. As IT transforms the workplace and work time, it also creates new divisions within the workforce and raises new issues of employee relations with which workers and management both must grapple.

McGrath and Houlihan[31] argue that "while it is possible to talk of 'telework' as a distinct trend, it is essential that this trend be seen in its proper context, as a subsidiary issue without the broader study of the changing nature of work organizations in contemporary society." They identify four types of teleworker: "homeworkers," those who work in "neighborhood work centers," "nomadic staff," and workers in "satellite offices."[32] Kraut categorizes telecommuters as "substitutors, self-employed, and supplementers" (p. 23). Olson[33] provides a typology of telecommuting workers based on the expertise involved. She distinguishes between "the professional, managerial, or technical" on the one hand and "the clerical, manufacturing, or semi-skilled" on the other. Rule and Attewell[34] distinguish telecommuting workers in terms of the work that they do: "non-transformative," "moderately transformative," and "highly transformative." Word processing that is a mechanical function belongs to the first category. Simple accounting practices, because they do not imply inferential thinking, belongs to the second category. Other practices that imply the ability to make choices about possible outcomes belong to this last category.

It is worth noting that freelancers—independent workers who are not employees of any firm—are a segment of the workforce that IT is making increasingly important. Such individuals may be classified as "self-employed" or "independent contractors," are not paid a salary, and are not always paid on a regular basis, but receive payments for jobs contracted with a firm. This means that they do not receive the benefits accorded regular employees, and they have no job security. At the end of a project, they may be offered another project, may be terminated, or else may have to look elsewhere for work until the company rehires them for another project. When the company is doing well, they are likely to be employed, but if it is downsizing its workforce, they will be the first to be sent away.[35] The appeal to economy-minded managers of using freelancers rather than regular workers and of transforming regular workers into freelance teleworkers is obvious. However, it is only an extreme form of the ways in which IT is creating new categories of worker, new divisions within the workplace, and new challenges for workers and managers alike.

The traditional office is fragmented along the lines of the telecommuting status of workers. Those who telecommute and those who do not constitute two groups of people at the workplace with different needs, which further contributes to the social fragmentation of the workplace. "There are two types of people basically at my company," one informant explained. There are "the engineers," who "can be anywhere, basically. There are some teams that go home and work, a tightly knit team. But for the engineers, there are no real reasons for working in the office." Then there are "the everybody else people," who are

> the programmers, developers, and the other people that include sales, technical support, customer support, people that run the network, and stuff like that. Those types of people . . . they sort of have to be in the office because, for instance, the sales obviously need to work together. The technical support people, the network guys, they have to be with the hardware, obviously, because they have to work with the physical equipment. (Male employee at Sun Microsystems)

There is thus a basic division between workers who are allowed to choose whether to telecommute or to take advantage of flextime and those whose status as a telecommuter or employee with regular hours is imposed on them. The basis for the division is usually the nature of the work involved. "Not everyone in the company is extended the privilege of working at home. Web development, you are working by yourself most of the time, there is some cooperation from working in the office and at home. There are certain groups that can work at home easier than others because of their job task," one informant said. Managers often cannot telecommute because coworkers depend on them for supervision. Secretaries need to be present in the office to process incoming calls. Some workers must use expensive and heavy equipment that the firm cannot afford to place in everyone's home. Other workers, by contrast, depend on IT whether they are in the office or not, and they therefore need not be in the office at all. In another firm,

> I think that it's mostly the nonengineers that work almost anywhere because those are the people that travel a lot. They are the ones on the trains or planes, going from place to place. They always have laptops and stuff configured in the laptops. Possibly, because the sales person, for instance, probably has to send some e-mails, whereas the engineer, to do his job, has to be connected to the network for the entire time. So that's probably a consideration. (Male employee at a Silicon valley IT firm)

Any division between those who are accorded flexibility in doing their jobs and those who are not leads to the temporal stratification of the workplace as individual workers show up at different times of the day or week and leave the premises at different times or do not appear at all: "At least in our place, we have several ways that we address the distance and traffic problem," one informant said. "The concept of flexible work hours or scattered work hours, people come to work based on the nature of what you have to do. Some people come at 8:00, 9:00 A.M., 1:00 P.M. depending on the nature of work, people are scattered. You don't have everyone coming to work at the same time."

There are both perceived advantages and perceived disadvantages to being on one side or the other of this division, however. Although the choice to telecommute or not is extended to some individuals, not everyone who could choose to do so sees the advantage of working at home. "I would rather go to the office to work because I feel more like working. I don't like to be at home all day. I would be more efficient working around people that have a more professional attire in the workplace." Some find that the convenience of not having to commute is offset by the lack of equipment at home to do the job well. "I think that for the nature of work that I am doing, we have to be in the office. We cannot afford to have three servers at home. We have to test a lot of things on the servers."

Conversely, some people work at home unwillingly, because of space constraints in the workplace. For them, telecommuting is not a desirable benefit to be taken advantage of, but a form of social exclusion and a career liability, since presence in the office may enhance one's possibility for promotion. Management, not the worker, decides who should have a permanent office, and it does so in order to accommodate its own needs, not the worker's. "I work at home once a week. That was the agreement. When the company started, they allowed people to do it because we did not have enough space," said a telecommuter.

Sometimes the distance of the residence of the worker from the workplace is the criterion that management uses to confer the choice of telecommuting on workers. "I think that one of our policies is that if anyone works past twenty miles of the campus, they have the ability to work at home. Anyone that works within twenty miles should stay on-site. If you work outside of twenty miles, you can have remote connections." Such criteria, while simple and clear-cut, can seem arbitrary.

What those who choose or are required to telecommute appreciate the most in this new digital labor regime is, not surprisingly, the flexibility of telework, which allows one to mix work with pleasure, domestic work with waged work, and household time with work time. "Recently, I have taken a laptop to my friend's house that has a network and DSL set up, and worked from her house. She is a computer programmer, actually technical support, but we are in the same line of work. She actually works for a different company," said a Yahoo technician.

There is at least one characteristic that seems to be singled out by managers and teleworkers alike that defines who is a candidate for telecommuting. The sociological literature and telecommuters interviewed for this study agree that telecommuting allows people with children to be able to shuffle their work time so as to be able to take care of their children's needs. It permits parents, particularly mothers, to stay at home and still work while raising children. In the traditional industrial setting, women with small children ended up either deciding to stay at home to care for them or having to make arrangements for day care and after-school care while risking the absence of parental presence that working entailed. Telecommuting has freed teleworkers from many of these concerns.

For me, even though my kids were thirteen and sixteen three years ago, during the day, I had all the time I needed to work, but it gave the freedom so that my kids would not have to carpool. I would not have to ask people to pick them up or whatever. During the day, if something came up, I could bring whatever to school. Before, I was not able to take them to school in the morning. They had to either take the bus or carpool. I spent a lot more time with them. My daughter had an accident last year. She is paranoid about driving right now, so I am the one who is driving her. If I were not telecommuting I would not be able to do that. Even though she is on campus, on weekends she comes home. When she goes to work I take her, especially in the summer. I have one car and my husband has the company car. For me, it does not pay to get another car just for the kids to drive. I save money by not having another car. (Female employee at the Marin County Assessor's Office)

Telecommuting enables women with small children to develop a schedule of work that is commensurate with their child-rearing responsibilities and aspirations. They work whenever the children are asleep, at day care, or at school. One interviewee said that she wakes up around four or five o'clock to do work before the kids wake up. She stops at seven to prepare the children for school, and she starts teleworking again at ten. She explained

If you have small children, you probably want to do some work, and then after they are at day care or school, you get some time to do your work. I think that's the beauty of the whole thing. That's why it is called the flexible work environment. Things that you never had a chance to do in the past, you can do those things, and then there is a good relationship between you and work. You feel good, and if you feel good, the managers feel good, and the firm will benefit. It is really a win-win thing. (Male manager at Quantum)

Although management often complains about the extra work they have to do to keep track of what telecommuters are doing, they tend to agree that this kind of work is beneficial to women with small children.

The first thing that comes to mind is the idea of women who happen to have young kids. In the past, they basically had limited choices. They could go to work and worry about their kids without really being productive. They could not go to work and then end up in the marketplace, losing a great deal of talents. By providing a flexible work environment for women, they are able to do the work and do it effectively while still supporting their kids, which is so key. I think society will end up benefiting from this. (Male employee at Quantum)

There is thus an implicitly gendered component to the ways in which some people are singled out for or allowed to choose telework. Because women who choose to become mothers tend to be identified by management as candidates for telecommuting, they are particularly exposed to one of the principal disadvantages that many informants discussed with regard to telecommuting: its effect on chances to advance within the organization. As Risman and Thomaskovic-Devey[36] argue in their study of firms headquartered in North Carolina, the introduction of microcomputers into the workplace exacerbates "current inequalities in the workplace," reproducing "the gender structure of society."[37]

The issue of who gets promoted becomes complex in regard to telecommuting because it implies the engineering of new rules, the ambiguity of old rules, and new modalities of worker–management relations. It entails new ways of evaluating performance and of assessing workers' fitness in the corporation. For example, the completion of a project on time, rather than showing up for work on time, is used to measure a telecommuter's performance. Telecommuting changes the rules of the work regime instituted by the Industrial Revolution: the rules identifying starting time, starting place, lunch time and its duration, ending time (what hours are routinely expected and what is extra), ending place (to ensure that the worker is at the workplace), behavioral etiquette (dress code, desk behavior, use of equipment), and visitation (to prevent friends from using the premises and wasting the employee's time).

These rules, which were made to regulate workers' behavior, to maintain order, to enhance productivity, and sustain professionalism, have been undermined with telecommuting, and conformity to them cannot be easily used as criteria for evaluation and promotion in the regime of labor practices instituted by IT. As one manager noted, however, "management sometimes, because they are unwilling to change with the times or because they have their own views of the work environment, may not agree" that new criteria are necessary, "and that creates problems with employees." Actual work practices and the criteria for advancement thus may not always be in synch.

There are other problems with regard to telecommuting and promotion, as well. Since telecommuting may not be allowed at every rank of the institution, promotion may mean surrendering ability to work as a telecommuter.[38] Workers are sometimes confronted with the choice between accepting a promotion with no telecommuting option or continuing the practice of telecommuting without promotion, and some workers would rather forgo a promotion if it means giving up the advantages of telecommuting.

> In our situation, there is appraiser 1, 2, 3 and then supervisor. I am 2. They said that appraiser 3's cannot telecommute because they review the work and they have to be in the office. They used to do that, but because there are different beliefs on telecommuting, there's a pull all of the time. Whenever a position comes up for appraiser 3...only two or three of us apply. One was told to apply because they wanted her for it. She applied and the only reason that she went ahead for the promotion was if she could telecommute, otherwise she did not want it. None of us wanted it. We did not want $100 a month more for it. We would rather have comfort. She got the position, but she could not telecommute, so she did not accept it. For me, I am five years away from retirement and I don't want to work much longer than that for only 5 percent more in salary. (Female employee at the County Assessor's Office)

The increased autonomy of the teleworker exemplified by this willingness to forego promotion is one indication of the way in which telecommuting dissolves the hierarchies of the traditional workplace. We are moving from a workforce discipline engineered by management and characteristic of the traditional industrial firm to a personal discipline set by the individual worker and characteristic of the IT firm. This comes about because teleworkers are not required to report for duty at the central workplace and are therefore left to manage their schedules as they see fit.

In this new regime, managers must rely on what one called "the trust factor." "It has surfaced to be a big player," he said. Managers need to be made to feel that they can trust digital workers to follow their own personal discipline, provided that the work is done competently and on time, instead of coercing them to do it. Conversely, when teleworkers feel they have earned that trust, one manager realized,

> They feel a sense of ownership when they do things. It's no longer the hierarchical way of doing things where you have the big boss where you do what needs to be done. People feel now they know what is expected of them, and it is something that they agree to because it makes sense from the bottom-line perspective. You end up having two major gains because of that. From my perspective, from what I saw in the marketplace, at least in Silicon Valley,

there was really added value to most firms doing business in that environment.

Another manager added,

At my work right now, most of my staff work pretty much any way they want as long as they have an understanding of the expected outcome. That's what is key, I think. There is also a major trust factor in comparison to the way things used to be. In other words, the hierarchical way of doing things has changed and what is now in the place, especially in Silicon Valley, is a very clear understanding of what is expected of the employees, and then confirmation between management and employees, and then execution by the employee in reaching the final goal. I think that those are key prerogatives that can enable us to make those things happen.

Earning management's trust, however, can seem difficult from the teleworker's perspective. Telecommuters complain that when they were working in the office, they did not have to prove to their managers that they were hard workers, even if they were not producing much. Their physical presence in the office was a clear sign that they were at work. With telecommuting, they feel that they have to prove that they are working hard, and they can do so mainly by raising their level of productivity. In the view of a telecommuter,

Until they trust you, you have to work like anyone else. Once they trust you, they trust that you know what you are doing and let you work alone. I have worked there for four years, so I was one of the first people to come in. After I had been there for three years, people had a good sense of what I was like and how interested in my work I was. I was genuinely interested in it. That's one of the facets of intellectual work. There are paying me for an extra piece, and in a certain way, they are paying me for a lot of artistic interpretation. They want my perspective, my code.

However, even though trust is a major factor in ensuring the productivity of teleworkers, management has also felt it has had to learn how to telemanage, to employ the resources of IT to reassert some form of control over workers whose labor is now disseminated in space and time. As one manager said, "I think that it takes more effort on the management's part, but I think that everyone realizes the benefit of the extra work in making that extra effort." Telemanaging has taken the form of instituting a regime of digital surveillance to ensure that the firm's work is not overshadowed by domestic work. As one manager puts it, "I work for Yahoo, and we all use Yahoo Messenger, so I can know exactly who's around and who is out to lunch by looking at my Yahoo Message window. That's how I often communicate with telecommuters." Another manager explained this regime in detail, emphasizing the ways in which management uses the surveillance capabilities of IT to regulate the practices of teleworkers:

> Our mandate...requires everyone that is using the flexible work environment to have some indication or communication of when they are commuting and how to get a hold of them. You are expected to receive your phone calls to do whatever needs to be done. You are not on vacation, you are working. It is not your day off or anything like that. You are working. Anything that could have happened at work will happen wherever you happen to be. That's one thing that we really try to emphasize. This is not your day off, you are working. You are just working in a different environment. You need to tell people very clearly the day you are off when you are telecommuting. This is how you get a hold of me. Sometimes we ask for a pager, home telephone number, cell phone, or whatever because we want to get a hold of you. It is a must. We have to. If it happens more than once that we are unable to get a hold of you and it is a pattern, then we need to take a look at that. Also, I want to make sure that tele-commuting is not for everyone....Some people choose not and that's OK with us too. We just want to provide flexibility and the oppor-tunity to choose to do whatever you want to do that can help you and help us.

The relations of management with telecommuters vary from one firm to another. Some are very informal, while others have more strict rules. The tendency, given time and experience, seems to be toward the imposition of more rules—at the cost of implicit expressions of trust. "We had very little restrictions on work hours and work days. We were strictly looking at the production. Is the work getting done?" one manager noted. However, he continued, "I think some people were trying to get second jobs squeezed in there and I felt that our work was maybe second to that. We did place some restrictions on it on both hours and days of the week." Tensions between workers and managers thus polarize over issues of trust versus surveillance.

Strategies for the digital workplace

Olson and Primps[39] have identified the three realms where IT is found to be of importance for telework. They see it as having mechanical, substitutive, and managerial roles. Mechanically, it is a tool that is used to process output, receive input, and retrieve data. This provides the communicational infrastructure that enables workers to interact at a distance with the central office and that allows managers the opportunity to monitor at distance the performance of the telecommuter. As we have seen, the possibilities that IT has begun to bring to fruition create new opportunities, new tensions, new problems, and new challenges for those who live in the digital city. In the digitized metropolis, that is the San Francisco Metropolitan Area, industry and the public sector have developed a number of different strategies for dealing with issues arising from the fragmentation of the workplace, the diffusion of work time, and the divisions within the workforce and between labor and management that the practice of telecommuting has created. They can be distributed analytically into six categories.

The first one, as we have already noted, is to make telecommuting subject to explicit rules that are part of the official relationship entered into by both workers and those who manage them. This strategy requires planning in order to anticipate the effects of telecommuting on tele-commuters and on those who remain in the central office, and how the work of the two will be integrated.

At my company, people sign a contract with the corporation that states what is expected of them. For instance, if you are out of the office, you are supposed to have some kind of paper that says how they can get a hold of you, where to reach you, when you are out to let people know that you are telecommuting that date. There is a process. It's not done ad hoc. There is a set of guidelines and pro-cesses that have been designed to make that happen.... We normally work with HR [human resources] and the legal offices in the corpor-ation, and we put together a package outlining exactly what needs to be done. People sign a contract in order to make that happen. There is a formal process because there are a lot of legal implications in doing that.... We require them to check their e-mails in the morning and before they quit work in the evening. If they are at home rather than in the field, we ask them to check their e-mail every three hours. We also call them when they are at home. (Male manager at Quantum)

The second strategy is an informal arrangement whereby telecommuting is done in the firm on a trial basis or in an ad hoc way to accommodate, at least for a period of time, those who for one reason or another cannot commute daily to the central workplace. The request by a digital worker to telecommute may be done because of illness, disability, or the need to care for a loved one at home. Sometimes it is a transitional practice that lasts a short period of time until the problem is resolved. But it can also be a more permanent change.

> I don't think they will allow an employee to telecommute without special circumstances. They want them to be here, talk to a lot of people initially, and learn. When they are on their feet, they can work by themselves and then throw in a day. I am sure after a person has been here for a while and really knows what's going on, it would be really easy to arrange for more. (Male employee at the County Assessor's Office)

The third strategy, in many ways the opposite of the first, is devised by the firm because telecommuting is strongly demanded by the workers. This strategy is based on trust, allowing telecommuters to do their work wherever they want to, and on the rationale that too much control may impede creativity and lead to the loss of employees. The following statement by a software engineer explains the circumstances that led him to request that he be allowed to telecommute:

> I live in Oakland. The driving is terrible. I commuted for two years, and it started to tire my body because I was spending so much time on the freeways. I decided that I could not take it anymore and told them I was going to quit. They liked my work enough that they tried to work something out where I could work at home three days a week. That worked for a while, then it changed to two days at the office, plus the job I was on required a cell phone and a pager. Once a week I had twenty-four hours of "on call," which means that there were 400 machines I was in charge of. If any of the machines broke down, it would page me every seven minutes for twenty-four hours. That was horrible. That got to me, and I decided that I could not take it anymore and decided to quit. They gave me a job to work at home as much as I want and trusted me to get the job done. I work on the infrastructure. I am on the team where I am writing the core software of the company, but I don't have to deal with the Web server side that has 400 machines.

Management is well aware that the failure to allow a worker to telecommute may end with the person leaving the firm. This may result in an abrupt halt in the work process. They also must take into account the possibility that the person may join a competitive firm, along with the costs associated with hiring a replacement, from advertising the job to interviewing candidates and training a new employee.

> Most of the folks, including myself, do not go to the office every day. Sometimes I work two days at home. I have a virtual office at my home. The company pays for a DSL line, and that provides me connectivity between my home and office. I have a laptop that I use in my office and virtual home office and I am able to do my work and do it effectively. I also extend that to my employees. Whatever I do, and I think that's a key factor to why the new ways of working have been successful, not only do we do that for management, but you also extend it to your employees as a way of showing added value. If you don't do that, then the productivity gain will not be as high as you like. Furthermore, you can end up losing an employee. In Silicon Valley, if you lose an employee, there is a tremendous cost that goes along with it. (Male manager at Quantum)

The fourth strategy is to allow a heterogeneity of work practices, with telecommuting being one among many. This happens in firms where unions oppose innovations based on IT as a way of preventing layoffs and as a way to prevent the dispersion of workers outside the central workplace, where they may not be so easily recruited by labor organizers. Away from the workplace, workers are also less likely to see their relations with management in class terms, since telecommuting may be the outcome of a negotiation that the worker might have initiated. Such a negotiation may also have been entered upon willingly to trade less money for more freedom. In such a context, where exploitation is not overt, there is less likelihood that union propaganda will find an audience. In some cases, therefore, management allows a variety of work practices to develop informally to accommodate union demands without having to make hard and fast policies in favor or against any practice in particular.

> It's politically really sensitive. We're involved—the city government has so many different unions. If there's benefits to be made...saying, "This is an official policy, and you can't do this," it will create so much infighting and tension and things like that. It's unfortunate

with thirty thousand employees. You couldn't do it [telecommuting] city-wide. People know it exists, but it's seen as something between you and your manager. So it's unofficial. We like to see it as a program for employees, but since there are so many city employees that could not take advantage of it, it ends up becoming a thorny issue. (Female employee at City Hall)

Such a strategy emphasizes the tendency of telecommuting to divide the workforce.

As we have seen, another critical issue in telework is that it suits some types of work better than others and thus tends to divide the work force, as well. On this basis, some firms purse a fifth strategy, explicitly prohibiting some workers and managers from telecommuting.

We have restricted telecommuting to journey-level people, not people who were new or in training and not supervisors, but to the appraiser 2, which is the journey level. We just restricted it to appraisers and not to anyone else in the staff because we felt that was probably more suitable to telecommute. We have had people who were telecommuters who were promoted to supervisors that have come off of telecommuting. They applied for that promotion knowing they would be coming off of telecommuting. It's been very fluid, and we have tried to be very flexible. One of the concerns that I had early on was the isolation of the workers. We were allowing people to telecommute five days a week. Beginning on July 1, 2001, we require the telecommuters to come in one day a week. It won't be the same day for all of them, it will be staggered. We are having a turnover of staff. We had a very stable experienced staff for a long time, and now we are having new, less experienced people come in. As I indicated before, one of the ways in which we expand our level of experience and skills is that it is passed on from one generation of appraisers to another. When you have all the experienced out in the homes, it is more difficult for that to happen. I want the newer people to receive the benefit of the experience of the older people. (Male manager at the County Assessor's Office)

The sixth strategy comes about when a firm lacks space to accommodate all the workers and is forced to employ telecommuting as a way of solving this space problem. Telecommuting is implemented here as an alternative to the construction of new facilities and is used as a way of minimizing costs.

We did not do that satellite office because we thought it was a better way to organize. We did it because we were running out of room here and we forced to do it. We were actually cut back on space that we had by the administrator's office. . . . I don't think it is the best way to organize. The communication is OK through telephone and e-mail, but it is not the same as being able to walk over to someone's desk and have a face-to-face conversation. (Male employee at Quantum)

This strategy is based not on the welfare of the telecommuter, but rather on securing the financial stability of the firm. As we have seen, it can force workers to telecommute against their will.

Partial digital decentralization/centralization

The Industrial Revolution centralized the workplace, requiring workers and management to be at the same workplace at the same time. It is frequently claimed that, in contrast, the digital revolution decentralizes, and that decentralization is an essential characteristic of the IT firm. As these strategies show, however, in each case, it might be equally accurate to refer to the process as partial centralization or networked recentralization in response to the fragmentation of the workplace, the dissemination of work time, and the challenges of managing digital workers, since while some aspects of digital work are decentralized, others are not.

Certainly, making telecommuting subject to explicit rules and limiting it to special circumstances are ways of asserting centralized control over the centrifugal effects of IT, and even honoring the wishes of employees who want to telecommute serves centralized administrative interests by limiting work interruptions, avoiding losses of personnel to competitors, and saving rehiring and training costs. Limiting the dispersion of workers outside the central workplace in order to preserve relations with powerful unions likewise is a far cry for total decentralization, while explicitly prohibiting some workers and managers from telecommuting and forcing workers to telecommute both depend on the assertion of central control.

Digital decentralization thus is not total, but always partial. Management continues to function as the networked coordinating mechanism in the operation of the workplace. Thus, virtualization does not entail the total elimination of centralization. Digital work may be decentralized, and even the administration of that work may be disseminated spatially and temporally, but what might be called the "political" component of digital work, the location of power, remains centralized at the heart of the disseminated network. There are various reasons why this is so. The central office is still the common meeting place for executives, the site where major technological equipment or components of the firm are located, the site where confidential archives that cannot be placed on the network are housed—it is the headquarters of the firm. Its centralization is selective or partial, too, however, because it does not have all the characteristics of the old, centralized firm. Partial digital decentralization and partial digital centralization are opposite sides of the same coin.

The original centralization of the office led to the development of forms of communication based on a mixture of proximity, physical access, body language, gossip, and content. With telecommuting, some of these aspects are not present, and therefore the communication pathways of the central office and the virtual office alike are hybridized, containing the old and the new, not as separate entities, but as engines joined in the production of a syncretistic outcome. On-line communication among coworkers is more subdued because it is more formal, and it is likely to be done for a purpose, not simply for gossiping. The pattern of intraoffice communication thus adapts itself to the virtual interaction of telecommuters. It is a system that is constantly being adapted to the ebbs and flows of the flexible copresence of telecommuters in the office.

(De)centralization is a hermeneutic issue because it is seen differently by different actors: the worker, the management, and the interpretive analyst. For the worker, it refers to the ability to work away from the main office. For the manager, it means managing at a distance and a new challenge to meet the new needs of the workplace. For the analyst, it is a new form of centralization—networked partial centralization—that consists in the reorganization of the workplace to reflect the new logic of the operation of the firm: partial decentralization.

Telecommuting and globalization

Global and local telecommuting contributes a wider dimension to the partial (de)centralization of the IT firm. The IT infrastructure of multinational firms allows local and overseas workers to communicate with each other and to maintain long-distance interactions under the aegis of different management units that themselves may be both physically dispersed and electronically networked. The practice of IT firms in Silicon Valley in outsourcing projects to Taiwanese or Indian employees and of receiving digitized drawings or products from them, modified to meet US standards, indicates how the office is virtualized, how the space of the office is extended to sites outside the United States, how the production of a specific item is globalized, and how the team that works on such a project is globalized. Technical teams made up of individuals who live in different countries and who cooperate in the development of electronic products have been a fixture in the way in which IT firms operate for some time. Telecommuters may be new recruits or current employees at the headquarters and overseas subsidiaries of these firms.

In a global network, the actors may move around as they maintain contacts with coworkers around the globe. As one informant noted,

> Only my boss, the person who writes my check, who I directly work with, is stationed in this area, but most of the time, I have no idea where he is. He travels so heavily. When I talk to him, the other day I talked to him, he was in Hawaii.

Global networks with people in fixed sites because they reside there thus can be contrasted with global networks made up of mobile agents. A local node may take on a global identity, and a global network may take on a local identity.

Telecommuting thus intersects with globalization in many different ways. Some telecommuters engage in global interaction as the essence of their main job. Individuals who live in Silicon Valley and work for overseas firms are in constant virtual interaction with their employer and coworkers, while managers of transnational corporations exchange notes and discuss matters with overseas counterparts and clients. In other cases, the global interaction is more sporadic. For example, a global telecommuter can function as a member of an international team for a specific project and thus must interact in the course of the assignment with overseas coworkers. Likewise, a freelancer may engage in global telecommuting occasionally whenever an opportunity presents itself.

Over the years, it is possible to map out the geographies of interaction among specific units of globalized firms and workers because of the long-term relations that have been established. One informant noted,

> On one of the projects that got me the position I have now, I wrote the software that allowed mail to go global, the translation of different languages. That was my work. After I wrote that, and was able to use it, I had frequent contact with people all over the world, mostly producers through Web page directories, and there is a server for every international country. For instance, there was a French server that had to use my software I was communicating with the whole time.

These global interactions are general when they occur for the exchange of information with no focus on interest, as one expects when employees call each other as part of the modus operandi of the firm. They are specific when, as in this case, specific units interact with each other because they are in the same line of work and they need each other's expertise.

Global processes initiated by teleworkers have different tempos and are related to the type of project that is undertaken. Some units have a rhythm different from the others and sometimes this creates disjuncture between the two, fragmenting the digital workplace globally. And while some global processes are work-related, others are not, at least not directly. Global processes are also stratified by ethnic origins, depending on the locations of these ethnics in the firm. These global ethnic relational flows do not have the same content or target. Some may be generated for personal or family reasons, while others are purely professional or technical relations between two IT centers such as Bangalore and Silicon Valley.

Computer-mediated telecommuting must be seen as a central channel or vessel that sustains the infrastructure of globalization because it processually connects territorially dispersed overseas sites. It globalizes the space of interaction of teleworkers because of the transnational expansion of the labor process it facilitates. It globalizes the local flow of time because of the different time zones the telecommuter must cross in the performance of his work. It globalizes the labor process itself because of the international team mobilized to participate in the production of goods via the expertise that each one brings to the successful completion of a project. In other words, telecommuting using the virtual mode of interaction made possible by IT is a pivotal mechanism of the globalization of locality. The digital city is made up of local institutions and practices with global reach, and telecommuting is a representative sample of such a reality.

Conclusion

The practice of telecommuting in the digital city involves spatial, temporal, and organizational dimensions. Telecommuting partially decentralizes the centralized, fixed sites of the industrial era, which are now networked and only partially centralized. It brings polyvalence and pluridimensionality to the workplace. It blurs the distinction between work time and all other categories of time, potentially even collapsing the two. Telecommuting also provides a new principle for hierarchization, discrimination, fragmentation, and tension in the (de)centralized work-place. It thus transforms the nature of labor and labor processes.

The Industrial Revolution extracted the worker from home and forced the household to restructure itself to account for time spent outside the home. The IT revolution brings the worker back home, forces the worker to resocialize the household, and forces the household to restructure itself again. The destructuring and restructuring of the workplace brings about the restructuring of domestic space and a resocialization of the worker to be able to function adequately in both. Telecommuting also expands the boundaries of the workplace beyond the home, disseminating it, in principle, anywhere, anytime, and to anyone, globally, because of the extraterritorial reach of virtual interactions that IT makes possible.

3
The Digital Office

The previous chapter examined the local and global parameters of telecommuting as a social practice within the context of IT. This chapter shifts the focus to the nascent institution that supports such a practice. With the advent of IT, the traditional office, which has been the backbone of industry, government agencies, and the academy, is going through a momentous transformational change. While a good deal of empirically grounded literature exists on the traditional office, the evolving literature on the digital office or virtual office is more timid in its claims, partly because it is made up in large part of impressionistic, futuristic, and speculative pronouncements. It is not easy to make sense of a large amount of this literature because of the lack of empirical data and case studies pertaining to specific areas that could sway an interpretive analyst in one direction or another.

Through research undertaken in Silicon Valley, this chapter builds on what is known of the digital office and attempts to describe the forms of practice that characterize it, the ways in which traditional offices acquire digitized components, the transformations wrought in the workplace by the advent of the digital office, the problems posed by digitization, and the digital office's global dimension. It is therefore studied as a dynamic component of the global digital city.

Theoretical conceptualizations of the digital office

Analysts have emphasized different dimensions of the digital office, depending on their approach. Sometimes they equate the concept with that of "virtual organization," emphasizing social relations more than contiguous space; other times with that of the "virtual store," stressing reduction in overhead costs; still other times with that of the "virtual factory," highlighting the role of smart machines in carrying out the production process through telemediated communications without the intervention of human actors; some even equate it with the concept "virtual teams" to express the dispersed location of actors, their on-line connectivity, and their collaboration through the Internet; and commonly, some identify it with the idea of the "home office" or the ability to create such an "informal office" wherever one can connect one's computer to the Internet. Because these analysts magnify different aspects of the question, they provide clues that indicate the social parameters of the whole structure of the digital office. They all agree that the digital office is a component of the virtual world.

For Nardi and O'Day[1] the virtual world is a "computer-based environment that mimics the ordinary, physical world we live in or imagine." They further identify what they consider to be the four main characteristics of the virtual world:

> the first is geography, the metaphor of connected places, and the participants' role as builders of new places and things. . . . The second characteristic is identity, the freedom of participants to choose how they will present themselves to others. The third property of virtual worlds is communication and awareness mechanisms to suit different styles and groupings of participants. The fourth is a rooted sense of community that can develop for long-term inhabitants.[2]

Some scholars place the emphasis on human agency in creating the digital office in the virtual world. Others stress its structural elements: the digital office is anywhere outside the formal central workplace where the worker is able to plug in a computer and carries out work. For Guiliano,[3] "portable terminals and computers, equipped with appropriate software and facilities for communication . . . create a 'virtual office,' which is essentially anywhere the worker happens to be." Others highlight the network aspect as the mechanism that makes the operation both realizable and efficient. For Handy,[4] "virtual organizations . . . do not need to have all the people, or sometimes any of the people, in one place in order to deliver their service. The organization exists, but you cannot see it. It is a network, not an office." Both Castells[5] and Gell and Cochrane[6] downplay the notion of physical place, however, emphasizing instead "networking tasks performed in distant locations" or "collaborative international networks linking people through integrated ICTs [Information and Communication Technology]." The same network-concept is understood under the notion of distributed work.[7] For Campbell and Grantham,[8] "distributed work can be defined as work activity conducted by groups or teams of people separated from each other in time and space, with advanced communication technologies being used to coordinate the work process taking place."

Mansell and Steinmueller[9] see the flexibility of logging in and logging out as a central element in identifying the nature of the digital office. Because of this flexibility, they see the shape and the parameters of the digital office as always changing. For them, the digital office or organization can be defined as a collaboration among actors, "carried out in an electronic environment, in which entry to, and exit from, the structure is flexible and determined on an 'as required' basis."

Instead of stressing human agency, as in one way or another these others do, however, Les Alberthal[10] stresses the impersonality of a structure of interaction maintained by automated smart machines that are able to speak to each other and to accomplish tasks without the mediation of human workers. He envisions the virtual factory concept as "a manufacturing arrangement in which intelligent agents...communicate on the Internet without the need for human intervention." He sees that as an antithesis to centralization and as contributing to the "dismantling of the Fordian Complex," the almost Panopticon-like supervision of production.

Emphasizing the overhead cost reduction factor, Derek Leebaert[11] sees the digital office as a competitor of the traditional office. He argues, for example, that "the virtual store can expand at the special speed conferred by not having to meet rent, inventory, and most overhead. Its challenge to mall-bound 'brick-and-mortar' commerce should provide one of the heavy-weight battles of the early twenty-first century."

Perhaps the best structural account of a digital office, however, is the one that emphasizes the dispersed nature of the organization, its on-line characteristics, and its lack of physical shape. Knoll and Jarvenpaa[12] come closest to such a definition when they note that "what is unique about the virtual forms, including virtual teams, is that the forms do not have physical instantiation; they do not exist except in a digital or electronic form."

The various aggregates and definitional fragments discussed above suggest ways to approach the task of characterizing the digital office by means of empirical research into its recent manifestations. This chapter uses the emphasis on both agency and structure to focus on the parameters of the organizational makeup of the digital office and how digital workers fit in this new environment. The hope is to shed light on another aspect of the global digital city. It is clear that the digital office comprises both a local and global element that indicate how the globalization process has penetrated far and wide into the daily life of the digital city.

The parameters of the digital office

Although analysts agree that the digital office is a component of the virtual world, what remains to be seen is how this is empirically the case in the digital city and what the parameters of the digital office actually are as it is evolving there. In this chapter, the concept of the digital office means two things. It refers to the digital office that operates outside the constraints of a central workplace, in a cyberspace in which management, coworkers, and clients interact mainly through on-line communication. It also refers to the digitized office that operates inside a central workplace (or transforms such a workplace) in which interaction is undertaken through both physical copresence and telemediated communication. In other words, the digital office may exist by itself in the virtual realm, or be embedded in the physical organization of the modern office. The study of the digital office will be carried out in this chapter through a focus on its double component, that is its virtual and nonvirtual aspects.

In some cases, I found that the digital office does not have a physical location where employees meet daily. Instead, they are engaged most of the time in virtual interaction as the main channel of doing business. An example of such a digital office is provided by a software engineer in Silicon Valley.

My roommate runs a technology magazine out of his apartment. Because of technology, he does not even have an office. He can spend an entire day behind a computer, not say a single word to anyone, and get a lot of work done. It is his magazine. He e-mails and uses the computer for everything. He sees the layouts that are e-mailed to him and e-mails back to them. He e-mails the printers—kind of solitary.

In other cases, I found that the digital office has a physical location within an organization that is being transformed in the way it does business because of the pervasive role of IT. The majority of large firms in Silicon Valley function in this mode as IT becomes a central mechanism accounting for global relations with subsidiaries, the dispersion of the workforce, and the flexibility of work time and workplace. Tapscott *et al.*[13] provide a good example of this mingling of both the real and the virtual in the operation of the firm. They note that "customers of the

Gap can buy clothes online; if they don't fit, then they can return items to the store. Or they can browse the Web at their leisure and take printouts of desired items to the store. Gap has even installed Web lounges in some stores, where customers can place orders."

Finally, I found that the digital office can be a component of an organization that is being reinforced by IT in its traditional physical operation. Here, IT is important, but not transformational.

As far as we are organized here, I think we are fairly more traditional than anything else. We have taken a pretty good look at virtual organizations. I am not sure we could do that in a wholesale manner where we had everyone working like that since we do have a lot of interface with local taxpayers. It is a little difficult for the taxpayer and the appraiser to get together. There is a little delay in communication there. I think that what we have done has been pretty successful. It has evolved from what we first started with to something that is better than what we first started with. We have had a lot of different challenges along the way. (Male manager at state government office)

There are three ways one could characterize the interweaving of the real and the virtual in the traditional office. The first is in terms of the structure of the organization. There are two different types of organization. In the first, the traditional office with the managers and the employees constitutes the main site of operation, to which is appended a little experiment materialized by the existence of a virtual organization that operates through the telecommuters and e-mail and all of that. In the second, the digital office is sitting on top of the traditional office, with different types of people doing different types of tasks. They are integrated physically only when they come to work. Otherwise, they interact via the mediation of the telephone or e-mail.

The second way to characterize the interweaving of the real and the virtual is in terms of how human agency brings about the digitizing of the office. The birth of the digital office may be the result of either management or employees or both advocating this mode of operation for the purpose of efficiency and practicality, or it may be a response to clients' expressed needs. Workers who have requested telecommuting were often behind the move for the virtualization of the office. Clients who have requested the services are also a source of incentive for the transformation of the office, not simply because of the competition factor, but also because of the de facto incremental virtualization of the world outside the office.

The third way of characterizing the interweaving of the virtual and the real in the digital office is in terms of the persistence of existing practices and habits. This may be a factor in the supremacy of the traditional firms over on-line experiments, even in Silicon Valley. The view expressed by informants is that the traditional office is not going to collapse, and that although some aspects will undergo change because of IT, some others will remain the same. As a worker from digital city hall noted,

Based on my experience, we have very little interaction with the taxpayers on-line. We have a few inquiries that come in via e-mail. There has been some talk doing e-filing in the future, and there are a couple of counties trying to do that. To be honest, we are waiting to see what their experience is. Let them be the first out on that one. For the most part, it is mostly traditional. Telephone contacts and letters is what our main correspondence with the taxpayers is.

In addition to the inertia inherent in existing ways of doing things, no matter how much cyberspace penetrates office work, the need to commute to a central location for some types of work will not disappear. However, the old routine of commuting every day to the office is no longer the pattern followed by some workers, mostly telecommuters.

I think the old traditional workplace concept is changing. People get in their cars or buses or however they get to work and traveling to their work location everyday is changing. I think that in some form it is always going to be there, but not in the same form as it was in the past. I think that you are always going to have some people who need to be in an office a certain period more of the time or utilize satellite offices more central to where they live. I think there will always be the concept of the main office that is the center of where everything emanates.

From a genealogical standpoint, there are diverse factors that explain the existence of the digital office. Some firms are created as virtual entities at the start and operate in this environment; others begin as "real" and are transformed to meet a different set of conditions; others are "real," but have virtual components that are intrinsically part of the operation, while others are "real" and selectively deploy virtuality to take care of specific projects, especially in the case of projects that involve international teams.

We are challenged in this chapter to find out to what extent "the traditional office might cease to be the center of people's working lives, of corporate identity, and of employee security."[14] It has become obvious thus far that a major difference exists between firms in which the physical presence of workers is essential for their operation because of the activities that require physical copresence and firms that engage in the production and analysis of knowledge, which are less rigid in their structural organization. While the former continues to maintain its traditional form, the latter can function with workers remaining outside the physical space of the central workplace. We need to inquire further, however, into how and to what extent traditional offices become digitized and the consequences of this transformation for the nature of the workplace in the digital city.

Project-induced virtuality

Virtuality may appear as a permanent component of a traditional firm or as a project-induced component. When it is project-induced, it indicates that one unit is driving the rest of the company because of the intensity in which IT is used there, while in the other units its use may be more sporadic. Project-induced virtuality thus is the manifestation of a transitional structure that is driving the rest of the firm. The following case, narrated by a freelancer in software implementation, is instructive and provides some clues on the operation of such a system:

"The most amazing project of my whole professional career... started about April.... I was asked to help install the system, which was developed by a team in Utah. And then that system was highly desired by another division of the firm that was located in Europe. Actually all over Europe. They were located in London, France, Spain, and Germany, the German being sort of a half simply because the product manager who was responsible for this product that this operating system was going to deliver was located in Germany.

"But only for this reason was this system going to be employed actually throughout Europe. The project consisted really of dealing with all the offices in those countries. So the first challenge immediately was how are we going to work with folks who are nine time zones removed from us? Especially for me—because I from Orem it was eight time zones. We had right from the beginning difficulty figuring out how we were going to do this project because we had no business hours in common—between eight o'clock in the morning here on the West Coast and five o'clock there was not a single business hour in common, so talking with them really required that I get up at six or seven o'clock in the morning and for them it means four o'clock in the afternoon or staying after five. But they really wanted the system and the people at Orem believed they could do it in a very short period of time, short meaning two months. When they say "do it," that meant they had to do some modifications to the applications and then come to Europe and then install it. They agreed, they said OK, they said we will be staying after five if you are willing to get up at six or seven, we will put up with the system. The first thing that I did, since all the people that I worked with were outside of the Bay Area, I had to spend 2 weeks in Orem, Utah to first get acquainted with this application. And then we requested the group from Germany— when I say "group," I mean the product manager and the technical manager—make a trip to Orem. These poor guys were in flight on Saturday and arrived at midnight, spent the Sunday just recovering from the trip, which they said was something like twenty hours because the planes were late.

"We grilled them for two days, Monday and Tuesday, for what it really was that they wanted from this application so that the modifications could be done. During these two days, my heart was going out to them because clearly a nine-hour difference, eight-hour difference for them meant that they had to think very hard when it was time for them to sleep. It was really a difficult time. There were young guys, probably in their early thirties, so actually they did not complain at all it actually went very well.

"They left Wednesday morning. That was at the end of April. Until June fifteenth, we had twice-a-week meetings at six or seven o'clock our time here in California and did the entire project over the phone and over the Internet, of course. I kept sending them material over the Internet, and we looked over these documents, and then on June fifteenth I went to Germany and the team came from Orem and we spent two weeks—we tested it and installed it. It seemed no different than if we were located here in California."

This example shows us how the traditional office can be the bedrock upon which virtual organizations take place. Here the digital office is made to operate to improve the performance of the traditional office through the existence of virtual teams. The digital office may come about through the collaboration through the Internet of individuals who are not attached to any traditional firm. It may also derive from individuals selected because of their expertise in various local and international units of the multinational firm. Sometimes, as in this case, a freelancer may be brought in to manage and provide leadership to this virtual team. Other times, the digital office is made up of individual workers who belong to different firms. The firms exist as traditional enterprises, but are linked to each other through these virtual teams.

Workplace expansion

A major characteristic of the ways in which the office becomes digitized and acquires a virtual component is the dispersion or expansion of the workplace because the workers involved may not be at the same location. It is precisely because they are dispersed, but connected through the Internet that the digital office is possible. Distributed work made possible by IT because it enables collaboration with workers in different sites is a major factor in the construction of the digital office.

The expansion of the workplace occurs spatially because of the various locations that serve as its niche, as we have seen in the analysis of telecommuting, but it also occurs temporally because of the pervasive nature of work, as we have also seen in regard to telecommuting. The time of work is expanded or made flexible to suit the domestic needs of the workers. Unlike office work that is continuous, telework can intertwine with domestic work.

Work expansion affects not only the central workplace, but also the satellite offices that form the matrix of the network. A digital office does not have the same boundaries one finds between headquarters and satellite offices because the participants operate along the borders of virtual space.

Work expansion can also be fragmented, because some units may be involved in local connections while others may not. The same can be said about the global relations of the firm, which implicate only some actors or units, and not all of them.

The expansion of the workplace also relates to the mobility of sites where the connection can be made. Collaboration via e-mail is one of the main means by which people relate to each other. So site expansion goes hand in hand with site connectivity. Space expansion may also occur because of a merger when a company acquires another firm. Here, virtual interaction may be necessary not only for intersite communication, but also because of the distance that separates both.

Units in a corporation that are not very involved in the digital office because of the kind of work they do may as a result feel isolated from the rest of the corporation. This is why the digital office may be seen as a new mode of incorporation that maintains and strengthens interoffice ties as well as ties among employees in distant places.

The expansion of the workplace through its virtual components that accounts for the rise of the digital office provides an opportunity to shift from the traditional to the virtual as needed. It also provides a way of enlarging one's network beyond the firm for which one works or the locality where one lives. In the following interview, a manager of a digital office elaborates on some of the intricacies associated with this new form of networked labor:

"I work generally as a project manager for an Internet company, and I have been doing this now for three or four years. Even in the last three years, I have seen a gigantic amount of change in how I work, and the primary difference is that, right now, for about two years now, 90 percent of my work is done from home. I work for XXX, by the way. It is an Internet connectivity provider that was brought by a Japanese NTT company and they are morphing now into a Web-hosting provider throughout the world. It is very much an Internet-based company with a presence all over the United States and in Europe right now. The company is headquartered in Denver, but with offices here on the Peninsula. People like me, and other employees, are primarily working from home right now. There are people who are full-time employees that have offices, which are locked and empty most of the time because they are working from home. The company has not yet adjusted to all of that. This is going so fast that they haven't developed policies of how long someone can be in the office before they are allowed to start sharing offices with others. There is a lot going on with people feeling some queasiness about window offices being empty. I can see that this has been a problem for the last nine months. I always felt that I could do just as good of a job from home.

"What it means now that it is completely unimportant where the resources are. The team I work with is spread all over the United States. We have people in Florida, Denver, Texas, and Washington, D.C. and really in all corners of the United States. Now I was actually given a project in Europe, London. This is just the beginning. I see the approach to this is no different. We have conference bridges, in which we meet regularly.

"The distance has not come in the way, but I have had interesting experiences in the last two months. I was given the project to launch a certain process that involved meeting large groups of people, approximately ten to fifteen, about every month. The manager, he was the vice president of the corporation, decided that to ensure success of this new process, the meeting be face to face. In order to do this, I think he purposefully skirted the issue of cost. He just said to go to these places and make sure that you are there in person.... Here you have this Internet company that has access to its own backbone network of high-speed circuits, and yet we were not utilizing teleconferencing, and people still feel like the best way is to meet in person.... We will not have been able to secure commitment to the process, at least not to the degree we were able to by bringing these people together and going through the requirements of the process and really going through the process itself. Usually it took about four or five hours in person. I learned from this that there are instances where you need to bring people face to face.

"Now that I have been watching it for a couple of months, and while it was good at the beginning, right now, the process is settled, and we can just as effectively do it over the phone, and people know each other and understood what the process is all about and there is that commitment, so they all ask that we don't travel and do it all over the phone despite the fact that they were given full reign of the expenses and would not have been told that they could not travel.

"One thing that is better for me right now, with all this, is that all of a sudden I have clients that are all over the United States. I work with people; they work for these companies, but they know that I can help them, and they call me from Florida and ask me to do work for them. Some of them I have never even met. So, all of a sudden, my reach has expanded tremendously without me doing anything about it. If I have a chunk of time available, and someone needs me, I can do work for people across the country, as opposed to before, when I did not have that reach. I only worked for people who were based here and who would send me elsewhere, like to New York or Japan, where I was not connected to my workplace with my laptop like I am right now. I had to come back to the mother office instead of doing all of my work here."

What the digital office allows as a flexible infrastructure is the ability to form virtual groups depending on specific needs and irrespective of locations. A digital office may be comprised of people who work at the same place or people in different workplace locations.

It is important to stress that the digital office is not necessarily a permanent fixture. Some come into being because of the strategic role of a manager or worker who must travel, and wherever this individual happens to be may revive a digital office for the purpose of carrying out functions far away from the central location of the firm. Through transfer, face-to-face interaction may be transformed into on-line interaction, and vice versa. Hence we see here how the traditional office may give birth to the digital office and how one is called to support the other or how their operations are intermingled for more efficiency. An employee who has moved to another site of the firm may continue to maintain frequent on-line business communication with his or her distant coworkers still in the previous location.

Virtual communication

In addition to the expansion of the workplace, the digital office is constructed by the migration of workers and managers to on-line communications that link one actor to others in preference over other forms of communication. For many, convenience is the principal attraction of the digital office, whether it is wholly virtual or embedded in the structure of the traditional office. Such workers compare the difficulty of communication by telephone and the easiness of sending them an e-mail.

For the office that I work with, we deal with a lot of insurance companies for the hospital. If we try to get through to them over the phone, it is impossible. We end up being on hold for about an hour and a half to two hours. With the Internet, we just e-mail them about the concerns with a certain patient, what we need, and they e-mail us right back. I think that it is a faster type of communication. (Female clerk at a hospital in San Francisco)

Another hospital worker explains why it is easier to e-mail than to telephone, especially if the parties are living in another state,

It depends on the type of insurance that the people have. With most insurance, if they deal with HMOs or PPOs, the companies are in San Francisco. It makes the job a little bit harder when they have out-of-state insurance because we have to do a whole lot more. We have to communicate with the neighboring insurance in San Francisco and then we have to contact their connection in another state, for example, New York. We have to connect from one to another.

The telephone is regarded as a hassle, not only because of the time zones that force one to do business with the East Coast at specific times, but also because the call may arrive at an inappropriate time. E-mail solves this problem, since the receiver is not obligated to read the message immediately. A hospital clerk in San Francisco said,

> With the telephone, you have to know when to call. E-mail makes things easier. When you call on the telephone, you have to be aware of the time difference. Sometimes, if there is a three-hour difference, like in Florida, they will close before we do. When our office is still open, their office is closed already. When we call, we cannot get ahold of anyone. Sometimes, first thing in the morning, when we come in, we have a lot of things pending. We go ahead and e-mail that stuff or we send it by way of the Internet. By the middle of the day, which is when they close, we get all of our responses back.

Interactive virtual communication has its challenges for virtual workers because it requires literacy skills, sometimes requires the time needed to wait for an answer, and can result in misunderstandings because of the inability to read expressive behavioral signs.

As we have seen with regard to telecommuting, some managers stress the importance of the informal communication that is missing in the formal operation of the digital office. They remind us of the role of gossip, which provides context for formal communications. Sometimes gossip is used as a trial balloon and at other times it prepares one for what will come next. In other words, through more formal on-line communications the information is provided, but in the absence of informal communications, the context that could help in its interpretation is absent.

On-line communication requires a different set of expectations, which do not correspond to the situation that prevails in oral communication. Reading the written line is different from reading the face of the person who expresses his or her thought through that line. Words are read without the ability to read the behavior that contextualizes them and that could give clues as to meanings. On-line communication also has contributed to a change in the style of communications, since they must be short and precise, well written, and clear to prevent confusion.

E-mail may be fast and convenient, but it does not supply all the benefits of face-to-face communication. While it is acceptable to stop and visit a coworker several times a day to engage in small talk, it is more difficult to do so in cyberspace because frequent e-mail is likely to be seen as unwanted distraction. "I have to be more to the point in my e-mails and in my telephone calls," one informant complained, "because I cannot just get up and go to the other person's office and say, 'Hey, I need this and this' and just chat about why, basically lay it out—this is why I need it."

Virtual interaction therefore is sometimes supplanted by more traditional physical interaction. Workers can employ one or another, or use one to complement the other. A female clerk at San Francisco City Hall said,

> In a conversation, you can cover a lot of the bases. In an e-mail, you really have to spell things out and be very descriptive to make sure that what you are trying to communicate is there, or there is a lot of misunderstanding. That happens a lot when I get requests or people are asking me something. I think it also has to do with a lack of their understanding of Web terminology or technology terminology. If they are asking for something, I have to go back. If it is something complicated, I usually get on the phone with them because it is easier to clarify exactly what you are trying to explain. Simultaneously, you can also pull it up on the screen and see what they are trying to refer you to. If it is a larger project, and they are trying to convey that through e-mail, I would say that at some point I would have to ask them to come into the office and ask them to go through it with me. I think you have to be extremely clear in your e-mail, because the communication breakdown is really easy.

Virtual communication is the major mode of interaction among digital workers. It expands their sphere of interaction and unlocks problems encountered in the traditional office, thus promoting the transition to the digital office.

Surveillance and control

The digital office has transformed the environment of the traditional office in a number of ways and has raised new problems for management and workers alike. One notable transformation involves the way in which the advent of the microcomputer has facilitated the existence of a new regime of remote surveillance through cyberspace. This form of surveillance at a distance is different from the traditional forms of surveillance at the workplace. The physical monitoring of the beginning and end time of the worker's day, the use of equipment for company work, and the monitoring of telephone conversations that relate to work cannot be done with the older methods. However, computer software allows management to be aware of the time workers are on-line or off-line and also to be able to read at a distance what is being processed. Although the worker has much control over the time and place of work, management is not totally in the dark about when and how their employees are working. Electronic surveillance in cyberspace allows management to regulate what it deems to be acceptable in work performance, producing results similar to off-line surveillance in the industrial firm.

Some programs used in the industry have the ability to send a constant stream of information to management about the work output of workers.

Whatever I post on the computer, my boss knows how much I have posted. For example, my sister, who deals with authorizations and referrals, she does that by way of e-mail to the insurance companies, the patients, or to the doctors' offices. When she does that, my manager also gets an e-mail. Whenever she sends an e-mail, my manager gets a response e-mail saying that an e-mail was sent by this person to this person at this time. They have records of what we do. We have access to her screen, and she has access to ours. So we can see what she is doing. My manager has the master system in her office, so you can see when the person from home is logged in and working. If she is not working, you would be able to tell. (A hospital clerk in San Francisco)

The surveillance of workers occurs not only by management, but also by the software engineer, a fairly recent development. Those engineers who are responsible for the maintenance of the e-mail boxes may at time invade one's privacy. Some workers are aware of this double mode of control. "I worked on e-mail, the company's mail system," one software engineer told me. "When you are writing an e-mail service and you are fixing people's mailboxes and doing different things, you occasionally have to go into people's mailboxes, and you get a small snapshot of what people are doing."

Software engineers, however, also fall under the new surveillance regime.

There is something called source control. Basically, if I want to edit, credit, or delete a source code or file in Yahoo, I check it out of the tree, work on it, and then check it back in. When I check it back in, my manager, just because it is good for him to know what's going on, a message is sent to him that the code or file has been modified, and who it has been modified by. I can also make comments. I feel that he is checking on me that way because he knows when I have not turned in something for a while because I am working on something big. He notices what's going on, but definitely not in a hello sort of way. He is just touching base to see what's going on and that's really the only way that I sense that anyone knows what's going on. Like I said, I create this unique software, and I have a whole mailing list of people that are dependent on my software. That's another way they can see what's going on, because every time I release something I send a message to everyone. (Male engineer at Yahoo)

Postperformance file access at a distance is another method used to ensure that digital work is produced according to a firm's standards. Since the servers are part of a central system of digital operation, such files can be recalled, accessed, and assessed. "I would say that the manager has more ways to check if you are doing efficiently. Now you have to log whatever you have done for the day to the computer, and the manager can easily access that," said a clerk at an IT firm.

The surveillance system not only identifies the absence of work or slow performance, but also stops and prevents illegitimate uses of the company's computer. Downloading large files for personal use or surfing the Internet for pornographic materials are instances that fall under most companies' surveillance: "If you are using the Internet to play music, it takes a lot of bandwidth out of mission-critical operations that the company needs. We filter things like that. We don't really give you a choice to download MP3 files or something like that, or video files." What is a legitimate use of the company's IT and what is not, however can be a matter of tension between workers and management, because the sort of practices that never were questioned in the traditional office may suddenly be prohibited in the digital office. One city worker asked,

How much is the city entitled to look at somebody's stuff and see if the people are breaking the laws if they are looking at things they shouldn't look at? Are they using the e-mail to buy things? I think everybody does. I'm not sure how much of that goes on, but it's just like using a phone. Yes, if my daughter is sick: am I going to call her at home and see how she is? Yes. Is that part of my job for the city? How much of that are we allowing to do and how much should we do and where is the line? What's proper use of city facilities and what's not?

With the telephone, it is necessary to ask for permission to use it for long distance calls because of the costs involved, but with the Internet there is no cost involved. It is clear that the same policies may not be transferred from the pre-Internet era to the Internet era. New rules for the digital office must be tailored to this specific genre of working environment.

The pace of digital work

As we have seen was the case with telecommuters who work outside the office, some office workers have remarked that with IT, the pace of work in the office has changed, that the work is done faster than before and that more output is requested by management. The microcomputer has led to an acceleration of the flow of work. Because the worker receives work from both cyberspace and the traditional office space, he or she is compelled to work in both worlds, which amounts to pressure to accomplish more. A clerical worker in San Francisco said,

> I think that we are clearly a lot more productive. We can produce a lot more much faster. It has not meant at all that the work has shrunk. The work has expanded much faster than the productivity. We are doing so much more in terms of thinking, trying to develop more stuff, and inventing new projects. Once we finish one project, there are five more waiting. We can do them faster, but it is exponential. The faster the computer gets, the more we are doing, the more paper we are generating, which is even more amazing, and the expectations are rising.

The constant on-line communication between the central workplace and telecommuters often brings about the mixed identity of an office that is in part traditional, but that has a digitized component. Telecommuters are thus a major aspect in the digitization of the office. One may speak of the routinization of virtualization through the work of telecommuters. One informant conveyed the mixed identity of her insurance office when she noted,

> There is already someone in the office working from home because she had twins. . . . We communicate with her through phone or by e-mail. Since she is home twenty-four hours a day—it is not a problem to communicate. . . . If we need anything, if our books don't match or we don't balance in our money, we can always give her a call and give her a date of service and see what insurance did or did not pay or whether we need to bill the patient or not.

As we have also seen in the discussion of telecommuting, because cyberspace is accessible from anywhere, including the home, some workers find themselves being constantly at work, not because they are paid to do so, but because they cannot refrain themselves from being on-line.

There is a very serious disadvantage for people like me who have a predisposition to be a workaholic. I sometimes lose myself too much in my work. Something starts to fascinate me or just makes me anxious, and I go for it, and since I don't have children, there is nothing to bring me back to real life, and I keep working into the wee hours of the night. I keep working and working, and it catches up to me sometimes, and I have the sense of being so exhausted and tired. Sometimes I have to have the courage to push back and tell them that they are loading too much on me and that I cannot handle this. People are accustomed to the fact that we take these projects, we just do them. It requires a skill to be able to put boundaries around your work and really manage your time. There are some people that are very good at that. For me, it is sometimes a problem. (A secretary in a state government office)

People say that the computer workday is very stressful. Much physical stress is involved in working on computers. Workers complain about stress on their arms and their eyes. There is psychological stress as well. Workers complain that they cannot work in peace because someone is always e-mailing them something. Someone's problem is always on the table because of e-mail. Even if they do not want to deal with it, someone has already invaded their privacy and troubled their work with their problems. Even if a worker chooses not to answer an e-mail immediately, he or she feels it will have to be answered later. Once the e-mail is delivered, a decision must be made whether or not to act on it.

The virtual world thus is continually affecting the real in a multitude of ways in the digital office. A manager complains about the amount of paper that is being used because of the computer. He sees the virtual as leading to the real for the full realization of virtual communication.

I do have an opinion on how much paper is produced by computers.... I don't think that it is saving any paper at all. I think that an awful lot of people have trouble reading documents on a monitor screen, and I think they just print it out. When they are done reading it, they just throw it away or recycle it. I think there's way much more paper being used now than there ever was before.

What happens when the computers break down?

The ways in which the virtual affects the real in the digital office become particularly apparent when the hardware that supports the virtual component breaks down. Digitization has brought a new dimension of chaos to the office because of the dependence of workers on the computer to carry out their work: processing documents, editing and correcting reports, retrieving files, interacting with coworkers and management, contacting clients—the list goes on. Although digitization makes people more efficient, it creates a chaotic situation when the computer is down. A number of digital workers belonging to different firms were asked to provide their assessment of this issue.

> My sister works in the office. She is responsible for referrals and authorizations for patients. Her work is strictly on the Internet. If the Internet goes down, everything just messes up. We communicate through the Internet with other doctors' offices and that's how we get patients to other doctors. Sometimes people will need to see another doctor, and for the insurance to pay for it, they need to have a referral. If the Internet goes down, we are unable to get the referral to the other office, and it is just complete chaos. (A hospital worker in San Francisco)

In firms that have backup power supplies in case the electricity goes out for a while, another mixed type of situation prevails. During the rolling blackouts in 2001 that affected Silicon Valley, workers had the issue on their minds and dealt with it in different ways. This programmer of Asian background relates his observation in this fashion:

> That actually happened last Thursday. I was actually curious about that because I was sitting there listening, and I heard a lot of people punching on the keyboard, and I was wondering what they were doing. I walked around and noticed a lot of people e-mailing, surfing the Web, and someone was instant messaging with a friend. The majority of people were still sitting around, talking to each other, waiting for the servers to come back up. A couple of people decided that it was a good time to run errands, so they slipped out. It certainly halts people who are coding at that time.

Some firms have developed a routine to deal with a system breakdown. Managers, in those circumstances, let people do as they please, depending on the amount of time that is needed before the system can return to normal.

> "This company is really good about that," one informant told me. "A lot of common sense goes into it. They will typically give us an estimated time of when the servers will come back up. The individual

can judge if they have time to go or not. If there are projects due or deadlines, and it is beyond your control, it's totally understood."

A manager who was at once in the midst of a breakdown felt that it was a chaotic and stressful moment she had to endure because there were so many workers who depended on her leadership at a moment when she was not in control of anything. She was herself dependent on the technical staff to bring the servers back and running.

If the computers were down, it was considered to be something really bad. The people who were impacted by it felt as if their tools were taken away, but the managers who are responsible for this, for the breakdowns or the operations of it, for them it was a major problem. They would not take it lightly. It was a total or complete emergency for them. Everything needed to stop for them until it was fixed. There was much apology afterward.

In offices where a large amount of work is done via word processing, a network breakdown may not cause work to stop, because the bulk of the work is probably not dependent on networks and can still be done. However, such a situation may generate more face-to-face interaction among workers and may require the reshuffling of the daily routine. A clerical worker in San Francisco said,

First of all, I cannot check my e-mail. The inbox would not be updated, so I would not bother checking that. I can continue on my work because most of my work is on my local machine, so I don't have to worry about accessing the network. I can connect to my local database and continue my work. I can always check in my work after the server is up. I think I can pretty much do what I have been doing. One thing is that if communication is down, I would talk to my manager more often. I would go to her desk more often to see what she needs to do.

In some instances, workers are allowed to go back home or do errands when their work depends on the running of the server. "It happened once. We took off. It is a consulting company. Everything is dependent on the network connection. We do all the research on the Internet, so all of us took off," said a technician in Silicon Valley.

Other times, people hang around until the server is fixed. Sometimes they are required to stay put by management. But if after a while the problem is not solved, management may give them a choice either to stay or go home.

The other day, for example, we had a PG&E problem. I think it happened last week at around 10:00 A.M. Of course, we all hoped that it was going to come up in an hour. At 10:00 A.M., everyone went outside, talked and gossiped, and did whatever people normally do in a circumstance like that. By lunchtime, we all went to lunch in the dark. By one o'clock, I left. I told most of my people to go home, because there was nothing to do. People were getting frustrated—they had things to do, and you can sense the frustration. I said, at least to my folks, that they could go home. There was no reason to stay here. I left. (A staff person at City Hall San Francisco)

Some managers tend to be creative when such a situation occurs, and workers may inform management about their ability to help in other domains until the server problem is solved. Since these professionals have deadlines to meet, they can decide on their own how they want to manage their time. A manager at an IT firm said,

If a system breaks down, and it is your system, which happens sometimes, or a hard drive just gives up or dies, but the person still has deliveries to make, most likely, whenever it happens they will come to me and tell me, after calling tech support. It is frustrating on the part of those folks. You may ask them to do something else. Most of my people are technical professionals. They do not just croak or anything like that. They are professionals, programmers, Web designers, IT professionals. If they can't do their work, most of them will go home and take off while the thing is being fixed. I wouldn't question them. They know I trust them. They know what I expect from them, and that is the key. If they want, they might decide to help colleagues or do something else. If you don't have your computer up and running, you are really in deep trouble. You feel completely lost. Hopefully, those things don't happen too often.

In the case of electricity failure, workers do whatever they can that do not require the use of the computer.

Usually the emergency generator goes on and it only lasts for a minute or two. For the sake of addressing the point, I think that people have work that they can do without electricity. Most people have what they call "rainy day work" set aside. They can simply get out a pencil and paper and do work that they have, assuming there is enough light here to do even that. (A staff person in Silicon Valley)

Such a situation provides an opportunity to rearrange one's schedule. If one goes back home, one may have to return later or the following morning to complete work that must meet a deadline. The schedule of the worker is affected, but not necessarily the performance of the firm. "If you have things to do, certain deliverables and the electricity goes out, you still have to do it. We don't tell people that, but it is understood. That's what creates the frustration," said a cyberworker.

In firms where some individuals use the computers and others do not, it is only those who do who are affected by the system breakdown. Such individuals may simply revert to the old ways to pursue their work. The breakdown simply re-traditionalizes the firm for a short period of time, thereby undoing its mixed form. These crisis moments upgrade the traditional modus operandi of the firm. "There is a lot of work not related to the computer that you still can do.... We can do it by hand. A lot of people are still sticking to the old. Especially the older people don't want to go to the computer," said one secretary.

If there is a system breakdown in a headquarters that shares files with subsidiary offices, then the subsidiaries are called upon to do what the people in the central office cannot do.

It was chaos. We were doing five or six jobs at the same time. We were answering phones, setting up appointments, helping patients into the office. Since usually we have a breakup of the doctors— I said that some doctors are located in the central office and some are at the others—the appointments are broken up as well. People who want appointments for a doctor in Mill Valley will call that office, versus a patient who wants an appointment in the central office, who will call the Pacific Heights office. When the computer system goes down, we make appointments for everyone. Instead of having ten incoming calls at the same time, we had twenty or thirty. Instead of having five to ten patients who wanted to be fit in that day, we had twenty-five or thirty patients who wanted to be fit in on that day. Our days were longer. Doctors had to work extra hours. The phone was ringing constantly off the hook. The paperwork was just enormous. Our own work, for example—I did not have a chance to touch billing that week because I was focusing on someone else's job, because we were short-staffed at the time. I was busy helping other people catch up with their stuff, so that my work load was starting to increase. Once that week was over, we had to come in and catch up with our stuff. It just made everything more hectic and longer. (A hospital staff worker in San Francisco)

The shifting from computer work to work done by hand necessarily slows down the process, because the traditional way is more time-consuming and less efficient. It also adds more labor time, since what has been written by hand may have to be entered in the computer files.

When the system is down, we are all stressed. My manager has to do everything she does on the Internet by hand. She has to write the referrals out by hand, mail and fax a copy of it to the other doctor's office. She has to fax it to the insurance company and mail a copy to the patient. For example, in the day, she can do two hundred referrals on the Internet. If the system is down, she will only be able to do fifty a day by hand. (A secretary at a hospital in San Francisco)

Some workers distinguish short breakdowns that last up to one hour from those that may take an entire morning or day. Of course, the strategies for coping with these different situations will be different. In any case, however, the return to one's routine requires compensating for lost time, even though the worker is not at fault for such a problem.

It depends how bad the system is when it goes down. Lately, we have been having a lot of the system just shutting down or our computers have been down. We have two offices, one in the Pacific Heights area and another in Mill Valley. In Mill Valley, the whole computer system has been down, so it has been our job to take care of their business as well. While we are taking care of their business by computers, they still have to take appointments by hand, because we use the computers to do that, too. There is always a backup system, but it always takes longer. (A hospital staff person in San Francisco)

I was curious to find out if the public sector follows the same routine as private firms when computer breakdowns occur. An informant from one of the city halls in Silicon Valley spoke of the experience of her building when an electric failure prevented them from pursuing their work.

But we did have one big outage in December, maybe it was two years ago. And the whole city experienced it. It was something that happened with PG&E down on the Peninsula. And what happened was, first of all, we couldn't stay in the building, because we don't own this particular building, and the landlords wanted us to leave for safety issues because all the lights were out and the backup lights went out. So it was virtually dark in here and really cold out. So we were all waiting out in the street so we could get back in. Nobody knew, of course. Some of us did stay and went out and came back after the power was back on. But really that's been the only experience we've had in that. It hasn't been an issue.

The phenomenon of computer breakdown shows the high level of vulnerability of the digital office in relation to the traditional office. It further shows how the traditional office continues to serve as a backup when the digital office cannot operate because of mechanical failure.

The transformative role of IT

The IT revolution also has transformed the office in ways that go beyond the development of new forms of surveillance, the increased pace of office life, and the disruption of the real component of the office by events such as breakdowns in the virtual component. The transformative role of IT also can be detected in broader changes in the corporate culture of the digitized office, in the increasing need for virtual management at a distance, in the loss of control by management over the space and time of work, and in what may be the most significant trend in the long run, the tendency of digitization to promote globalization.

Corporate culture

Perhaps the most pervasive areas where IT is transformative are in the ways in which telecommuting changes the operational structure of the firm: first, because different units are affected differently; and second, because in each unit not everyone is allowed to telecommute. What is being produced in the telecommuting units is a corporate culture that is nomadic in contrast to the sedentary corporate culture of the traditional and modern office.

The multiple ecologies of the firm are emphasized and forced to interact by telecommuting. Multiple ecologies are created because of diverse telecommuting practices. For example, each unit may develop its own telecommuting programs. As we have seen, some units may allow workers to telecommute on a full-time basis, others only for specific projects, and still others on a part-time basis. When this experimentation is carried out in a unit, the other units are also undergoing some form of adjustment brought about by the fact they must interact with the telecommuters. In other words, telecommuting in one unit may affect other units, as well, because nontelecommuters must engage in virtual interaction in order to interact with telecommuters. Furthermore, in the telecommuting units themselves, not everyone is allowed to participate. Those who are not allowed to telecommute must adjust to the activities of those who are allowed. They are participating in a nomadic culture even though they are themselves sedentary. Telecommuting requires or implies the redefinition of everyone's job description.

The transformation of corporate culture by IT is also seen in the transformation of relations between the headquarters and the various sites where telecommuting occurs—satellites or subsidiary offices, drop-in centers, homes, and mobile workplaces. As IT fragments the infrastructure of the digital office, the concept of a "headquarters" itself changes. In Silicon Valley, the headquarters often is conceived of as the "corporate campus," for example in the case of larger firms such as Sun Microsystems, Cisco Systems, and Microsoft.[15]

> The concept of campus is really a set of buildings. For instance, where we are, which is the headquarters of the corporation, we have, I believe, a campus consisting of twelve buildings with three cafeterias. . . . The word "campus" probably derives from the university concept as it simulates academic activities found on any university campus. . . . We go to classes every day. I have classes scheduled every day of my work. These are technical classes. We have training on everything, human resources, learning to behave, learning how to write or read better English, learning a different language, and technical training. Then we give you certificates if you pass. (A manager in an IT firm in Silicon Valley)

This reconceptualization of the corporate headquarters as a "campus" reflects a somewhat less stratified, more diverse, and less industrialized conception of the contemporary workplace and the corporate culture of the firm. In this environment, the headquarters is seen as reminiscent of a university campus. It refers to a site with several buildings where new employees are socialized in the ways of the corporation. The firm is identified with a specific site. One speaks of the "Cisco campus" or the "Microsoft campus." It also emphasizes that teaching and research take place there and lead to some kind of formal recognition, such as a diploma or new product discoveries. Employees attend classes there to enhance their performances on the job. In addition, it implicitly valorizes the interactive social life among employees that shapes their distinct identity as part of the same corporation and that distinguishes them from other industrial groups. And finally, it projects an academic image to attract college graduates and ease their transition to industrial labor.

Virtual management at a distance

IT requires that management be done at distance. Managing at a distance means managing the workforce not just at the workplace, but also outside the workplace. It is not simply enough to learn how to manage at a distance, it is also important to learn how to coordinate the labor produced at the workplace with the labor produced elsewhere.

In the traditional workplace, the contiguousness of space makes it possible for management to achieve employee efficiency via surveillance and control. In the virtual domain, however, surveillance and control cannot be done in the old-fashioned way. As we have seen, control is often replaced by trust and surveillance may be done sporadically electronically, but has its limitations.

Virtuality thus has caused a redefinition of the job of the manager and brings a new dynamic in the authority structure of the office. The hierarchical structure that was prevalent in the traditional office is being replaced by a centrarchy in the digital office, and the manager has progressed from one who controls knowledge and choreographs the employees' work to achieve a specific outcome to one who coordinates diverse sources of outputs because he or she does not control or understand the specialized knowledge generated by subalterns.

This involves not simply more work for the manager as he or she moves from face-to-face interaction to virtual interaction, but also longer hours to accommodate telecommuters. More IT learning is called for in order to keep up with the pace of the production of specialized knowledge by subaltern workers such as programmers.

Flexible space and time

Although a few people, such as the receptionist and managers, maintain their offices on-site, as we have seen, with telecommuting there is a reduction in the space used in the office. As more workers work at home, there is less need to use their cubicles. This free space requires the organization of use.

Some workers may no longer have a special office, but occupy whatever office is available when they show up. They usually sit wherever they can when they come back, wherever there is a free computer. A telecommuter said,

> I am one that does not have a telephone. When I come into the office, I scout for an empty cube. I am allowed to take any empty cube that's available, and I use that phone, even though I don't have a voice mail, to make outgoing calls. If I am here during the day, I can tell people to call me at a certain number, and that's my number for the day.

Virtuality thus makes place irrelevant to the production of output. Even in the office, one can enter virtuality anywhere there is a computer or a plug. The order of space is not as fixed as it once was. This space is always being made and unmade—sometimes without the consent of management. The spatial order of the office infrastructure was created by management to carry out a specific mission or goal. In the digital office, management loses control over that space of interaction.

As we have seen, with the fragmentation of the workforce of the digital office, management loses its traditional control over the time of work, as well. Time no longer is marked out by a schedule that regiments the life of the worker from the moment of arrival at the centralized office until the moment of departure. The elasticity of the office workday creates shifts that expand the time of the workday. It creates an unpredictable population density as people are available on-line and off-line. The digital office juxtaposes the logic of regimented work with the regime of unregimented work, telecommuters with nontelecommuters, and physical presence with virtual presence.

Globalization

When the digital office fragments into one or more entities that are virtual or may become virtual, the virtual component of the digital office tends to emphasize the possibilities of interactions not previously available to the traditional firm. IT tends to give the firm a more global orientation. An office may become a global entity even if not all units are involved in global connections. A firm may be globally connected because of the global profile of one of its units, and not its entire network of units. The globalization of the outlook of the firm thus is a tendency inherent in IT.

The office has been slowly transformed by the use of telecommunications, beginning with the ordinary telephone, then the facsimile, voice mail, and now the microcomputer. These devices have expanded the spatial sphere of the modern office and contributed to the globalization of its undertakings. They contribute to the reshaping of the space of interaction of the firm, the physical form of the office, and to the global expansion of the office. The office has become a node in a global network of transactional relations.

However, the traditional office may be global only in its virtual manifestation, and not in its traditional manifestation. Some corporations have a global architecture because of the physical locations of their offices, the kinds of activities undertaken there, and the equipment found there. A computer technician said,

We are in thirty-five countries as a corporation. We are in most of the states like New Jersey, Texas, and Oregon. These places are what I mainly call sales offices. We have the corporation here in Milpitas; then we have what is called the hubs, major hubs, which are in Colorado Springs, Ireland, and Singapore. Those are major places, which are duplications of our headquarters in regard to technical resources and IT-related resources and tools.

In its physical setting, the office may be stratified in terms of status, expertise, or functions, but this stratification cannot be transferred to the digital office, since it tends to transcend this geographical specificity. The result can be a mixing of the global and local in which the digital office is the transitional component between the two and in which the traditional office is inhabited by pockets of transitional digital offices that are globalized and globalizing. In Silicon Valley, where the majority of those who participate in digital offices are also employees of brick-and-mortar enterprises, workers move back and forth from the virtual to the real and from the local to the global. Some spend more time interacting physically with local folks, while others spend more with employees in distant locations. A manager of an IT firm said,

In Europe, we have branches in France, Germany, Switzerland, England. On average, I spend more time interacting with the local people than with the others. Besides conference calling, we interact primarily by e-mail. E-mail is really our life blood, e-mail and voice mail. If there is something to be done, you can drop someone a voice mail or write an e-mail, or both. Then they will get back to you. We are able to communicate effectively and extensively in order to get things done.

These globalizing tendencies produce the variable geometry of global interactive virtual time. For example, global time is affected by local time. Although the operation of the digital office can be done irrespective of the time zones, in practice, for some interactive virtual communication, at least, one must pay attention to time. So we have a global process that penetrates time zones and that places international actors in different temporal situations. The scheduling of virtual interactive time cannot be done in a temporal vacuum. An engineer at Quantum said,

Because I am closer to work, I can go to headquarters. If you were in New York, or some place else, we also have a collaboration in which we rent videoconferencing with AT&T and you can go to an AT&T office close to you and do it. You don't have to go to a Quantum site to do it. The reverse is true if you deal with APAC. I know they have conference calls at least once a week with Europe and APAC. I do most of my conference calls with Europe at home at 7:00 or 7:30 A.M. If it is video conferencing, which is different, I have to go somewhere. I will either have to go to my office or go home and come back. If there is an audio conference, I will most likely do it at home. Before I go to dinner, I will do my conference call with APAC.

Globality not only mixes global time with local time, but also global inter-action with local time and local interaction with global time: "I have two days with conference calls. One day is for Europe, normally on Wednesday, which I usually do pretty early in the morning," said a manager.

Because it must occur across time zones, global interaction often becomes a succession of time shifts in the production of an outcome. An individual works on a project, e-mails it to a team member before he goes to bed, and receives the new product in the morning, after the other person had worked on it during the interim period.

Basically, you are able to work around the clock, if you are e-mailing or something like that. You are in constant communication with what's going on with your group members. Should there be a team in a different time region, you are able to work around the clock. We have that at Sun. We have a team in the U.S. working with a team in India. A lot of times there is a lot of interaction going on there. Everyone can access the same files around the clock. (A male engineer at Sun Microsystems)

The deployment of virtual global interaction has different shapes depending on goals pursued from the unit level to a much larger universe. This has an elastic or flexible composition.

We try to minimize video or audio conference calling, because as a courtesy, we would rather not have people come early or late. We have certain conference calling on a weekly basis, but the bulk of the people—unless it is an all-hands meeting, which gathers the entire IT organization from a world-wide perspective—what we try to do, and this is normally once a month, is to gather everyone in the U.S. and combine them with Europe. It's not that bad. Everyone can make the sacrifice and we'll have something separate with APAC at another time. (A manager at Quantum)

The digital office is seldom without physical interaction, however. In most of the cases studied here, some form of physical or face-to-face interaction takes place at some point. This happens sometimes in the beginning of the project, or toward the end of it to ensure that the whole thing is coherent. Sometimes a manager visits the troops wherever they might be to bring a human element to the process.

In my case, because of my job, you have people throughout the enterprise, so it is good to establish that face contact, the human bonding. When you are far away, you cannot really do things too much in the context of the U.S. You are a global firm and you have people that work for you all over the place. So being able to see what's going on, listening to them once in a while, and also being able to establish a stronger relationship with your business users are really key factors to keep in mind. (A manager at Quantum)

In addition, not all digitized firms are routinely engaged in global transactions. Digitization does not mean ipso facto globalization. For such firms, global interactions are incidental because the kind of work they do implies more local interaction. "We are local government. Occasionally, we have taxpayers that live out of state or out of the country and occasionally we do have to contact them, but it is not the rule. Usually the taxpayers are within the county, or within the Bay Area. We are not very global," said a state government manager.

Some firms are global by entropy. They are not fully engaged in transnational interaction to sustain their undertakings, but rather open a window to the world so that global actors can access whatever they have to offer. "We have a virtual library where we put out our materials. Not as much is in it as we would like, but we have various folders in our servers that people can open up and research," said a manager in Silicon Valley.

Conclusion

The digital office is a privileged site that unveils the extent of the ramifications of the transformations being wrought by the information revolution. It shows how place has become less central than space, and it indicates the momentous changes in the workplace brought about by IT: mobility and flexibility of work sites and the globalization that the Internet makes possible. The digital office has multiple shapes, from the modern digitized type to the mainly virtual form. In some instances, it is a traditional office with virtual components and is being transformed or reinforced by IT, while in other cases it does not operate out of a central, formal workplace at all. Thus the digital office seldom displays a permanent shape because its configuration varies with participants and with time. In addition, its shape is protean because the virtual and nonvirtual components of the digital office are so integrated that people move from one to the other without being aware that they are shifting their mode of operation.

Virtuality provides an alternative mode of social interaction and has become a major variable for social and global integration. IT has contributed to the remaking of the dynamics of the digitized office because of the fluidity of the transnational relations it nurtures, the new paths of communication it sustains inside and outside the central workplace, and the flexibility and mobility it affords digital workers.

4
Virtual City Hall: The Governance of Local E-Government

The study of the digital city would be incomplete without an analysis of the governance of a virtual city hall, including its digital management and its relations with the urban citizenry. City hall as the visible face of government at the local level is an important locus of study that can help us understand how virtuality and globalization are inscribed in this local site of global practice. One informant noted,

> There are three different phases to e-government. One is just the putting up of static information on the Web page. Almost every government is at that point. I think we are limited by bandwidth issues at this point, but I definitely think it weighs towards "we are all putting information out there, help yourself to it." It tends towards the transparency of the government and it starts to move away from "OK, we only work from 8 to 5." The second phase is putting up transaction and e-commerce sites. For example, we have on-line filing of business taxes, registration payment on-line, other taxes, and what not. I think that there is another stage to e-government, which is to fundamentally change the way we do business. Right now, I think that most of the use of the Web mirrors the hierarchical structure, and I think that the real power of the Internet is to break down those structures.... Instead of being tempted by putting a Web interface on an existing process, this should be an opportunity for the government to look at the ways of reengineering the process.

The study of the effect of IT on city hall has been carried out on various levels: with a focus on the role of city Web sites in providing information to the citizenry, the enhancement of participatory democracy through on-line interaction of city employees with urban residents, and the provision and administration of digital services to the local community.[1]

Web sites both provide public information to residents that have access to the Internet and also hide controversial documents from them. Privacy concerns and potential legal challenges have led city officials to select the kinds of materials they deem necessary and safe to place on the Web. Davis[2] argues that "not only are public officials placing on the Net favorable material about themselves, but they are also attempting to restrict access to other bits of information they don't wish the public to have." However, Mansell and Steinmueller[3] state that "the existence of Web sites provides little insight into the range of organizational dynamics that underpins the new virtual community strategies. It merely points to the probable existence of such dynamics."

Much effort has been expended to show that the use of the Internet by city hall provides a new avenue for facilitating democratic practices.[4] Some analysts see it as a tool for the strengthening of democracy, for establishing electronic campaigns, for processing digital voting, for monitoring performances, for regulating behaviors and controlling practices at a distance, and for expanding the practices of participatory democracy in the public sphere in general.[5] In contrast, the Internet is also seen by other observers as a hindrance to participatory democracy. For example, Richard Davis[6] argues that "one way the Internet may actually reduce public participation is through its requirement of technological competence in order to become involved in public opinion expression or even voting." For still other commentators, "computing has been a politically conservative technological innovation" because "the primary political effect of these information systems is to reinforce existing patterns of power and influence within the government."[7]

Some studies argue that the use of the Internet by city hall enhances and facilitates the administration of city services by making them available on-line, while others stress that it is a tool used by city officials to entice foreign business to invest and international tourists to visit the city.[8] As Mansell and Steinmueller[9] have found, "some administrations are interested in providing access to municipal services using the Internet, including the potential to apply for permits, query municipal databases… and provide information about the availability and conditions of municipal services of all types." They further argue that "a major driving force in the development of municipal Web sites is the widespread belief of public administrations that they should take responsibility for representing their communities to the rest of the world in ways that reflect the diversity of local social and cultural resources." In this way, the use of the digitization of city hall is seen as a possible engine of growth and as a mechanism that further sustains the globalization of the city.[10] Instead of following these approaches, this chapter explains the social transformation of city hall brought about by the creation of a virtual component, a virtual city hall. After a brief history of the virtualization of city hall, it examines how the IT team and its Webmasters have become important players in the organizational politics of the city hall and the digital city. They help represent city hall and its policies to both the citizenry and the organization, and thus are responsible for the appearance of the digital city in cyberspace. The chapter examines the content and structure of the digital city on the Web as represented by the digital city hall. Digitization has allowed city hall both to improve the access of citizens to their government and to shield information from the citizenry in new ways, and the chapter examines the ways in which IT has transformed the communications between the digital city hall and the citizens of the digital city. It also explores the limitations of the Web for the implementation of democratic politics. Finally, it examines the globalization of city hall and explains how virtualization is a central factor in that process.

A history of a virtual city hall

The history of the process of digitization of one city hall in the metropolitan Bay Area sheds light on the evolving culture of the institution and explains how some of the IT problems the institution is facing can be traced back to that earlier period of its formation. The introduction of the computer in the workplace was a slow process and done on a step-by-step basis, partly because staff training was selective, partly because the microcomputer was not made available to all the employees, and partly because of the diversity of software used. The history of the digitization of city hall thus is in synergy with the history of the microcomputer itself, at least the history of its availability to the public. When the city started using its mainframe, and training its employees for digital work, it was not clear that the microcomputer—or for that matter, the Internet—was going to be soon made available to the public.

An employee who has played a key role in the implementation of city hall's IT policies recalls the phases in the evolution of the digitization of city hall. She does not speak as an observer, but as someone who has participated in every phase of the process. In other words, this history is told by an insider who reflects on what her team has accomplished thus far.

Before we were a department, we were a little section in the controller's office, a little information division of the controller till not that long ago. It wasn't until maybe ten years ago. And we had the mainframe, that's what gave us control. It's when we had one computer and we had the computer—we were the high priestess of the computer, and you couldn't do any computing except to go through us. We were the intermediaries, and that gave us a measure of control de facto, irrespective of what anyone might want to do.

But then, PCs came along, and we suddenly realized that people felt empowered. Like any place, people like that. You want to have your own PC at your own desk. Even if it is less efficient. You don't want to have to be a slave to a big computer. Everyone wants control. That happens at a bigger level—even the departments feel like they want to own their own system, even if it's on the mainframe—you make a point that it belongs to you. It's your data.

In the city, since the departments are so loosely configured originally, it's been particularly hard, in my opinion, to impose—and they started buying their computers independently. Then we came along with COIT—and its predecessor, the Electronic Information Steering Committee—and tried to impose standards.

I was here when we first did the survey, trying to get things— things were out of control. We did a survey of all the different kinds of hardware about fifteen to twenty years ago, and we had a 147 different brands of equipment. And then we said, "We need a standard." So we had Wang chosen as the midrange standard, as the standard database. At one point it looked like midranges were going to go away. Later on, nothing but the client server, maybe the mainframe would go on, and we'd standardize. And we are still trying to standardize. We've had several generations of this. It's not going to happen. The reason that it's difficult is that the standards came along long after everyone was already doing their own thing, and people like local control.

The virtualization of city hall evolved as a result of its adjustment to the ongoing digitization of the world and the need to synchronize the delivery of its services with the expectations of the local population. One informant describes the trials and tribulations of the early period of computer use by city employees:

I am going back to 1994 in that time frame. The intent was that we are going to try out this thing called the Web. We are going to dabble in it and see if it has any relative value. And once government employees got their feet wet, they were all of a sudden in the pond.

The formal digitization of city hall required that, after a period of trials and errors, a new administrative structure be put in place to coordinate this effort. The city at first appointed an advisory commission composed of insider managers and outsider technicians to make recommendations on how to proceed with the digitalization of its operations. In that sense, once the decision was made to virtualize aspects of the workload of employees, digitization was planned ahead of time and did not come about in a haphazard manner. However, since departments were left with the freedom to experiment with new software and hardware that met their particular computing needs, the administrative process overall was not in perfect synchronization with the implementation process in particular situations.

With the production of IT policies, a new administrative supervisory structure emerged that oversees the process and ensures its smooth deployment. An external committee evaluates performances and makes policy recommendations, and an internal committee serves as an advisory board to the mayor's office, the board of supervisors, and to the city hall telecommunications and information services. While the telecommunications unit coordinates the technical aspects of the IT infrastructure for the whole operation of city hall, the mayor's office and the board of supervisors each have their own IT unit and their own political agenda for posting things on the Web. The existence of these polar IT entities contributes to the fragmentation of the digital infrastructure because of their different orientations, agendas, and administrative goals.

Coordination by telecommunications and information services does not mean lateral integration of software and vertical control, but rather insures the interoperability of the system. Control still remains in the hands of each agency, which explains the diversity of the software used, policies on posting, access to materials, and the visual presentation of information.

Perhaps what makes the digital experiment unique was that early on, the so-called "Sunshine Ordinances"[11] inscribed the availability of documents on the Net as one of the tenets of the city's public policy. City hall was mandated by this ordinance to provide information on-line to the public and to ensure that the implementation of new applications would be accompanied by public access, so that the population may scrutinize what is being done, e-mail their comments, or request services. The ordinance does not describe in detail what digitization would entail in its diverse forms, but rather concentrates on the politics of access. Not only would people be able to read city documents on the Net, but services would also be provided on-line, and overall this would make the affairs of the city more transparent for citizens' scrutiny.

As might be expected, the decision to put things on the Web initially met with opposition. As one informant put it, "We could not be too burdensome in the beginning because there was resistance to it. I knew this was going to be a hated project." Some resistance stemmed from the prospect of making sensitive information available for public scrutiny, and some from the work required not only to post, but also to archive, to order, and to position the information.

Because the various departments were not provided with instructions on how to implement their IT programs when city hall made the decision to enter the virtual sphere, each unit developed its own way of interacting with its own public and strategies to meet the expected desires of that public. In the process, some departments began to feel that they were losing their autonomy, thanks to links with other departments and the ease with which the public can access their information—they felt that they could no longer "possess" their materials. Conversely, other departments were to become more autonomous because they have their own constituencies and are more likely to interact with them than with other departments.

> We were having a problem this morning we were discussing. One of the departments sees itself as its own entity. It doesn't even want to backlink its Web site to the rest of CitySpan. [They say:] "People come to this department and they don't really care that it's part of the city government. They come to us for what we do." And they don't want anyone to know they are part of city government. It's absurd to me. But we're running into that—over and over. (A City Hall employee)

As we have seen throughout our examination of the digital city, digitization tends to create new constellations and associations, but it also fosters a significant amount of fragmentation.

Although there was an ongoing discussion among the administrative staff to ensure some form of standardization, in practice, because departments were left with the freedom to experiment as they pleased with new software, even that goal has not been attained. The desire of the IT staff for standardization could not be fulfilled because of market pressure and also because of the way the purchase of software drove the purchase of hardware. Since departments buy software that suits their needs, the process of standardization in this environment could not be pursued from the top or from any specific position in this networking architecture: "Now that there's off-the-shelf software, you buy the package. When you buy the package, you buy the hardware to support the package. So we've got a proliferation of midrange equipment. And we're just cramming it into the room, with the mainframe. And my hopes of ever standardizing have gone out the window a long time ago," said an IT technician.

The role of the IT staff has been transformed somewhat over the years because of the availability of ready-made software. Since this costs less and since departments have different needs, and hence different hardware, the role of the IT staff has shifted from programming to ensuring the smoothness of connectivity, that is, to making sure that the computers are able to speak to each other in order to facilitate office interaction. The goal is no longer to achieve homogeneity of hardware and software at city hall, but rather to ensure their interoperability so that the computers can interface. As an informant puts it, "the real challenge is to get everything talking to each other, but not to get everyone using the same thing."

When the research for this book was undertaken in 2000, the city was about to implement a unifying policy so that coordination of the various units with different computer systems could bring about some form of interoperability or at least resolve some computer-interface problems.

But all of a sudden, everything's gotta go. Many government entities, including San Francisco, are taking a step back right now. We're in the process of hiring, what we're calling a citizen technology manager, which will be responsible for our Web site, our e-government initiatives, and our cable TV station. And the intent is that we will be bringing together a unit; we will be establishing those policies, particularly in the e-government arena, and we'll be codifying many things that are kind of informal at the moment. (A female manager at City Hall)

While most people think that the microcomputer has led to more decentralization because of the autonomy it provides its users, people at city hall believe it has created more centralization within the larger decentralization scheme. It has also created new power centers because it has elevated the status of the IT team and key digital workers. They have become power brokers, because theirs is a key unit that links all the units to each other.

The micropolitics of city hall's Web sites

Web sites constitute one locus where the micropolitics of city hall as an institution is played out because Web sites empower some individuals, undermine others, and reposition still others. Because of their central position as a result of the information-communications system they control, the Webmaster team has become an alternative power center vis-à-vis the formal power center. Politics is waged at two levels to ensure that the Web site projects accurately reflect the identity of each department and that its structural role in comparison to other units is not overshadowed.

The design of the Web page that is supposed to project the identity of the city is done in different ways throughout the Bay Area. Rarely is it the outcome of discussion and input from all concerned employees. This is due to the fact that people may not have clear ideas to offer or simply because this is supposed to be someone else's job. Such input is sometimes provided when the right incentive is given: "When we did a first draft of the Web site and we put it up, we have about fourteen people in our department, and I sent it out to them, and I proposed to give a gift certificate to all the people who offered feedback. It was just a drawing to get people interested in it. I got some good responses," said one manager.

Strategies used in the creation and maintenance of a city Web site include hiring an outside expert to be in charge of this venture or recruiting someone from another department with the right expertise to do it. Of course, with job done in-house, the city may save money, and that's often an incentive to proceed in this fashion.

The role of the IT staff is to advise the units on how to present their material to be posted. This constitutes a major form of virtual interaction between the IT staff and the other departments. The Webmasters may influence the item before it reaches them and therefore are not obliged to edit it at a later stage. The advice is not so much about content, but rather about designing or redesigning a Web site, for example to make it more attractive, more colorful, and friendlier to the public. Such a task may be undertaken to project a certain perception of the department, to make things more accessible to the public, and ultimately to make city bureaucracy more efficient.

Since the content of the items is not prepared by the Webmasters, the relations between the IT department and other departments are not always harmonious. Such a tension is related to the fact that the Webmasters may not be able to post things on time, which may affect the effectiveness of the agency. The time when such items must be posted may also depend on public expectations, and this varies from one department to another. Webmasters are the employees who facilitate the interface between the citizenry and city hall. A Webmaster said,

> We have to have all of the meetings up there, by Thursday afternoon. If we don't have them up, we hear from the board of supervisors, "Why don't we have them up?" Or, "There's a broken link here." There's a lot of pressure to get that stuff up there, because that's what the public wants. For example, that one from the planning department must be up by Friday afternoon so people can look at it— people are counting on it, to be able to look at it over the weekend. So it needs to get up—and it's a drag for us, because if we don't get it till five o'clock, we have to stay and do it.

Relations between the IT team and other departments may also be strained because the Webmasters need to do simple editing to get rid of sensitive material or even censor the postings to remove items that should not be posted for legal reasons. In theory, all the documents produced by city hall are supposed to be posted on the Web, but in fact, only some are made available on-line. Those that are available are general documents that do not foster any potential legal problems for city hall. There may be disagreements on what constitutes a potentially troublesome document. Is it the information it contains, the possibility for a misreading and misinterpretation of its intent, or the possibility that it might fuel a controversy or even be used against the city?

As a general rule, the Webmasters are not supposed to change the content of what the departments send in, but as the last people to see the texts before they become public, they have the task of ensuring that the text is fine. One Webmaster has the following to say about her role:

> We don't really control their content. We organize it for them, we put it up in a certain way, and follow these Web standards to try to get them up in there, organize them so that people can find them as quickly as possible. We take what they give us and put it into the structure. And day-to-day press releases and agendas and things, we don't touch them.
>
> In fairness, we do gross level of content review. For example, we are not going to let anybody put some copyrighted information out on the Web if we know that's copyrighted information. But in terms of how the department functions and how it wants to appear to

the constituencies it serves, that's entirely within that department's domain. We're facilitators, but we're not policy makers.

Nevertheless, Webmasters wield real power. This comes not so much from editing and censoring content as from assigning relative values to what gets posted. They are subtly producing knowledge, projecting a specific view of city hall, and in the process, they make what are actually political and policy decisions. A Webmaster thus in effect becomes a virtual mayor because of the knowledge they control and the dependence of other parts of the city administration on their services.

Webmasters also have an active role in determining how items get posted on the Web. Webmasters help departments make sense of what they want to communicate to the public, often working with them before they post on the Web. The Webmasters' influence can be either in the process of preparing the text or after the text is completed and in need of editing. A Webmaster said,

> And we give guidance to these departments, again trying to arrange their sites in a more service-oriented view. So when a department comes to me and says, "Here's our organizational charts, here's where the buttons need to be," and we're like, "That doesn't make sense to a user. Let me make sense to you instead." But as a citizen, I don't care what department handles dog licenses; I just want to get a dog license. So we help—I won't use the word "reorganize"—we present it, but we don't change the content.

The Webmasters thus also represent the users of the Web site to the city departments that serve them, soliciting items that may be of interest to the public and making access to that information easier.

> In a subtle way, we almost become the citizen. We have to imagine, "I'm a citizen. I don't care about all these departments. I don't care about all this. I want to find what I want to find." So specific content, no, but in a way, we do drive how it's organized, and it's very service-oriented. I at least hope it's very service-oriented. What we're really trying to do is—and we say this all the time—"I'm the dumb citizen. I don't know anything about my local government, and I want to find this." How am I going to hit my home page and get to that information quickly without taking up this whole department hierarchy? So in that sense, we do have a kind of overview in terms of driving the way a citizen is going to experience their government.

So I think what we have to do, and I think what the mayor and the policy makers, at least I hope, are relying on us as a Web group to do, is to make it easily accessible for the constituents, whether they be citizens—residential citizens or business citizens—or even other government entities. I think that's what they are relying on us to do. We try to be agnostic in terms of politics. Our goal is to provide a useful resource for those that are using it. (A Webmaster at City Hall)

While each agency targets its own public, the Webmasters are in the business of constructing a much larger public, based on their reading of residents' needs and the logic of the site. The general view of city administrators is that there is a public out there eager to find out what the current policies are and what the city is doing to improve the quality of life for urban residents. The information is provided on the Web to meet the expectations of constituencies and people who want to do business with the city. For example, the Web site receives and posts answers to citizens' questions.

These are real questions. These are the ones we actually had on the Web and we get real ones: "I have a dog next door that is barking a lot. Who do I contact?" And we forward it on to the correct department. For the most part, what we try to do with questions like that is we try not to answer them ourselves. If we know a department has the expertise or if a question crosses department lines, we try to send it out to them, and not try to answer them. And again, they know the content. They know the rules and the regulations. But nobody controls whether the Bay is fresh water or salt water, so we have to come up with that ourselves. So we do know . . . mostly, what we try to do is to know who handles the power. (A manager at City Hall)

Although the Webmasters and the IT staff are on a different footing in city hall than the public relations staff, who are the public faces of the institution, they nevertheless project the image of the institution in cyberspace. Thus, although the Webmasters frequently represent the needs of the citizens to the various departments of the city hall and stand at an important node in the political and policy process in that sense, at a switching or distribution point, the process of representation runs both ways. The architectural design of the city Web sites, in particular, reflects more what the organization wants to tell the people than what the patrons want to know about the institution. The Webmasters create a hierarchy of sites on the Web, a city hall in miniature, or a cybercity hall. The positioning of icons, their forms, size, and colors are a visual expression of the power hierarchy and administrative services offered by the city.

> And the perceptions when you do come into the home page, there are three little buttons: mayor, board of supervisors.... they are not big like on some sites, like in New York City, where all you see is [then mayor Rudolph] Guiliani: There he is. Obviously, he controls New York. But San Francisco doesn't have that kind of centralization, so you know, the little buttons down there are equal in size.... So in a way, the perception—when people come into our Web site—I think, is not of a strongly centralized government. (A Webmaster at City Hall)

In organizing the Web site, the Webmasters think of the users, the information they want to create or convey to them, and the logic necessary to make that information easily accessible. There are several types of patrons that they have in mind, including citizens who request services both from private and public access; ordinary people who want to familiarize themselves with city hall; students, researchers, and politicians who are asking for specialized information; city hall employees who need to look up files for the use of their departments, or research questions they could not answer, or connect someone with another agency; those adults who would prefer not to use the computer and continue to do business by coming to city hall, who need to be referred to specific physical sites; those who occasionally use the computer to request information; the younger generation who feels more comfortable doing business on-line—in essence, anyone who has access to computers. At least, that is the projected goal.

As this list suggests, the digitization of city hall serves the needs of not only the citizenry, but also those of city workers and departmental agencies. Documents posted on the city Web pages allow city hall employees to find out what information other departments have and this contributes to interdepartment interaction. In this context, some see the Internet as a tool that fosters greater integration of city hall and that facilitates collaboration as city officials use the intranet to request comments before they post things or before certain decisions are made.

> And we've been putting things on the Web site to allow people from different departments to talk to each other, because you know we are also physically scattered. I mean it's a small city, but still, we have a lot of different locations. We're putting stuff on the Web site that

will allow the departments to see what the other departments are doing. And we all never get together. So in that sense, it's fostering communications and a rapport. And I think that having the Web site will foster the communication—we had put up a discussion group, which we hadn't done before. We're putting up the project plans, and everyone can see it. Before, only a few people who were on the project could see it. So there's the potential that it can actually help foster these relationships. (A Webmaster at City Hall)

The Internet also has affected the way city hall lobbyists go about their activities. Instead of calling each activist or sympathizer one at a time, it is much simpler and cheaper to send an e-mail invitation to all of them at once. Lobbyists use the Internet to rally their troops in order to influence and shape local policies to the advantages of their constituencies. City hall employees do the same thing. It is easy to send one e-mail to a number of people alerting them to meetings or hearings that may concern their interests. "CityWatch—people being about to watch the board of supervisors meetings on-line. . . . If you go talk to XXX, from the mayor's office, about disability, he's got a list on his site of all the meetings, and he rallies his troops. They all go down there whenever the board of supervisors meets to discuss things that may concern them," said one manager at City Hall.

The content and structure of the digital city on the Web

The digital city hall as it appears on the Web has a specific content and a specific structure. The content is defined by what is made easily available, what is made available only if citizens exercise some effort, and what is withheld. It is also defined by what is permanent and what is constantly changing. The structure is defined by the links made available within and beyond city hall itself and within and beyond the city itself.

All information offered on the Web does not have the same weight or status. Some of it is legal and provides the procedures, applications, and parameters of ordinances and jurisdictional matters. Some of it is purely informational and does not remain there for long. Some needs to be updated to reflect current policies of the city. Updating in some cases also means upgrading, because new items are introduced and old ones are eliminated. Likewise, updating can mean that new links that did not exist before are now added to the Web page. So updating refers to new information, the repositioning of files, elimination or archiving of files, or to the addition of new links to sites that may be useful to the urban resident.

Some departments already have forms up. I believe you can get forms up for some departments. County clerk, I believe they have forms up. Fictitious business names, things like that. Those are the kinds of things that are up there. I don't know what kind of departments they have up. The information I have on my table does not say on-line. Eventually—this is still a work in progress—we are going to continue to upgrade this as it goes on. (Staff employee at City Hall)

On the Web sites there are also documents that are archived and not subject to change. This is the fate of a good chunk of legal texts and ordinances that serve as references to onlookers. Information originally is posted for a certain period of time. Once it has spent the length of time required, it may be archived as part of the history of the city. Those who are interested in such information may access it on the Web. The archiving of documents is not left to the Webmaster's judgment, but is done according to a set of city policies.

The city attorney actually decided to set up a template for our reten-tion policy. Departments have some ability to decide how long they want to keep things. There are some legal requirements. I think most things are two years. The controller requires that... certain financial documents be kept twenty years. The city attorney makes sure that every department, because of Sunshine, has a record retention policy. (Staff employee at San Francisco City Hall)

In addition, "In November 1999, the city voted to enact a more extensive sunshine ordinance, and part of that ordinance required city adminis-trators to develop and create and maintain an index of city records." Archiving documents forces the departments to put some order in their day-to-day activities and makes it easier for both employees and citizenry to access these materials easily.

Of course, archiving and maintaining access to materials can be costly: "You know how we used to have a time limit on data—on how long we retained it? And now if we are retaining it forever, that is a sig-nificant financial cost to the government. Not that I'm saying that we shouldn't do it, but it's just something that we need to be aware of."

In contrast to archived documents, there are also posted documents whose contents change through the updating and upgrading mechan-isms. Some documents remain where they have been placed because of their strategic importance for reflecting an agency's mandate, while other documents can be moved to other locations or archived while still available to patrons. There are various reasons why a document may be moved elsewhere.

Some documents are placed on the Web for a shorter period of time because they reflect a transitional moment of decision-making. One may think of documents prepared to commemorate a specific event in the history of the city. This information is provided, but is subject to change before the next cycle. Other documents are placed there on a permanent basis because they reflect core values and policies of the city.

Some documents are made available to the public because they provide legal or policy information. Other documents may be available, but are not placed on the Web because of the sensitive material they contain or because they can be used to challenge city practices or to fuel legal charges against the city. Individuals who are aware of their existence may request them, otherwise they cannot routinely be accessed on the Web.

Archived information is not necessarily on the Web, but must be requested by the public if they know about its availability. Since this information is not likely to be delivered on the spot, the interim period allows time to review the document and take appropriate steps to reduce potential problems.

Well, first of all, they don't have to get it back within a business day. Some information is not easy to get your hands on. If it's a piece of paper, they can go into a file and get it. There's something called an immediate disclosure request, and I forget what the requirement for that is, but sometimes they might say they have ten business days. This was just legislation that was passed originally by a couple supervisors and then the city voted to enhance it. I know people are not happy about it. For the most part, there are a few departments where these gadflies are here, you know, and actually it's practically harassment. For most of the things on our Web site, I don't think that anyone is ever going to ask for this information. (A clerical worker at San Francisco City Hall)

Information or documents judged by city hall or a department to be confidential will not be available on the Web. Such documents will not be forwarded to a Webmaster, but will remain in the office that generates it. In this specific aspect, both the traditional and the on-line methods of archiving information are used for somewhat different purposes.

There are documents that are confidential. For the city attorney... there is confidentiality. I've been advised by the city attorney that people can put up files and say these are the files we have. They don't necessarily have to give them if they're confidential, however one of the departments... office of city complaints... I mean this is very threatening to people because sometimes there is actual fear. There's fear of retaliation. There's all kinds things, so in this particular office, they didn't even want to put certain files up. I say that, you know, that's not up to me, its up to you if you want to put them there. My assignment is just to have this thing created and ask you to give me the information in a universal way that is going to fit. But I don't decide on the content to put up. (A staff person at City Hall)

The right to decide what is public and what is confidential is not always left to the interpretation of city government. Politicians and activists may challenge such policies and get things resolved through the judiciary system: "We get into this gray area because the public is trying to force out information that they are not necessarily entitled to, but it becomes political—its not legal. It could get down into a legal issue," said a City Hall employee.

Sometimes files are made confidential because angry citizens who are aware of the existence of sensitive documents want to use them against the city government and request them to boost their own case. A secretary at San Francisco City Hall said,

Somebody who used to work for the medical examiner started their own cremation business. And they had given out contracts to outside vendors—or not vendors, but providers. They contracted out the cremation. This is pretty down-to-earth. They contracted out the cremation. The city then decided that they would take it back and do it themselves.

But anyway this person was very angry... and somehow had instigated an investigation of someone, and they wanted the files. And the police department and district attorney had said they were not entitled to the files. This person then sent a request to me saying that he wanted to file a complaint to the Sunshine Ordinance task force, and he then told me that he had filed a suit. Well, I had said that if you had come to me originally, you know, maybe we could have worked something out. This was just too big of an issue. This was really too serious. Sometimes somebody goes to a counter and somebody said they were too busy and they wouldn't give them a document. Somebody calls me, and I would either call them up and say can you give them that document. You can charge them if you want, you can charge them ten cents, but unless it's confidential, they're entitled to know.

The question of access has always been problematic, especially when the city is dealing with sensitive negotiations. While in the name of open government it is important that the citizenry be aware of every move the city government is making, it can also be counterproductive if the information is leaked to the public before a deal is made. In other words, early access may also undermine the productivity of a negotiation process.

The presumption of the law is that nothing is confidential unless you can prove that there's a reason. The Sunshine Law obviously is because government should be conducted in public and people are entitled to public documents and blah blah blah. And that's true, but one of the problems and where this started was a few years ago, when Viacom, the cable company, was negotiating a new contract and I can't... I am involved with so many projects: It became from Viacom to TCI to TCI to TNT Broadband. But they were negotiating a new contract. The *Bay Guardian* [newspaper] wanted the information. They wanted to know what the negotiations were. Well, you know, when you are in negotiations, that's part of the deal... we don't give away if you are going to get the best deal for the city. The *Guardian* is contending that they [the city's negotiators] are not getting the best deal for the city. The city attorney's office is contending we cannot get the best deal. So they are contending that there are some areas that need to be done in private. And when they are finished with it, there also was a push... to force out the scoring list. You know, there are points on both sides? You know they want to find out: Was this a fair process? (A San Francisco City Hall employee)

There are things that the city would not put on the Web, such as personnel files, even though people have in the past requested them. The distinction between public documents and personnel documents has been clear, despite challenges to open them up to the public: "Most documents do not have to be confidential. There are certain things that I think the public is not entitled to. I don't think they are entitled to personnel files. I think personnel matters are private. But it's increasingly moved. The line has moved. What is in the public's interest and what is not?," said a San Francisco City Hall staff.

The structure of the digital city hall consists in part of the relation between internal and external networks—between the city hall's intranet and the Internet as a whole. The city government employs an internal network, an intranet, to integrate its political apparatus and its administrative processes in the virtual realm, two spheres that do not entirely coincide. While the Internet is used to communicate with the public, the city hall intranet is used for internal communication among city employees. In order to protect and safeguard its political and administrative practices, the digital city hall makes special efforts to ensure that the public does not access this private network.

> Our Web site is geared toward city employees, and we don't advertise it outside because it would end up being a source of frustration. If noncity employees got to this Web site and said, "Oh, I want this benefit, too."...There are a lot of people and organizations that work for the city and yet they're not city employees—like the California Academy of Sciences, for example. It's a delicate situation. (A San Francisco City Hall staff)

Intranet e-mail has become the main form of communication among workers because it is easy, fast, and secure. It is used more often than the telephone, and it has become the unobstructive way to discuss things with coworkers: "Well, I would say e-mail communication is very—that's really the mode of communication: It's e-mail. I would say that's where two-way communications does occur, and that's made our lives a lot easier. Because we are a kind of satellite office with our main office, which is at Eleventh and Grove Streets. E-mail is the main form of communication, more than the telephone. And that is the centerpiece," said a San Francisco City Hall staff.

Just as on the Internet, on the intranet, city hall employees move easily between the real and the virtual. One comes to rescue the other. One is used to access the other, which shows how the use of these two media is intertwined.

> If I'm on the phone with somebody, and they say, "How can I find this information?" you know, I could say, "Well, you know, you can actually go to this page." And I could be on the phone with them and tell them, you know, what the URL is, and then I can pretty much navigate them through, you know, what they're looking for while I'm on the phone with them. So...it's a kind of a combination of both things. (A clerical worker at City Hall)

The intranet allows a greater social integration of digital workers in the social structure of the workplace at city hall because of the digital, interactive communication that it allows, the greater knowledge of the environment that it facilitates, and the breakdown of departmental boundaries that it fuels.

At the same time, the Internet allows the virtual city hall to provide citizens with access to certain parts of the virtual system while prohibiting access to others. The structure of the digital city hall on the Web thus also consists in part of the ways in which Web sites developed by a department are linked to the main Web site and the ways in which, from the main Web site, one may access the diverse units of city government. The architecture of these links gives a sense of the relative importance of the various units. A link may be made of sublinks that provide a choice to visit other units in this networking architecture. "This Web site is only limited to city employees. I mean we have a CitySpan site, which I can use to get information as a city employee, and I use that, as well as other people use that. And our site is on the main city site, as well. There's a link to it." The Internet both enhances the citizen's knowledge of city hall practices and makes city hall employees more accessible to the public. The Internet and intranet must thus be seen as the private and public communication tools that serve as the conduits through which the virtualization of city hall is effected.

Of course, links to Web pages also connect both citizens and the digital city hall to Internet resources beyond the city. Because some city services are also sponsored by the federal or state government, linkage can be made to these other institutions, as well. The assembling of all the items in one Web site facilitates the introduction to on-line services offered by city hall. The main preoccupation of Webmasters maximizing the effectiveness of this structure is: what is the best way to present the information so that it can be easily accessible, the architecture of icons is easily understood, and the information provided is accurate and useful?

Communicating with the citizenry

The following emails give a glimpse of the contents of the on-line interaction between the virtual city hall and the citizenry:

Subject: Title Search
Date: 6/26/01 8:59 AM
Is it possible to search the County (Property Tax) Assessor's records on-line to determine who holds title to a particular property?

Subject: Re: Title Search
Sent: Tuesday, June 26, 2001 10:21 AM
Don't believe they are there yet. Call Assessor at xxx–xxxx. Sorry for possibly putting you in voice-mail hell but that's all I know. Administrative number is xxx–xxxx if you get nowhere with other number.

Subject: Re: Title Search
Date: 6/26/01 1:36 PM
Thanks for your prompt reply.

Subject: Sunshine Index Comment
Date: 5/30/01 7:25 AM
Desperately trying to get records of my employment with SFUSD
in 1970 and 1971. Have had no luck with the school district or the IRS.
Must document my employment in order to retire from teaching in Denver
so that I can care for my aging parents. My name at the time:———.
SS:———.
Thanks.

Subject: Re: Sunshine Index Comment
Date: 6/30/01 4:09 PM
You might try the California State Retirement Office. They should have
a record of your employment from the monthly contributions. Let us
know if that works or doesn't.

Subject: Thanks
Date: 5/30/01 9:37 PM
Thanks so much for the help. I'll try the California State Retirement
Office and get back to you if I get stumped again.

Subject: Police record
Date: 5/8/01 10:58 AM
I am a San Francisco native currently residing in Nuremberg, Germany.
I need my police record—or lack of one—to show the government here
that I have no convictions in order to obtain my residence and work
permits so that I can continue to teach English.

Please let me know what information you need from me to complete
this transaction.
Thank you for your cooperation, and I look forward to hearing from you.

Communication between citizens and government institutions is
a major aspect of the Internet as an enabler of democratic practices.
Legitimate queries that people could ask over the phone now come in
through the Internet. In this sense, too, digitization is transforming the
modus operandi of city hall.

We actually only have one e-mail box for the Webmaster and for
people who don't know where to write, they write to us. And it's
amazing the range of queries. [laughing] From "Where can I can get
free English as a second language lessons?" or . . . we've been getting
a lot of inquiries about jury duty lately. They know it's really serious.
They've been living out of the country—"Can you please forward

this to the jury commissioner?" There's obviously an unappreciated need, or an unmet need, for that one particular function. Not a lot of traffic ticket stuff, which I thought we'd be getting a lot of—I know people are really anxious—or would really like to be able to pay your tickets online. But a ton related to the jury thing, which is really just informational and easy to do, since it's not money related. So I think we just push them, encourage them to put up something that is more interactive then they've already got. (A staff person at San Francisco City Hall)

Despite the availability of some services on the Web, some people prefer to talk to someone, either on the phone or by visiting city hall. Some do this simply because they are not at ease with the computer.

If I'm Joe Citizen and it just makes me furious to get voice mail instead of a live person to get me information that I need to conduct my city business. I mean I'm a taxpayer—I'm paying for these services. I don't want to have to go to through six different menus and all that kind of stuff. You need someone there to humanize the face of government. Obviously I have a prejudice. (A secretary at San Francisco City Hall)

The inability to conduct interactive communication in real time is a technological problem that is yet to be solved. There is a significant lapse of time between the moment the e-mail is sent out and the moment when the message is read and a reply provided. "I wouldn't necessarily say it's one-way. It's one-way inasmuch as any kind of advertising is one-way. But there is ample opportunity for people to respond back if they have questions or to get more information." Until the time gap between query and response is closed, city employees and citizens alike will have no other alternative than to live with the disaggregation of the time of querying from the time of answering.

Well, I'm always pushing for two-way things, and I design the feedback forms. And we have a feedback form if you want to write a comment. And I don't know if they ever answer it or not. I don't have control over that. But it gives people what they want. They want to be able to communicate—sometimes they just want to write to us, from people all over the world. We're known to the world because it's a world-famous city, and people . . . they want to know how many bikes are in Golden Gate Park. To me, it's something that I think will come more and more and become a communication and dialogue back and forth between the departments and the people that are using their services. (A manager at San Francisco City Hall)

The tendency of digitization, however, is to replace immediate contacts with Web-mediated interactions.

As part of our Web site, in the beginning there is a part to click for e-mail. What happens is I get all sorts of requests for information, instead of going to our department they are coming to me, and I have become a Dear Abby for information, which is kind of fun. You know, it's kind of interesting. And people say—you know, someone in my family just died, and I need to find out what property they own, and is it on-line? So now this e-mail thing is kind of taking the place of the old telephone call. (A San Francisco City Hall staff)

In fact, the tendency toward Web-mediated interaction can be so strong that some employees of digital city hall even use immediate contacts to send citizens to the Web: "When they call me, I just say Web access and I give them the Web address, and they go directly to the Web site. And I never hear back from them, and that's generally a sign for me that says they got everything they needed on the Web and they're moving forward," said a secretary at San Francisco City Hall.

What has changed in the interaction between an office unit and the taxpayer who is interacting with city hall thus is the increase in computer-mediated interaction and also the spread of such interactions. Instead of a citizen asking a question, receiving an answer, and then moving on, the interaction may last an entire day or week as the e-mails arrive and require answers and other e-mails follow. The result is a sort of detached intimacy.

Somebody taught school in the early '70s and they needed to look into their retirement, and they didn't know how to do that, and I wrote back and said you need to call the Board of Education, and here is the phone number, good luck. Then they wrote me back the other day, and said, "I did what you suggested." I mean, we do, we have these little relationships. (A staff person at San Francisco City Hall)

The combination of telephone and Internet is the preferred mode of interaction at city hall. This combination is natural, but is also required by those who want human interaction and those who are computer illiterate or who do not have a computer or access to the Internet. As one informant described being on the phone,

I'm giving them the information to help them access [the Web]. I will say to most of them, "Here's what you should do. If you have no success, let me know." And I'll do that. But I would be spending all my time being a switchboard operator. The one that called me back who wanted in the information from the '70s, I gave her a phone number, they called her back right away, she spoke to someone in classified, but they haven't gotten back to her. Would I forward this message again? No, because I wouldn't know who to call. If its something I can do like that (snap). . . . And I said to her, you need to call this person back. I think that's obvious. You need to call that person back. I wouldn't even know who to call. But it provides some kind of human contact, it helps the issue. Somebody is helping them, as opposed to just being lost.

The e-mails force employees to get acquainted with other department Web sites so that they may refer people to them if asked. "Somebody wrote me today, 'How do I get a copy of a marriage license? I've looked at the city Web site and somehow I can't figure this out.' And I told them, here is the Web site, go to the county clerk, it depends on what kind of marriage license you want, there's confidential, blah blah blah."

In sum, what is emerging in practice as the virtual city hall communicates with the citizenry is not the total replacement of one form of communication by another—telephone access, voice mail, and face-to-face versus on-line—but a multichannel environment in which a taxpayer can use a number of ways to access city government, one for some services and another for other services, or all of them as complementary mechanisms of communications.

Well, I think what's going to be eventually evolved is that the Web is one channel for delivery of services. Another channel might be the telephone. You know, whether it's an automated voice response system or actually talking to a real person. And clearly, the personal touch, going down to an office, is not going to go away. So I think there's going to be a multichannel for the delivery of services, and it's going to depend on a lot of characteristics of the person using the service— how they choose to interact with the government. I think down the line it's government's responsibility to provide the multichannels. (A manager at San Francisco City Hall)

In this multi-channel environment, the various complementary possibilities for communication will end up being a natural way of doing business for both the city employee and the taxpayer. No matter what, some communication media will be more efficient than others, depending on what is sought.

As a citizen, there are times when I want to talk to a person. They will put up frequently asked questions, but my question may not be on the list. I have to talk to somebody. They cannot possibly provide every bit of information that a citizen is going to need on the Web. They can't think about all of them. You're going to meet my unique situation, or another unique situation, or whatever it is. So you're almost going to need to have the brick and mortar in places, as well as the on-line version. There's no way one can substitute for the other, but it can supplement; it can be a good frontline. Most typically find information on the Web.... "Good, I don't have to inundate Animal Care and Control with these questions. But now I have got this unique situation where the neighbor's snake ate my Chihuahua. What do I do? Get another one?" So I don't see the Web replacing, I see it possibly becoming more powerful, but never replacing going down and talking to people and having people available who have the knowledge and know all the ends and outs and the exceptions to the rules to which they might not be close to. (A manager at San Francisco City Hall)

Limits of the Web for democratic practices

Despite all the magic of the Web, it has its limits in what it can do to enhance democratic politics. It does not eliminate the need for the human touch. Some information still needs to be given out through face-to-face communication.

And there are a lot of departments that you actually need human beings involved with. I mean, obviously our favorite, Animal Care and Control. I mean, a computer is not going to find my dog if he runs away—maybe soon, but not now. Places like the Department of Human Services, I mean, if I were having problems with welfare, I wouldn't want to rely on a machine. There is always a human factor. Human beings don't always want to rely on machines. There's a lot of government that deals with things...Recreation and Parks Department. I mean a computer can't grow a tree, or mow...well, mow the lawn, maybe. There's a lot of things that you still need the other part for, and a lot of departments that handle things are very human-oriented. You can't put it on the Web. I mean you just can't do it. So I don't see one surpassing the other. (A female resident of San Francisco)

As we have seen, the Web produces one-way communications, not interactive communications in real time, and this irritates some people.

Also, the Web is not an equal-opportunity medium. It facilitates and empowers those who can access it for information and networking, and it places the unconnected in a disadvantageous position because it excludes them. It ends up enhancing the power of the powerful and disempowering the poor.

However, that may be changing. As one informant noted, "We are getting e-mails from some semiliterate people. Not people who don't have the punctuation right, but really the grammar! Just lately, I've gotten ones that I can barely understand, which suggests that someone from a different socioeconomic group is getting access to a PC somewhere." Public access to the Internet may narrow the so-called "digital divide" somewhat. Transactions with the city are sometimes done through the use of public computers, that is computers in public places such as public libraries that are made available to users.

Did you hear about the homeless people? Apparently they line up here outside the public library before it opens and go racing upstairs the minute it opens to check their e-mail. So they have e-mail accounts. There's a huge line every time you go to the library here, the main library right down the street. There's a large number of terminals, but there's always a line, especially around lunchtime. You have to wait at least fifteen minutes. (A manager at San Francisco City Hall)

One obstacle to access that city hall confronts is the need for on-line services to be accessible by the disabled. This may require the purchase of new equipment tailored to the need of this segment of the population and extra work that may be needed in terms of reformatting so that the information can be made accessible to them.

Well, I think there are certain citizens here who have easier access to the Web than a lot of the other citizens. And that is an issue that we have actually started to look at, not even just economic, but also compliance with disability issues and what not. That's a tough question. I think we try to look at it as being, as the Web being an enhancement and not a replacement to services that already exist. But I couldn't say whether that is a bad thing. (A staff person at San Francisco City Hall)

In addition to these limitations on the ability of the Web and the virtual city hall to enhance the democratic process, the "information" provided by the virtual city hall needs to be treated with a certain amount of skepticism by all who can access it. How do users separate institutional public relations (PR), objective information about the organization, political spin concerning internal events, and responses to events that the city hall does not initiate? Does the Web really capture the political and administrative process, or it is mainly about results—that is, only results are posted and not the content or the process that leads to such results. It seems unlikely that the digital city hall represented on the Web will capture or make accessible the informal processes that lie behind formal policies. The nature of the Internet also would seem to limit the modalities of discourse that are mapped onto the Internet or translated to suit the logic of the Internet. A broad spectrum of people with a diversity of often conflicting interests can access the virtual city hall, and that accessibility seems to make it difficult or impossible to tailor a message to address a specific audience.

Digitization and globalization

Virtual city hall has not simply a local, but also a global dimension. This global aspect is manifest in terms of services, policies, governmental relations, economic transactions, social interactions, and cultural practices. On-line services are provided to taxpayers who live abroad, to tourists who want to visit the city, to investors who need information, and to foreign agencies that seek transnational collaboration. Governmental relations are forged and maintained through the mechanisms of trade and sister cities. Since the tax base of the city depends on the performance of the local economy, of which the hotel industry is a significant part, the city engages in international advertising in order to attract tourists and foreign investors. The existence of ethnic enclaves also drives the city's global interactions and transnational cultural practices. The city tends to develop amicable relationships with countries whose immigrants live in the city. The celebration of ethnic holidays and holy days provides a peak time for these on-line activities of globalization.

The virtual city hall is one conduit through which the globalization of the daily practices of city hall is effected. Virtual activities that include extraterritorial sites and agents feed back to formal activities or are the mechanisms through which they are conducted. Since those who live outside the boundaries of the city cannot engage in face-to-face encounters with employees of city hall, they do so through on-line communication and interaction. Cyberspace thus is the privileged site for global communication that sustains the global transactions of city hall.

The globalization process fragments the virtual city hall because each unit develops global interactions with different actors, based on the kind of services each is able to provide. In that scheme, some units may be more global on a daily or routine basis than others that cater more to the local population. For example, the department that provides services to the homeless and needy is exclusively geared toward the local population, while the mayor's office must deal with foreign relations as well. Digitization also fragments locality because of the different temporal flows and rhythms of the virtual activities it induces. Some departments are routinely involved in global interaction, while others do so at certain peak periods. For example, because citizens overseas want to vote, the unit in charge of elections is more involved in virtual international relations during periods of electoral campaigns than during in-between dormant periods.

We are approaching an era in which a unit may interact more or as much with other extraterritorial units in the cyberspatial circuit or network than with other departments of city hall. This double integration of the cyberspace circuit and the local circuit rearticulates local relationships and in a sense remakes city hall because it integrates the virtual with the real.

City hall is involved in two mechanisms of digital globalization: front linking and backlinking. "Frontlinking" refers to the process whereby a unit of city hall engages in global interaction as part of the operation of the unit. As an official puts it, "I envision us working more with appropriate offices at the state and national levels than I would with our office right across the hallway because that's who we need to work with, the foreign business, for instance, whatever the case may be." "Backlinking" refers to the process whereby city hall engages in a global operation for the sake of enhancing the activities of an entity in the city. For example, it may interact with the homeland of an ethnopolis or chronopolis as a way of maintaining good relations with such an ethnic community. Likewise city hall may engage in transglobal relations for the purpose of helping some business groups.

Conclusion

The digitization of city hall is a work in progress that began as experiments carried out in specific units, then became official policy of the city in the hope of better serving the people, and now offers the prospect of providing fluid interactivity with them. It is a work in progress because the equipment still does not allow a two-way interaction in real time, because the organizational makeup of city hall does not yet fully correspond to the logic of virtuality, and because the public does not yet really relate to the institution in a way that promotes the virtual sphere as an electronic agora. The general view among the staff is that there will be more proliferation of software, more variety of equipment from one department to another, and that the IT environment of city hall will not become more stable until a panoply of hardware and software still in production in Silicon Valley becomes available.

5
Virtual Diasporas and Cyberspace

An important aspect of the digital city is the malleable virtual space that serves as its infrastructure. To map out a sociological dimension of that cyberspace, the focus of this chapter is on one of its components, virtual diasporic space.[1] It is assumed here that the digital city houses lattices of cross-border virtual spatial circuits, and it is not the purpose of this chapter to enumerate or even analyze the properties of them all. By focusing on one of them—virtual diasporic space—including its global apparatus, we will begin to understand its operation and importance in the sustenance of the digital city. The digital city is a multiplex node in a transnational circuit of virtual and nonvirtual nodes, each serving as a pole for distinct social groups and formations. A virtual diaspora is a pole of an existing diaspora. Virtual diasporic space provides us a good entry point to penetrate and conceptualize the characteristics and modus operandi of a virtual diaspora.

Because of past segregation practices, diasporas occupy specific physical niches in the city. With the advent of modern ITs, however, one witnesses the rise of groups of immigrants who organize communities based on their ability to navigate in the ethereal space of on-line communications, not on the principle of physical location. I hasten to say that the global city is traversed by or houses more than one cyberspace, and virtual diasporic space is one of them. It is important to understand the operation of this space and its globality, because it helps explain how the internal politics of many nations is becoming globalized in ways that transform the national into the transnational. This chapter therefore approaches the e-space of virtual diasporas via a focus on the transnational political activities of virtual diasporas.

The virtual space of the city, because it comprises different spatial circuits, can be either the initial site where the main actors establish

125

themselves and penetrate the space of the digital city, an intermediate site where information is reconducted to other nodes, or an unimportant site because of the size, nonstrategic status, or marginal position of the actors. For this analysis, I have selected two intermediate points in virtual diasporic space that shed light on the importance of the other sites, as well. Both had nodes in Silicon Valley: the circuit through which the transnational Chinese virtual diaspora participated in the democracy movement that culminated in the events of Tiananmen Square and the circuit through which the transnational Haitian virtual diaspora participated in the polarization of Haitian national politics after the second election of Jean Bertrand Aristide.

Although I recognize both the local and global aspects of cyberspace, I will concentrate here on its global dimension to accentuate the global parameters of action of the digital city, seen more as a process than as a place. Global connections can be more productive than local ones because of the knowledge that can thus be gained. Hence, diasporas have their own rationale that explains why they connect locally or globally in order to achieve an expected outcome. In so doing, global/local virtual diasporic spaces are made and remade. For example, going global can be a strategy used in order to be efficient locally. The goal here is to show how a diasporic individual or community can be the embodied site that links to other nodes that make operative or sustain the transnational circuit of virtual nodes. To do so, I will begin by explaining the concepts of "virtual immigration" and "virtual diaspora" and the relations of one to the other.

Virtual immigration

Immigration, like any social process, can become virtualized within a virtual world. If one is to speak of a virtual diaspora, one must be able to explain how it is related to immigration. In reality, one cannot speak of diaspora without thinking about immigration. Can virtual diaspora exist without real immigration?

The concept of "virtual immigration" refers to a new type of immigration that is undertaken without physical movement. The migrant does not have to leave his or her place of residence to acquire such a status. Such a person may belong simultaneously to an existing neighborhood community at home and to a virtual community on which his or her livelihood depends. Everard[2] proposes that "new forms of virtual labour migration are emerging with knowledge workers in one country being employed directly by knowledge clients in another without physical relocation taking place." Diasporans no longer need to rely on specific places and times to engage in border-crossing activities because they can access the network wherever they happen to be and at any time that is convenient to them. In particular, telecommuting, by combining both flexiplace and flextime, enhances the ability of diasporans to participate in virtual diasporic circuits by circumventing time zones, domesticating labor time, and hegemonizing diasporic time in their daily practice.

Virtual labor migration thus occurs whenever an individual in one country is contracted to do work for a firm in another country. Such jobs used to be given to immigrants, but now they are offered to virtual immigrants. Although the first—immigration—entails physical movement from one place to another, the other—virtual immigration—implies only connectivity. Virtual migration decouples movement from place to place and recouples it with connectivity in cyberspace.

Coyle[3] discusses the rise of virtual immigration in terms of its effect on the economy. She notes that "the combination of computer technology and cheap telecommunications means the industrial world has 'virtual' immigration. Any direct investment by a Western company in the Third World is a partial substitute for importing cheap labour."

Virtual labor immigration displays unique characteristics. Unlike real immigration, it does not entail uprootedness and separation from the place of residence and family. However, it entails reliance on an external entity for one's economic welfare and participation in a virtual transnational circuit of interaction for the purpose of the production of output.

More broadly, in virtual immigration, through the mediation of IT, people can be actively engaged in the functioning of foreign institutions for the sake of achieving their own personal or group goals. This definition emphasizes the transnational dimension of the process, the connectivity factor that makes the experience possible, and the profits gained from an external source upon which one's social well-being depends. Virtual immigration is undertaken by two groups of people: those who have not traveled abroad, but are nevertheless connected to other people, groups, or firms transnationally, and members of the diaspora who have returned home, but are still involved in cross-border transactions essential to their welfare.

One may then ask: what are the relationships between virtual immigrations and virtual diasporas? Can the one exist without the other? One should not confuse these two concepts, because they belong to different conceptual domains. While virtual immigration does not necessarily presuppose immigration, a virtual diaspora does not exist without a real diaspora. This does not preclude integration of nondiasporic people into a diaspora. They are integrated as "others," and not as members of the diaspora, because the diaspora identity (virtual or real) is specific to those who have experienced dispersion. The only exception to that rule refers to dediasporized individuals, those who at one point lived in the diaspora and had returned home and reacquired their nationality and citizenship. One may speak of them as a dediasporized diaspora.

The virtual diaspora

The literature on cyberspace provides some clues as to how we should approach the concept of a virtual diaspora. Cyberspace has been seen as parallel, different, expanded, polar, interstitial, augmented space, or as a flow. What one takes to be the identity of cyberspace is likely to be important in characterizing the identity of virtual diasporas.

The conception of cyberspace as space parallel to and different from physical space of everyday interaction is sustained by two observations. Looking at the phenomenon from a legal standpoint, Johnson and Post[4] propose that "a new boundary, made up of the screens and passwords that separate the virtual world from the 'real world' of atoms, emerges." For them, this new boundary implies the existence of a "distinct cyberspace that needs new law and legal institution of its own."[5] They refer to new phenomena in cyberspace that have "no clear parallel in the non-virtual world."[6] In the same vein, Burrows[7] speaks of cyberspace as a "digitised parallel world."

The opposite view of cyberspace is provided by Bennahum,[8] who sees it as being made by a "set of different communications tools" that allow more emphasis either on the rights of the individual (private), such as e-mail, or the rights of society (public), such as Usenet news. For him, "cyberspace is part of the real world."

In a somewhat different perspective that comports well with this notion, cyberspace is seen as constructed space for the purpose of achieving in the cyberworld what one could not do in the real world. In this scheme, cyberspace is an extension or virtual representation of the real world and is constructed to help resolve problems that could not be resolved through the traditional means of the real world. Benedikt[9] speaks of the designers who "will be rerealizing in a virtual world many vital aspects of the physical world."

Conceived of in this way, cyberspace can also be seen in dialectical tension with the visible world. One then speaks of the appropriation or even colonization of one by the other. For example, Schiller[10] argues that "far from delivering us into a high-tech Eden, in fact, cyberspace itself is being rapidly colonized by the familiar workings of the market system."

As I argued in the opening chapter, however, the most comprehensive way of viewing the relations between the digital realm of cyberspace and the real is to see them not simply as different, parallel worlds, or as simply implicated in each other in some way, but as poles divided and connected by a continuum, and therefore as extensions of each other. However, even at its polar extreme, Cyberspace is not monolithic, but rather is made of a plurality of virtual spaces. As Benedikt[11] argues, there are "different kinds of cyberspaces, each with its own overall culture, appearance, lore, and law."

In this chapter, I argue that virtual diasporic space is that particular region of cyberspace that provides a virtual spatial infrastructure for diasporans to engage in on-line communications for the real-world benefit of themselves, the homeland, and the host land, a virtual corridor that links diasporic groups or individuals to each other, the homeland, the host land, and other international entities. Such virtual interactions can be with members of the diasporic group living in the same foreign country or in other countries, with individuals or entities in the homeland, or with others in the host land and elsewhere. What these groups have in common is that they belong to the same homeland and they have the capacity to unmake and remake themselves. Virtual diasporic space connects virtual national spaces (including local and regional spaces), virtual transnational spaces, and virtual global spaces. The parameters of such spaces can be mapped out because these spaces are constituted by human agents engaged in computer-mediated communications who live in specific places and who penetrate or participate in them from specific sites.

A virtual diaspora thus is the cyberexpansion of a real diaspora. We have said that no virtual diaspora can exist without real-life diasporas, and in this sense it, too, like the space that it inhabits, a virtual diaspora is not a separate entity, but rather a pole on a continuum. While actual diasporas are essential to the infrastructures that produce virtual diasporas, Elkins[12] sees virtual diasporas as strengthening real diasporas. In this light, he writes that,

> as these virtual ethnic communities take form and become more visible to their members or to observers, they offer opportunities to existing ethnic communities to consolidate their diaspora and to facilitate the identities and behavior so difficult to sustain over the generations when small enclaves have been isolated to one degree or another within other societies.

On-line with other compatriots, they address issues pertaining to their country of origin, issues that may be of little interest to others. Their diasporic status provides them a common ground to discuss matters related to the well-being of their community and the welfare of their country. Matei and Ball-Rokeach[13] note that "a consistent theme that emerged...was that online connections link our respondents to people and institutions of similar ethnicity or countries of origin."

The concept of a diaspora has its pristine and archetypal meanings inscribed in the early dispersion of the Jewish people.[14] Its principal meaning is "dispersion," but in this specific experience it entails notions of "persecution," "migration," "exile," "faith in and national connection to the homeland," and a longing for "return," a longing often expressed among Western European Jews in the phrase "Next year in Jerusalem." In the great majority of migrations, however, the components of persecution and faith are less prominent, and the term "diaspora" is now used to refer to all individuals who live outside their ancestral homeland. "Diaspora" therefore must be seen sociologically as a generic term serving as an umbrella covering different subsets of immigrant groups—exiles and others whose involuntary migration is caused by religious, gendered, and/ or political persecution and those whose voluntary migration is undertaken for the purpose of enriching their lives and reuniting their families. In this expanded definition, the criterion is migration to and/or residence in a foreign country or being the descendant of an immigrant family. By this definition, we tacitly recognize that some individuals have become diasporans not because they have migrated to another territory, but simply because of the redrawing of the national borders.

Conceived of in this way, the adjectives "diasporan" and "diasporic" refer to the identity of different groups of people who maintain different types of relationships to their homeland and their host land. The most recent typology of diasporic communities distributes them into six distinct, but not mutually exclusive categories,[15] identified on the basis of their global relations: the *ethnopole* (such as, for example, Japantown in San Francisco), in which ethnicity is central to social identity and governs the logic of the place of residence; the *chronopole* (such as, for example, the Orthodox Jewish community or the Muslim community in New York), in which community time has a different rhythm than that of mainstream society because the homeland calendar they use in matters of religious practices gives a distinct cadence to their weekly cycles (Saturday, for example, being the peak day of the week, instead of Christian Sunday); the *panethnopole* (such as, for example, the Mission district in San Francisco, which houses Spanish-speaking immigrants from various Latin American countries), in which groups share contiguous space with other regional groups who speak the same language; the *technopole* (such as the Indian community in Fremont, Silicon Valley), in which immigration and relocation are largely influenced by the level of technical skills of the individuals involved; the *liminal transnational community* (such as, for example, the Haitian refugee community in Guantanamo in the 1990s), in which their transitional status between homeland and host land causes problems; and the *creolopole* (such as, for example, the descendants of colonial Anglos and slaves), in which communities maintain only symbolic relations with the homeland.

The concept of a virtual diaspora is not used here to refer to an additional type among the subsets mentioned above, however, but rather as an extension of the other types from the pole of real diasporas into cyberspace. So we are not talking about fixed categories or fixed identities with regard to virtual diasporas, but about flexible entities whose members display flexible and changeable identities as they migrate from one virtual space to another, belonging to and participating in more than one virtual diasporic space. For example, one may express unorthodox political views using a virtual identity that one might not venture to express with and among friends, or dare to betray at all when in one's *propria personna*.

Cyberspace thus is now a medium used by diasporic activists to intervene in the affairs of the homeland on behalf of the opposition. That is why as national governments spend an ordinate amount of money to develop telecommunications capabilities, to create Web sites, and in some cases to provide on-line services to citizens, they are also concerned about on-line diasporic activities that may undermine their political basis of support. New capabilities are being developed to monitor these activities and to gather intelligence.

Virtual diasporas are not identical to real diasporas because they inhabit distinct, although connected conceptual universes and because their identities display different characteristics. The size of a virtual diaspora, including its composition and the geography of its location, is not a duplicate of the real diaspora. Because of this difference of group cohesion, real and virtual diasporas engage in different social dynamics. For example, while a real diaspora may inhabit a city, and even an enclave within a city, but be dispersed otherwise, a virtual diaspora inhabits its own virtual space, even though it may have a dispersed membership. Before the advent of the personal computer, diasporans may have had extralocal connections through the telephone, a *one-to-one* mode of communication, but now the computer allows them to have *one-to-many* communications in real time.

Just as real diasporas include diverse communities of interests, virtual diasporas are not monolithic entities, either. Virtual diasporic space is not ideologically homogeneous. Every diasporic group tends to generate a plurality of virtual diasporas around areas of interest, such as religion, politics, gender, professions, and the like. Since the membership comes from the same pool, these virtual diasporas tend to be made up of intersecting circuits that crisscross one another while maintaining their distinct purposes.

As a result of this blurring of boundaries, the borders of identity among the various forms of virtual diaspora expressed in one group blur, as well. The same must be said about the relations between a virtual diaspora and a real diaspora. Virtual diasporas allow individuals to exhibit short-term identities that may complement or contradict their long-term identities as expressed in reality, and virtual identities may even sometimes incarnate themselves in reality. A short-term virtual identity is contingent upon and may shift because of the composition of the virtual group, its ideological orientation, its social fragmentation, and the content and nature of the virtual discussion underway. The resulting inconsistency was observed by Rai: "the same textual construction of the diaspora can at the same time enable these diasporas to be for 'affirmative action' in the United States and be against 'reservations' in India, to lobby for a tolerant pluralism in the West, and also support a narrow sectarism in the East."[16] Elkins[17] refers to this bundling and unbundling process as "the opportunity to be different people in different settings." The logic that may be prevalent in one setting may be somewhat different in another setting.

Human agency is what links the identities of real and virtual diasporans because it produces both. The individual person wears a different mask to perform the self in each of these contexts. For Elkins,[18] "historical instances of bundling and unbundling have eventually allowed many people to be comfortable with the concept and reality of multiple identities." While human agency is firmly bundled in the reality of daily life, it unbundles and rebundles itself to participate in the ephemerality of virtual diasporic circuits.

While the diasporic individual is the subject that links virtual and real diasporic life, diasporic media such as ethnic newspapers and television link the two publics together. Elkins[19] refers to these mass media as "targeted or addressable" media because they cater to "homogeneous audiences," that is, to the diasporic community. Their homogeneity inheres in their belonging to the same national community. These on-line and off-line diasporic media are the conduit through which both real and virtual diasporas are fed. Because these texts are written in the national language of the group (French, Spanish, Creole, and so on) and discuss matters pertaining to the life of diasporans and homeland people, they serve as a main supply source of commentary on the country for the diaspora. They shape the opinions of the targeted public and their content is shaped by diasporic interaction.

Virtual diasporic space as networked space

The ways in which the boundaries of identities and social groups blur and shift in virtual diasporas force us to reposition the concept of a real diaspora in relation to the concept of a virtual diaspora. While a real diaspora implies the homeland as one pole and a host land as another, a virtual diaspora implies the homeland and host land as nodes in a network of nodes. A node in a virtual network can be said to be "flat" or "deep." A network is flat when it is constituted by the association of individuals acting simply as such. In contrast, the membership of a deep network is in constant interaction with subgroups of which they are members and which they may be said to represent, an interaction that may influence their contribution to the network. Thus, in a flat node, the person may simply represent himself or herself, while in a deep node, he or she may serve as the spokesperson for a group.

By referring to virtual diasporic space as networked space, we want to indicate that a network does not imply that all the nodes are active, but rather that they are potentially capable of being reactivated. In a network, there are degrees of participation, and there may be layers of subnetworks that feed the main virtual diasporic circuit. One can think of networks of activated nodes, networks of activated and inactivated nodes, more activated than inactivated nodes, or more inactivated than activated nodes, or the spatial circuits of activated nodes as dependent upon the rhythms of interaction. In addition, as we have seen, virtual diasporic spaces are not monolithic. That means they are made up of a plurality of virtual spatial circuits. This plurality is fed by different levels of technology available to nodes (availability of computers and compatible software), different levels of appropriation and use of technology (computer skills to navigate the realm of on-line communications), and different levels of connectivity (slow modem versus fast speed connections). Virtual diasporic space thus has a variable architecture that reflects a diversified and heterogeneous universe constituted of multiple smaller networks that have their ways of behaving vis-à-vis the total network.

The virtual spatial shape of the network changes depending on the actors involved. In other words, the shape of the total network may not materialize because some possible members never connect with it. Also, the total global shape may remain the same, but the hierarchy or shape of subnetworks may change and therefore change the dynamics of the global system. The dynamics of the main virtual diasporic circuit may be subverted or influenced by what goes on in the subset of networks attached to a specific central node.

The global-spatial shape also changes in terms of depth. Not all the interconnected nodes have the same status. Because of their position in the circuit and the subset of networks they command, some are more influential than others that do not penetrate the circuit with the same intensity or simply because they encounter technical or infrastructural problems of interconnectivity.

A major shortcoming in the study of networks is the neglect of the temporal factor. This neglect tends to position nodes as equal entities instead of unequal sites. Adding history to the dynamics of sites provides clues as to the identity of such sites. Each node can have its own genealogy in its relations with other nodes and perhaps with the global network.

Adding history to the dynamics of virtual diasporic spaces allows us to see the processes by which they are assembled and by which they change. These include the process of aggregation when the sites are interconnected and telecommunication between them takes place; the process of attachment when a subset of networks or individuals is connected to a main node for the purpose of communication; the process of detachment or isolation when a main node or subsets of networks or individuals disconnects from the network momentarily or permanently; the process of combination when two or more nodes collapse into one as a result of strategic alliance; the process of flexible membership when a node may be invited to participate from time to time in the network without being a permanent member of it; and the process of delayed connectivity when one cannot immediately access the virtual diasporic circuit because the computer is down or because of time zone differences. Time zones do not impede global connectivity, but they do impede availability because the message may be received when the person is asleep.

The total network is made global because it is globally connected, but not all the players are directly connected to each other, because smaller subsets of networks are connected to different nodes. The spatial direction of the global network is molded by the whole group or influenced by the leadership. Since the initiators may have their own agenda, this bias of orientation may give a specific identity to the virtual global-spatial process itself. Networks are not neutral entities. They are led and structured by participants or the leaders that comprise them. In each locality, the use of IT may contribute either to reinforcing the existing hierarchical system, undermining existing hierarchies (collapsing, resisting, creating an alternative form), or rearranging the *rapport de force*.

Virtual diasporic space and transnational politics

To say that the networks and circuits of virtual diasporic spaces are not neutral thus is simply to recognize that a principal component of their effect is political—political especially in the sense that virtual diasporas affect the politics of their home nations, as well as participating in the politics of host nations. Those who have studied the role of traditional immigrants in American society have tended to focus on the immigrants' loyalty to the United States and their efforts to influence US foreign policy. They have tended to see the political activities of traditional immigrants in terms of the expression of democratic rights that provide a needed balance to mainstream democratic practices, and more recently, those who use the diasporic approach have argued that immigrant lobbies are the channels through which immigrants participate in the political life of the nation and that they actually promote American democracy in their homeland societies. This literature was developed in the context of the Cold War and was necessarily influenced by that context.[20]

This literature, however, deals with real diasporas, and not virtual diasporas. The political effect of virtual diasporas goes beyond the promotion of American interests and extends to the globalization of the national politics of all nations, democratic and otherwise, developed and developing. Virtual diasporas help make national politics transnational, complicating the politics of both homeland and host land. These unseen actors contribute their own visions of politics, which are influenced by their life abroad and which may not coincide to the perspectives or aspirations of those in the homeland. Virtual diasporans, like real diasporans, develop their own political stances on issues that concern their countries of origin, views that may not correspond to the official policies of either the homeland nation or the host nation. But the IT revolution allows virtual diasporans to intervene directly and immediately in the politics of both. Thus, diasporic Web sites sometimes display propagandistic materials in support of political parties or factions that the host country and the homeland country alike want to suppress. Or they may support movements opposed by one or the other, the host or the homeland. In all cases, they pluralize or extend a pluralistic approach to the politics of both. The transnational politics of virtual diasporas thus complicates international relations.

The channels afforded by virtual diasporas may serve as the means by which local conflicts are both exacerbated and resolved, not only because the diasporans bring a larger view of social reality to the issues, but because they may feed information or interpretations to homeland actors through on-line communications. Thus, for example, in a conflict that opposes the United States to a homeland, the diaspora may serve as a go-between passing information through on-line communications between political actors in the United States and abroad.

Virtual diasporas thus contribute to the deterritorialization of the nation. Like real diasporas, they disassociate the nation, with its border, from its citizenry. As groups of persons who do not relinquish their rights to intervene in homeland's affairs, virtual diasporans constitute a force to be reckoned with as they may undermine or strengthen the stability of the national state.

Virtual diasporic spaces can function as archival sites. Unlike real diasporas, which may not leave any written trace of their political activities because of the orality that face-to-face interaction entails, virtual diasporas produce texts that can be accessed and studied years later. Such spaces are sites of memory where past activities can be recalled. These two sites— virtual and real—can be combined to understand the totality of the diasporic experience.

The globalization of national politics in and by means of virtual diasporic space, and its transformation into transnational politics, can be witnessed in this archive in two instances in which virtual diasporas played a significant role: the Chinese democracy movement that culminated in the events in Tiananmen Square in 1989 and the polarization of Haitian politics with the second election of Jean Bertrand Aristide in 2001. They illustrate the ways in which spatial national boundaries, which have always been artificial or conventional and materialized through the division and separation of physical space, social status, and identity, are transmuted and transgressed by the ability of virtual diasporas to traverse the nodes and circuits of cyberspace.

The virtual space of the digital city is linked to a series of global virtual spaces that define the arena of political engagement for virtual diasporans: the translocal, the transnational, and the transglobal. The translocal translates activities that occur at a single territorial site; the transnational expresses the extension of the local through transborder practices to other nations; while the global circumscribes an even larger set of territories. The virtual diaspora inhabits all three.

The 1989 Tiananmen Square prodemocracy student movement is a good example of how a virtual diaspora located in a variety of translocal sites worldwide penetrates the national politics of a homeland. The virtual diaspora influenced real-time politics at home by supporting students' views, by engaging a wider circle of the diaspora in homeland affairs, by putting people in contact with folks at home, by advising on courses of action, by sending money to dissidents, and even by encouraging diasporic students to return to be part of the movement. Virtual connections with the diaspora short-circuited the ability of the Chinese authorities to censor transnational conversations and provided access to a solidarity group outside the country capable of lobbying in their respective places of residence on behalf of the students and engaging other non-Chinese activist groups in the process. The virtual diaspora also effectively combined their efforts with the real diasporas to lobby government officials in their host lands on behalf of the homeland movement. Such virtual circuits strengthened the position of the students because of the support coming from abroad.

The role of Hong Kong University students in channeling funds and ideas to the prodemocracy student movement is well documented by Zhao.[21] According to Yi Mu and Thompson,

> Widespread sympathy was also shown through support demonstrations around the world both by overseas Chinese communities and by the natives of the countries in which they took place.... At the same time, Chinese students abroad tried to collect funds to help defray publication and medical expenses incurred by the student protestors and also as a reserve fund for emergencies. In North America, U.S. and Canadian citizens donated money generously and spontaneously.[22]

In the era of the technology-induced virtuality, the Tiananmen Square prodemocracy student movement shows that democracy is a dual project driven by both face-to-face and technology-mediated communications. The real and the virtual are part of the same frame of reference to the extent that the real influences the virtual and the virtual influences the shapes of the real. They are in synergy with each other.

At a time when the Internet was not yet made available to the public—something that happened in 1994—Tiananmen Square dissidents made use of the limited availability of this telemediated mode of communication. Miles remarks that "a few dissidents even had access to fax machines... A few of those affiliated with academic institutions could use the Internet, the computer network that allows millions of computer users around the world to exchange uncensored information instantaneously at minimal cost."[23]

The computer printouts communicated information from conversations between the diaspora and the dissidents, ideas sent by the diaspora from their in-group discussions outside the borders of the Chinese state, and texts sent out by the dissidents either to inform the diaspora or simply to request their opinions about strategies of action. In this atmosphere, it is not easy to identify the place of origin of a specific idea because it could originate from any node in the transnational circuit. Virtual conversation between two nodes or more served to shape the content of printouts made available electronically to activists and potential dissidents.

The virtual diaspora did not simply influence the ideology of the revolt and strategies of action, it also recruited new dissidents, thereby enlarging the size of the group through the same process of e-mailing texts to friends and family members, encouraging them to support the movement. Diasporans also lobbied their respective governments to intercede on behalf of the democracy movement in China. They organized and engaged in demonstrations supporting the movement in the homeland and urging the US government to support their cause.

The intensive virtual communication between the diaspora and the homeland prodemocracy movement led to migration in both directions: diasporic students returned home to be part of the movement or simply because they were homesick and longed to be in the middle of the action, and homeland students joining the diasporans in exile because they were afraid that they would be arrested and because when the movement was quashed they had to seek asylum elsewhere to prevent arrest or death. The success of the revolt would have led to the migration of more diasporic students to the homeland, and the revolt's failure drove more people to exit the country and join the diaspora.[24] What began with virtual communications for a just cause at home thus ended with virtual communications in search of sponsors/money in the diaspora for eventual emigration to a safe place.

In the Chinese case, one may identify three distinct periods of virtuality, each with its own agenda and intensity and each affecting the local community differently. The *precrisis period* is characterized by individual linkages for the purpose of maintaining family relationships and supporting local development projects. These are ad hoc virtual communications that do not immediately involve the politics of the homeland. The *crisis period* is when virtual communications are at their peak. The communications include more people in the network, participants are more active in contributing whatever they can to the process, and central issues of national politics are at stake. What makes such a situation a virtual and real crisis is that dissidents are operating both in reality and in virtuality and the source of their action may come from either pole. The situation becomes more volatile because of the number of invisible virtual diasporans who are intervening in the politics of the state. The decline or *postcrisis period* is a period of disengagement for some, demobilization for others, and longing for emotional support for still others.

The diverse Chinese communities in the United States participated at multiple levels in this transnational intervention into homeland politics, partly because Internet use was not that widespread, but was confined mostly to universities, other research institutions, business organizations, and the military. Other factors also explain this fragmented participation, including the non-Chinese origin of some recent Chinese migrations. I am referring to immigrants who came to the United States from Malaysia, Singapore, Vietnam, the Philippines, and South Korea. In Silicon Valley, individuals had access to computers and used them to send messages to Beijing encouraging the students, providing them with ideas, strategies, and advice, and sending them money in some cases. In return, the students informed them about the course of events at home. But diasporans also provided information on how the events were seen and interpreted abroad and did their best to enlarge the size of non-Chinese sympathizers by lobbying their representatives, by recruiting activists from other ethnic groups, and by mobilizing the local media as a way of shaping public opinion about the prodemocracy student movement.

In the Chinese case, therefore, one may speak of a crisscrossing circuit that links a virtual diaspora to the homeland. When Silicon Valley—based students from Hong Kong learned that money was needed to support student protesters, they located intermediaries to deliver funds to students. Here was an excellent example of how a circuit feeds one of its nodes.

Although the prodemocracy student movement provides us with a few clues and early signs of how the Chinese diaspora used the Internet and fax machines to convey their ideas to dissidents, they had only a moderate effect on the movement's trajectory. Access to the Internet was limited on both sides to those who worked in educational institutions and business corporations.

Virtual diasporic space: The Silicon Valley and Port-au-Prince circuit

The effect of the Internet on the transnationalization of politics by virtual diasporas is emphasized by the case of Haiti in 2001, when Jean Bertrand Aristide was inaugurated a second time as president of Haiti and the country became politically polarized. One executive in Silicon Valley helped the regime financially, gave it access to US representatives from California, and attended the inauguration festivities in Port-au-Prince. He had steadfastly enrolled Haitians in Silicon Valley to endorse the Aristide campaign by organizing meetings and introducing people to one another for the purpose of establishing a pro-Aristide group in the Bay Area. Most of these local interactions were done via e-mail with exhibits appended in attachment files, and sometimes by telephone and fax.

Transnational communication between Aristide supporters in the valley and in Haiti was necessary to discuss ideas at the local level. The Silicon Valley leader became involved in other national activist networks with tentacles across the United States and in Haiti, France, Canada, and the Dominican Republic. These circuits were engaged in different activities: support for Haiti in the US Congress, cooperation with Canada for police training, cooperation with France for public transportation projects, and tackling the Haitian immigration problem in the Dominican Republic. For the most part, these were closed conversations. On one occasion, a Washington group decided to publish an editorial favorable to Haiti in one of the American newspapers. The draft was crafted in Washington, DC and sent via e-mail to members of the group for their reaction. The text was edited through this process as some people reacted against some language while others added ideas. Even though I am not a member of the network, I was contacted for advice that was passed along to the draftsman.

The political polarization problem was exacerbated by the virtual transnational circuit, which operated at different levels and which reproduced in virtuality what also existed in reality. The opposition parties have had their own representatives in the valley and use the Internet to engage in similar interactions with associates both in Haiti and abroad. Virtuality thus expands the problem of political polarization from the national to the transnational arena and complicates the possibility of its resolution.

Conclusion

The Tiananmen Square and the Port-au-Prince cases allow us to begin to understand the ways in which virtual diasporic space is critical to the transnational politics of conflict and cooperation. To begin with, as we saw in the instance of Tiananmen Square, the diasporans encouraged instead of discouraged the local population to take immediate action. This rationale was based on their experience abroad and their understanding of the positive outcome for society of democratic politics. Likewise, although the diaspora has had reservations about Aristide's democratic practices, it was partly the negative perception of the Aristide administration carried out through e-mails and bulletin board discussions that finally eroded Aristide's basis of popularity.

During the early phase of the identification of the issue, the diaspora helps identify points of contention. A problem may be identified in virtuality, discussed there, and a number of people who see it that way may enroll there in informal political efforts to resolve it before it is presented *in vivo* as a problem. In fact, virtuality is adding a dimension to the dynamics of informal political association. Issues are often discussed informally in virtual networks before their resolution is sought out in the formal political sector. This is a different issue than the use of computer simulation *in vitro* before the actual test *in vivo*, a process in which ideas are formally circulated for the purpose of getting people's reaction, and if everything is fine, one may pass on to action. Informal political association in cyberspace does not entail any planning, but comes out as a result of on-line informal discussion, while simulations are fully conceived in reality, but are placed in virtuality for testing before returning to reality for implementation. One thus may speak also of the circulation of opinions among network participants in the formulation of the identity of the problem. In virtuality, the identity of the problem may change because each participant may reframe it, add new elements to its problematization, complicate the avenues for its resolution, and blur its actual contents and boundaries.

In addition to contributing to the way in which political issues are framed, virtual diasporas also can contribute to ways to address them. If a tactic cannot be fully developed through face-to-face communication, bringing it to the virtual arena, such as when a draft is circulated, before it is published in a newspaper, allows the diaspora to participate in the process, as we saw in the case of the Haitian diaspora.

In the arena of transnational conflict, virtuality also can complicate the ways in which issues are addressed. Even when agreements are arrived at, virtual discussion can undermine them. Sometimes no agreement is possible because through the virtual routes new dimensions are added to the problem. It is like simultaneously conducting a formal conversation in real space, one in which people are polite and refrain from abusive language, and an informal conversation in cyberspace, one in which the rules of etiquette are less likely to be respected. The conversation at one level can impede progress at another level. In the intersection of ordinary national politics with the transnational politics of virtual diasporas, we are dealing with two crisscrossing publics with different dynamics that are unique to each because of their different composition and the different rules of interaction and etiquette.

Because identities are fluid in cyberspace, on-line interactions cannot be taken at face value and frequently require interpretation. Different entry points in the network can serve as front sites behind which hide other networks. So the first layer of conversation is backed up by a second layer that comprises the subset network to which a participant may belong. Things are not always what they seem. To understand the role of a participant in a discussion group, one may have to dig deeper into the subgroup that shapes his or her understanding of things. Entry points are stopping points because they stop the circulation of the interaction at this juncture, providing their own contribution by way of reinterpreting or reshaping it and moving it along to others. They are distinct sites for the mapping of cyberspace.

Also, in on-line interactions, the participation of each individual does not have the same value. The nodes with subsets have more value because they are sustained by subsets and therefore are in an advantageous position vis-à-vis those who do not. Likewise, not all discussions in virtuality have the same value. That depends upon the identity of the virtual group. In some, all the members are known to each other. In others, some members are known and others are not. In still other groups, some individuals may hide their identities by providing false identities. Finally, one must also pay attention to the level of forcefulness in on-line interaction. Some ideas are advanced as trial balloons, others are fixed ideas for which no negotiation is sought, and still others are presented in a give-and-take spirit.

The temporality of cyberspace must also be taken into consideration. Differential times of access pose problems for the interaction of virtual diasporans around the world with groups in the homeland. Time hierarchizes the priorities of participants' involvement. For some, the interaction may be the most important conversation of the day, but for others it may not. Interpreting the ways in which virtual diasporic space may influence transnational conflict thus entails paying attention to time, as well.

6
Virtual Time: The Processuality of the Cyberweek

Just as virtual space serves as one aspect of the infrastructure of the digital city and serves as the site of its characteristic social formations, virtual time rhythms the practices of the digital city's inhabitants in ways related to, yet different from, the rhythms imposed by the temporal conventions of the real city. Virtuality thus requires a reconceptualization of time and the various units of the civil calendar—the day, week, month, and year. It requires a concept of virtual time, as distinguished from both so-called "real" or "objective" time and from the divisions of the civil and religious calendars.[1] Here, to map out the sociological dimension of virtual time in the digital city, I select the virtual week as the unit of analysis—the cyberweek. Unlike the civil week, the cyberweek is characterized by what might be called "cybertiming" and "flextiming," consequences of the ways in which computers have modified both when and where work and nonwork activities are carried out.

This chapter examines how these two processes compress and expand the week, blurring the distinction between work time and leisure time, household and workplace, and the public and domestic spheres of the digital city. In the cyberweek, virtual time manifests itself through the collapse of temporal boundaries and the compression of time-distance. Cybertiming blurs the boundaries between the work week and the weekend and between daytime and nighttime, and, by undermining the conventional definition of work, reinvents the borders of the civil week. Flextiming likewise affects the content, linearity, and borders of the civil week, time zones, and real-time schedules, both synchronizing and desynchronizing the connectivity of the local and the global.

The civil week is organized along several axes that give it its stability, channel its deployment, and spatialize its content: These are the differentiations of space (the workplace versus the home), the divisions of time (work time versus rest time), the temporal harmonization of collective activities (people doing the same types of work at the same time), the linearity of chronological order (the work week versus the weekend), the temporality of physical presence (face-to-face interaction in the carrying out of activities), and the policing of time through the surveillance of the diverse boundaries of the civil day and civil week (blue laws, firm schedules, and the temporal regimentation of society).

The cyberweek is organized along a different set of axes: *hybridity* (real time is mixed with virtual time as people move back and forth from one type to another in the process of completing a specific task), *multiplicity* (one has different temporalities to choose from), *ubiquity*, "going everywhere" by using the Internet as "the network of all networks"[2] (one is able to accomplish a task in a continuous time period despite the vagaries of different time zones), *flexibility* (the work can be done at any place, and interconnectivity can occur at any time), *recombination* (several tasks can be accomplished at the same time), *compression* (one can squeeze a week's time into a few days), *expansion* (a task that can be done in a week may now be spread beyond the boundaries of the civil week), *telepresence*[3] (one can replace or substitute virtual presence for physical presence), and *telespatiality* (one can indicate the role of human agency in the transnationalizing and globalizing of cyberspace).

Processuality characterizes the cyberweek and virtual time as products of sociotechnological relations. Processuality is understood here phenomenologically, as the deployment of social action whereby one step leads to the next in a logical-structural order. Such a structure of action may have a forward or a backward orientation. The processuality of the cyberweek appears in the unfolding, motions, and parameters of this chronodigital order. As the linear deployment of social action, processuality implies that human agency, through computer connectivity, is central in the production of cybertime. This chapter explores and examines various ways in which this processuality, in its backward and forward expressions, deploys itself in human experience. Although processuality tends to be linear in the civil week, in the cyberweek it is both linear and nonlinear because of the possibility to archive, recall, and reorder things according to a different chronology. It is the logic of cybertime, the time of virtual time.

Virtual time and the cyberweek

"Virtual time" is a universal time that provides global alternatives to the regular and traditional clock in terms of units of measurement. Hiltz and Turoff emphasize that unlike the telephone, which "requires people to be available at the same time... the computer... allows individuals the freedom to choose their own time of interaction."[4] "Virtual time" thus refers to a number of disparate realities. For some, the best example is time spent logged onto the Internet.[5] There has been considerable disagreement over whether what has been called "Internet time" is an actual phenomenon or an evanescent buzzword.

Whatever the outcome of that debate, this chapter concentrates on a different, more general set of issues pertaining to the conceptualization of virtual time inside the cyberweek and the civil week—on virtual time as such. By "virtual time," we refer to the sociotechnological production, inscription, mediation, experience, and embodiment of time. The traditional clock provides us with an electronic measurement of time. The computer, by contrast, is a high-tech mechanism through which electronic time is produced and the conduit through which such a time is circulated, manipulated, and oriented. The machine does not simply allow us to experience electronic time, but also makes it possible for us to do so whenever we think it is appropriate. It makes possible the characteristic processuality of cybertime, the processuality of the cyberweek.

It is possible to model the cyberweek as it functions in the digital city in three different ways in relation to the calendrical civil week, which continues to be a fundamental temporal pivot of civil society in real time—the "parallel week," the "auxiliary week," and the "interactional week." In them, the cyberweek is conceptualized as parallel to, supplementary to, or complementary to the civil week.

In the "parallel week" model, the cyberweek is theorized in processual terms as having its own logic and mode of operation. This is so because it operates in the world of virtuality, which has a dynamic, intrinsic to its own internal mechanisms. This frame of reference focuses attention on the technology of that logic: How time, which is already an abstract phenomenon, is virtualized, the role of human agency in such an endeavor, and the ways in which the boundaries of such a week become fluid. In such a model, one conceives of the possibility for an individual to carry out some of his or her activities in cyberspace.

In the "auxiliary or dependent" model, the cyberweek is conceived of as an appendage to the civil week and therefore does not have an independent life or a structure of its own. It is called upon to help with deficiencies in the civil week. In processual terms, it can be seen as an enclave, marginal to or an expansion of the week, or simply as a mechanism that helps the civil week achieve its full potentialities. As such, it can be understood through the logic of the civil week that feeds and regulates it.

In the "interactional week" model, the focus is on the processual relations between the cyberweek and the civil week and how human agency moves back and forth from one to the other. In this model, the cyberweek is seen as inseparable from the civil week, since both are complementary to each other. The metaphor that one uses here is again that of two poles on a continuum, whereby they interact with each other and reciprocally feed each other.

Although each model emphasizes a different aspect of the cyberweek, the interactional week in fact encompasses the salient points of the other two. The interactional week emphasizes the role of the subject in the making and consumption of cybertime, as in the first model. In such a frame, time is subjectified because the individual subject composes the boundaries of temporal units and also moves from an objective fixed week with fixed boundaries to a weekless week whose temporality is inherently flexible and globalized.

The model of the interactional week also expresses a hybrid logic because of the time zones it crosses for the purpose of interaction or reinforcement of local time. Its hybridity comes about as the result of the process of the mixing of global with local time in the various corridors of the information superhighway of interconnectivity. It thus incorporates features found in both the "auxiliary or dependent" and "interactional week" models.

As the interactional model suggests, the cyberweek is not separate from the civil week, but rather is a continuing 168-hour time period that is activated through technological means and that is amalgamated with the civil week through a Web of individual and corporate times. As a result, it is probably more appropriate to speak not of "technological time," but of "technological times" in reference to the cyberweek. This dependence and interactivity evokes the limitations of virtual time's localized temporal globality.

However, as a pole on a continuum opposite to the civil week, the cyberweek does not necessarily follow the logic of the deployment of the civil week in terms of the boundaries of days, the division of the day into daytime and nighttime, and the location of the weekend at the end of the work week. The cyberweek not only contributes to the contraction and expansion of the week, but also has a virtual identity with its inherent logic.

Understood in terms of this model, then, a cyberweek is a set of times electronically produced through the intervention of human agency— measured with no reference to the rotation of the moon or the sun—all of which are equivalent and contained in linear or nonlinear sequences, or in both, in a flexible, cyclical temporal domain. The logic of the cyber-week can be fully understood by seeing it as comprising "virtual days" and by locating it inside a "virtual month" in a "virtual year" cycle.

The collapse of temporal boundaries

The processual logic of virtual time emphasizes flux, temporal flows, motion, speed, and direction in the temporal connections between two or more sites through the medium of high technology. In cybertime, temporal boundaries collapse "because the many different time zones of the globe interpenetrate continuously within and between cities."[6] As Moss puts it in reference to the concept of what constitutes a city, "the operational boundaries of a city are no longer defined by geography or law, but by the reach of phone lines and computer networks."[7] Cybertime ignores time zones, penetrates them, circulates between them, links them to each other, and, in the process, transforms the circuit into a homogeneous temporal terrain. However, cybertime does not eliminate some of the practical problems of communications associated with time zones. For example, they constitute a main headache for workers in the digital city, not in terms of e-mailing information to persons who work in a different time zone, but in terms of interacting with them in real time. While the computer allows the Internet connection, it is, however, in no position to ensure the availability of the interlocutor.

For example, a computer programmer in Silicon Valley discusses the kind of problems that may arise when people who live in different time zones attempt to communicate with each other through the use of the Internet and explains how he copes with time zones.

What does the digital day look like when you have to communicate with people outside of the U.S.?

It depends on where they are. The time shift is a big consideration. Often, if you are as far away as Asia or Europe, a lot of times you will send an e-mail and they will be asleep. They will respond at the beginning of their work day when I get off of work. So it's kind of difficult to communicate with people across the sea. For instance, in Europe, I think there are a certain amount of strategically placed offices. In Spain, there is a two-hour buffer at the beginning and ending of the work day where the Spanish and the U.S. overlap and there is open communication. That's basically why I think that most of the work is done out of Santa Clara and why they don't distribute around the world, because it's difficult to communicate.

Furthermore, cybertime—in each local site—ignores local time. The message is delivered no matter what time it is at the receiving end: daytime, nighttime, working-hours time, rest time. As a transnational and global circuit, it collapses the temporalities of these local categories. It competes with the neat categories sustained by the organization of local times and ends up hybridizing them by subverting or mixing them. In this new temporal regime, as Negroponte puts it "Sunday is not so different from Monday."[8]

These temporal boundaries do not refer exclusively to time zones. They also refer to the diverse local temporal boundaries that separate one human activity from another, for example, work time from lunch time, school time from rest time, church time from entertainment time, and dinnertime from sleeping time. All of these activities are locally temporized and can be retemporized by cybertime.

Cybertemporal penetration indicates that there is a fixed point from which the message starts, there is a trajectory, and there is a receiving end. It is the sending site that disturbs other sites, penetrates their temporal sphere, and influences or even reshapes local orders. So the temporal flow is directional and indicates the order of its motion.

As paradoxical as this may sound, cybertime's temporal flows are not themselves in temporal motion. They are grounded in specific sites of sending and receiving along its trajectory. Precisely because this transcendent global metatime also is always localized, cybertime can traverse all local times, and local times can be diffused into transcendent cybertime.[9] Because it is time experienced by the subject, cybertime always has some local content: It refers to and consolidates a local reality. It is time used to do everyday things. One connects to the Internet, for example, for the purpose of accomplishing quotidian things for oneself like chatting with a friend or shopping on-line. However, cybertime also allows an expansion of the local, linking it to or making it part of the global. Through such a technological means, the local not only penetrates the global, but expands itself beyond its natural boundaries.

For example, the recent project of the US Department of Defense to allow Americans stationed overseas to vote in presidential elections through the use of the Internet will allow an act accomplished overseas to be counted as a local act by counting telepresence as a form of or an equivalent to physical presence.[10] Through its connection to the electronic superhighway, the city, state, and national citizenship becomes transnational and global. This is not seen as an intrusion into the space of a foreign state, but rather as a cyberextension of the space of the nation.

The compression of time–distance

One of the characteristics of cybertime thus is to compress the distance between two sites, to reduce the time it takes to communicate with someone in another site because of the instantaneousness of the process, and to produce telepresence without physical presence. This separates the physical presence from the telepresence and at once localizes and transnationalizes or even globalizes cybertime.

Such a compression of distance enhances and hegemonizes cybertime over local time, decreases the importance of distance in matters related to communication, and desynchronizes telepresence and physical presence. It does not eliminate distance, but makes it less of an obstacle. Through the Internet, telepresence can be achieved no matter how great the physical or geographical distance is between both subjects.

The compression of distance makes possible the relocation of the global inside the local and the local inside the global. In other words, "there" is "here," and "here" can be "there," as well. The receiver may find himself or herself inside the temporal matrix of the sender for the purpose of communicating. Here, telepresence means more than just teleproximity, because it insinuates cybertemporal expansion and one's contribution to the prevailing logic of the network. As Giddens puts it, these "disembedding mechanisms...lift our social activity from localized contexts, reorganizing social relations across large time and space distances."[11]

Information technology has led not only to the collapse of temporal boundaries, but also to industrial adjustment because of the pervasive use of cybertime. For example, Hepworth remarks that

> We are now witnessing the "collapse" of these temporal boundaries in the international equities market. The superficial expression of this "collapse" is recent changes in the trading hours of different stock markets: the London trading floor now opens thirty minutes earlier (at 9:00 A.M.), and the American and New York stock exchanges are examining the feasibility of twenty-four-hour or round-the-clock trading....These changes have, however, resulted from...the use of information and communications technology by financial institutions.[12]

Cybertiming the civil week

The interaction of one type of week with another has been common in the United States and elsewhere for many centuries and manifests itself in the relation among and between the civil week with the Christian,

Muslim and Jewish weeks. Various calendrical weeks are in competition with each other because they are used by various segments of the population in the same place. The cyberweek thus is one additional type of week in the plurality of weeks that already exist in multicultural America. These religion-based weeks compete with the civil week for recognition, if not for hegemony, but the nature of the competition between the civil week and the cyberweek is yet to be determined. In some respects, the cyberweek transcends the civil week; in others, it can justly be seen as a prolongation or a cyberexpansion of the civil week; and in still other contexts, it implodes inside and transforms the civil week, as we will see below.

While the other weeks—civil, religious, or ethnic—are regulated either by the state or by the church, the cyberweek, which operates in the cyberworld, is not constrained by any institution or external entity, but rather is self-controlled and enjoys much freedom to make or remake itself. Because its deployment depends solely on individual will and action, it has no prescribed day of rest or worship, as in the case of the other types of weeks. In the nonvirtual world, the day of rest or worship is what separates one week from another and is the culmination of the work week. What kind of week is it without a day of rest or a day of congregational prayer? The cyberweek, as a continuing week, is one such week.

Because the cyberweek has no fixed beginning or ending, it does not follow the logic of any of these other weeks. It may start or end at any time. While its boundaries can be agreed upon in a case of contractual agreements or can follow those of the civil week, they may also be informal, as in the case of self-employment.

The virtual week is made up of virtual days. However, unlike the Jewish or Muslim day, which begins at sundown, or the Christian or civil day, which begins at midnight (in the Gregorian calendar) or at noon (in the Julian calendar), the virtual day may start at any time, and in this sense it may be seen as an *artificial day*—a day that contrasts to the *natural day* that is based on either solar or lunar motions. In the same way that the Jewish day does not coincide with the civil day, the cyberday may or may not coincide with the civil day, even though the latter may provide it with its temporal boundaries. It follows also that in the same way that the Muslim week does not coincide with the civil week, the cyberweek may or may not coincide with it, either.

Cybertime affects both the quantity of work performed in the digital city and the quality of life there. It affects the quantity of work because of the expansion of working hours and the quality of life because of the freedom to pick and choose where and at what time one would do the work. In the nonvirtual world, one finds five work days plus the weekend, which is different from the rest of the week. Cybertime reconfigures that order by blurring the distinction between the work days and the weekend because it is so easy to open the computer on Sunday morning and get back to work. This blurring of the boundaries between the work week and weekend is exacerbated by the presence of the global, which also turns it more and more into a continuing week. Because e-mail may penetrate one's time zone at any time to deliver its message, and because the receiver can immediately provide a reply, the global constantly implodes inside the local.[13]

It alters the work day, as well. Since the work can be done at any time at home or in the workplace, it decompresses the day of work that used to be compressed between 8:00 AM and 5:00 PM, allows for more choice between virtual and real time and place of work, makes possible greater connectivity, and decreases the need for interface interaction through the usual meeting in a specific place. One can work not only from 8:00 AM to 5:00 PM, but also early in the morning and late at night because the workplace, for some, is no longer located in a fixed geographic space separate from the home. Cybertime also blurs the very definition of work because workplace tasks can now become housework.

The cyberweek, however, does not undo the traditional civil week. It simply allows a greater disconnection between the conventional and individual practices in a way that cannot be easily regulated because of the interstitiality of behavioral practices.

The cyberweek changes the order of work for some by decreasing the Monday workload. In some lines of employment, the expectation in the civil week was that much of the work that was not done the previous week must be done on Monday. As work is done on weekends at home, this tends to alleviate part of the burden, but as people become more accessible through the cyberworld, new workload may be added through weekend connectivity. This lack of specificity of Sunday in the cyberworld as a day of rest or worship turns the work week in cyberspace into a continuing week. Although the precise medical implications of this temporal transformation are yet to be substantiated, one may nevertheless speculate that for this category of individual professional workers, the role of Monday as the peak day for cardiac arrest may be diminishing over time as a result of a different rescheduling of the cyberweek.

More radically, however, the cyberweek has tended to deregulate the order of the work week. One of the main roles of the civil week is to regulate the public sphere by way of assigning times when public work can be done. It does so for all individuals, irrespective of gender and race. This brings some order to society, at least in the compartmentalization of daytime. Industrialization has had a destabilizing effect on the civil day and week because of the necessity of night and day shifts to feed the needs of the workplace. In response, work-time regulation often was negotiated by managers and unionists through labor-relations disputes. Now, however, we enter a period when such schedules, because they are individualized in some firms, leave no room for external regulation. Perhaps the new paradox is that such work—more, and at different times, than before—is done by some teleworkers not because they are forced to do it, but simply because they enjoy doing it, even though they are not necessarily paid for this extra labor. In other words, paid or not, they do it for their own enjoyment, as part of self-learning, or as a way of increasing output needed to be successful in the workplace.[14] It is a way of improving one's skills, maintaining good relations with management, and engaging in overtime activities because of the lure of extra money down the road as a result of one's acquisition of these extra skills.

Cybertime thus simultaneously transgresses and thereby reinscribes in altered form the borders of the working week, the borders of the weekend, and the borders of the civil week itself. Consequently, as paradoxical as it may sound, cybertime reinvents the civil week by shedding light on the day of rest: Although one is restricted from engaging in public work that prevents others from resting or worshipping in places that have developed Sunday legislation, one is not prevented, however, from doing work at home, even if it is computer work. The public aspect of the civil week is underlined to the extent that such work annoys others. In the cyber regime, work that once belonged to the public sphere and therefore fell under the constraints of Sunday legislation has now fallen under the private sphere.

Flextiming the civil week

Cybertiming is but one aspect of flextiming the civil week, since the latter was in use even before the existence and spread of the former. Flextime, in the case of the digital city's telecommuters, refers to the process by which work that used to be done at a conventional workplace can now be carried out elsewhere (locational flexibility) and at a time of their choice (temporal flexibility). Flextiming also refers in its traditional meaning to the ability of industry to reconstruct its formal time by allowing employees more freedom in the organization of their working hours or by coupling virtual time with real time in the delivery of services or the production of goods. Flextiming affects the routine of the civil week in these two arenas. The time of work no longer needs to coincide with the hours of the working day. By shifting working time inside and outside the traditional working day, flextiming allows for much more flexibility at the workplace.[15] Work time does not need to coincide with one's presence at the workplace, hence the split between work and workplace and the recognition and inclusion of home as formal workplace, as well. Time allocated for work at the workplace can now be spent for leisure, and leisure time can be spent to produce labor output. The identity of the working hours of the day can be disrupted to insert leisure time, and the continuity of leisure can be disrupted to insert labor time. Flextime disrupts the clear separation between leisure time or weekends and labor time in ways different from the disruption that occurred earlier with the advent of the Industrial Revolution.

The second aspect of the phenomenon is the reconstitution of the civil week by way of the reconstruction of labor time. Instead of an objective definition of labor time as fixed in a specific place within specific working-day hours, now one gets a subjective definition of labor time dependent on the subject's way of organizing his or her weekly schedule. This labor time can expand to include the prelabor time (between 6:00 AM and 8:00 AM), the postlabor time (after 5:00 PM), domestic labor time (Saturday), or even nonlabor time (Sunday).

Flextime also works toward an expansion of the week as it happens when labor that is supposed to be done in one week is completed instead in another week. It crosses the borders of the civil week. In this sense, there may be no necessary coincidence between the work week and the work itself. We have seen a similar thing with the day. As the work of a week spills into another week, the boundaries of the civil week become blurred for those involved.

Flextime also works toward a compression of the work week into fewer days. Instead of the regular five days, the week can be reduced to longer hours per day and fewer days. This can lead to an expansion of leisure time or an expansion of the weekend.

Q: Do digital workers in your firm compress sometimes their work week, and how do they do it?

A: I have seen people do that before. In the contract it says that they are paying me for this job forty hours a week. So I have seen people do things where they will work their forty hours in a few days. They will work like four (twelve-hour) days. That, of course, is a little harder when you have to go into the office every day. That's why my situation is really unique because no one will notice if I am not working. Whereas, if you are in the office, people will see that you are not there. (Interview with a manager of a computer firm in Silicon Valley)

By allowing the relocation of public work time inside private household time, flextiming also helps define the secular identity of the civil week by way of delimiting the identity of the day of rest. Since Sunday legislation regulates public life via negative laws—what not to do—flextime like cybertime, allows one to work at home on Sunday, thereby reducing the jurisdiction of the blue laws. Flextime shows how Sunday legislation projects Sunday as a day of nonpublic labor for some (Christians), a day that is not to be confused with a nonlabor day.

Flextiming is carried out not only inside the civil week, but also inside the cyberweek. In fact, flextime is a fundamental characteristic of the cyberweek. The cyberweek's deployment depends on flextime because of the flexibility and elasticity of interconnectivity and also because of the need of the individual to juggle between real time and virtual time given the actual constraints of civil society.

Behavioral decoupling of time zones

Virtual time results in the behavioral decoupling of time zones: An individual who lives in a specific time zone adjusts his or her social activities to the rhythm of life in another time zone. Behavioral decoupling means living one's life as if one were elsewhere. As a consequence, personal temporality is in disharmony with the local temporality, but in harmony with the temporality of a distant place. Although such a disharmony has always existed in the realm of religious practices, whereby the temporality of religious rituals and celebrations may follow a church calendar (as in the case of Jewish and Muslim celebrations), the connection with the homeland has been of a spiritual nature. IT has made it possible for individuals in one time zone who live according to the time of another time zone to maintain electronic connectivity with those who live elsewhere. The novelty here is the passage from a situation of unmediated connectivity to one of electronic connectivity.

Virtual time thus annihilates time zones without annihilating the social processes that emanate from time zones. While the local system continues to organize itself according to the time zone it is in, individuals and groups demarcate a different time through the use of the Internet. What results is a multiplicity of temporal disharmonies and subsequent back-and-forth movements whereby two discordant times are integrated into the life of even those who are not themselves subject to virtual time. Thus, cybertime imposes itself as the dominant time that regulates the local social structure. The following teleworker reflects on the effect of IT on everyday life and time fragmentation both at the workplace and at home:

> I was employed at [XYZ Securities], a small broker dealer in San Diego, California where I worked on the trading desk, which was directly related to Wall Street and the *New York Times* schedule. The working hours began in San Diego at 6:00 A.M. and ended at 2:00 P.M. My job required me to arrive at 6: 00 A.M., but the strangest thing is that the rest of the company—everyone outside of the trading desk—would work a normal hour, maybe from 8:00 A.M. to 4:00 P.M. or sometimes even 9:00 A.M. to 5:00 P.M. But the people in the trading room would work from 6:00 A.M. to 2:00 P.M., leaving early every single day. I guess one of the side effects of the time difference inside of the company was that the people working until 4:00 or 5:00 P.M. were a little ambivalent. The people who had to stay until 5:00 P.M. and saw people leaving at 2:00 P.M., didn't know what was going on. They didn't realize that we got in at 6:00 A.M., or they thought it was by choice we were in the office at six in the morning. I was lucky because it was something that I only did for a couple of months each year as a summer internship. So I had to adapt to a schedule months at a time, but it was not something that I had to keep permanently in my life. But those who did, it seemed to me, had an opposite rhythm than most people. They weren't able to go out late at night.

What is indicated here is how the use of the Internet fragments the local workplace into groups of individuals with different temporal rhythms of work: those who must follow the New York schedules and those who follow the local time as the parameter for their work. This decoupling of time zones resonates inside the local firm and creates time fragmentation among workers. As a consequence of this temporal disjuncture at the workplace, the household also becomes the site where time fragmentation is experienced. As a teleworker from the San Francisco Bay Area explained,

"People with that kind of schedule couldn't meet for dinner at 6:00 P.M. because they had to be in bed at 9:00 P.M., or they couldn't really spend much time with me outside of that, even though I was involved in that time. It seems like I adapted a little more. I was used to having later nights, and because most of my friends finished work at 5:00 P.M., I would have four hours during the day to sleep when I returned from work, and then see my friends or family after that time. This would cause an even worse effect, since I would be up all night after having slept a short nap during the day, and then in the morning I would be exhausted. That continued throughout the whole summer. I can't really imagine what it would be like to work like that throughout the entire four quarters of the market and have a family outside of that. There were some brokers on the trading desk who wouldn't necessarily go home: they'd leave the office at 2:00 P.M., but then they would have three or four hours until their family got home. Some people would be fortunate enough to go play golf or something else together. Even though they weren't necessarily friends, it was more convenient to socialize with people who have the same schedule. I guess a small community did develop because restaurants would have happy hours right after work for people working with the stock market—specifically for that. So workers started to all mingle together, but not any type of genuine friendship, just a commonality of having this amount of time together. But the strangest thing was having different time schedules within the company. For example, you would have a company meeting or a company lunch, and you're working on the trading desk, and you can't take a lunch break because the market doesn't close, so you have to eat at your desk. There may be some great company lunch at twelve, but it's the peak of the market at the time, and there's no way you are going to leave to go have a luncheon, so you don't show up. Meanwhile, the rest of the employees have this negative attitude, like, 'Oh, you don't come to the company lunches, you don't do things like that.' And it is just continuous like that. Another thing about this environment is that you work very hard continuously, and it's not something that finishes at 2:00 P.M.; there is a lot of preparation that goes on before and after hours. So you are there at 6:00 A.M. when the market opens, but before the market opens, you have to prepare some paperwork, so that means being in the office at 5:30 A.M. And to be there at 5:30, that requires leaving the home early."

This temporal disharmony is also seen within a given household when one partner works according to the cadence of local time and the other according to that of another time zone.[16] What is reported above is not an exceptional case, but is the lifestyle of an ever-growing population of chronospatial workers. Shapiro and Neaubauer[17] note that:

A recent article on the Style Pages of the *New York Times*, "The Los Angeles Life on New York Time," describes "a small army of Los Angeles residents" who awake at 3:00 A.M. in order to be at work at 5:00 A.M.[18] The rest of their schedule is similarly out of synch with that of the other L.A. residents—lunch at 9:00, happy hour at 2:00, bed at 8:00. These people are "stockbrokers, bankers, lawyers and news and entertainment people whose professional lives are keyed to New York and other Eastern cities." . . . To the extent that work relations depend on speed and the timing of communications, geographic space dissolves in favor of what Virilio[19] has called chronospace.

The Internet has contributed to a temporally fractured workplace with individuals participating in cohorts based on whether or not their work time is in harmony with time at another location. Such a disjuncture allows those whose schedule follows another time instead of the local time to engage in activities, develop comradeships, and be at odds—timewise—with other employees. One consequence of this work arrangement is that these two cohorts may not be available or even on the premises at the same time to participate in corporate functions that require the presence of every employee. As some of these people leave home earlier than the rest of the family and come back home earlier, their schedule is at odds with those of their household mates, as well.

Temporal unevenness

In addition to these disharmonies, digitization has brought with it unevennesses in the distribution of the work process that are reminiscent of the traditional workplace. These forms of multiple temporality come about in various ways: with peak and nonpeak work time, with the shift from digital to nondigital work, with temporality that is contracted or expanded because of equipment problems (nonavailability of servers or inability to connect to the Internet), and with a mazeway of digital temporality that is a function of flexiplace/flextime arrangement, and global connections. As one city hall elections worker put it, "It's difficult to say, because there are certain times when basically a lot of the work is kind of as-I-have-time-to-do-it kind of thing. It's a pretty much a pretty good mix of everything as, you know, as the election comes closer they'll be more and more campaigning questions, from, you know, people that are running for office."

Digitization has not done away with the reality and practice of peak time. What it has done is to redistribute it. This redistribution may coincide with the traditional peak time, and in this case it enhances it, facilitates it, and may make it more stressful, not necessarily because of added work, but because it requires one to shift one's posture from traditional to digital technologies.

The source of that peak time is not located in virtuality, but in the reality of one's daily life. Cyclical events in the life of the firm, for example, feed peak time periods that resonate in more digital activity among office workers and telecommuters. These peak digital periods are distributed across the day, the week, the month, and the year. They are distributed unevenly because they may affect one department more than another. For example, in an election season, the department at city hall in charge of the process is more affected with e-mail queries than others. As a San Francisco City Hall employee stated:

> I had some really kind of angry citizens come in that wanted to get a referendum started when the Board of Supervisors passed the sex-change legislation, and they didn't like that, so they wanted all kinds of information about starting a referendum, so I gave them the information that they needed, and at that point, it's in their hands to, you know, continue with the process.

Time fragmentation as a result of the combination of traditional and digital shift in one's work and telecommuting is a foundational element in the temporal digital architecture of the workplace. Digitization has allowed people to do linear work, work embedded in the logic of the modern industry, in a nonlinear fashion, or even to carry out multiple tasks at the same time, because the microcomputer allows this kind of flexibility.

Real-time schedules and virtual time

Although it is obvious that virtual time has quickened the pace of time in virtuality because it reduces distance, it is important to address not only the issue of contraction of real time, but also of its manipulation. For example, through contraction, virtual time speeds up the mail delivery system through instantaneous e-mail and in the process provides a new identity to the regular mail delivery system, which, in comparison, is referred to as "snail mail" to express its lack of speed because of the geographical distance it must travel, the physical transportation of the courier, and the scheduling of its delivery.

Virtual time makes possible the manipulation of real time by decompressing and deprocessing its linearity. It changes, for example, the temporal logic of scheduling. The notion of a schedule implies the organization of time in concrete units following a linear order of things.[20] Schedules imply the imposition of a regimen, as in the case of industrial work, because of its disciplinary goal.[21] This imposition can be a negotiated process whereby a fixed outcome ensues, or a proposed temporal unit can be submitted by a subaltern and meet the acquiescence of the other party. In all these forms of scheduling, there is one aspect that remains the same: that is, the fixation of a specific time. Before the advent of the Internet, one had to deal with these schedules at the appropriate time. If not, one misses out. Traditional schedules are like television schedules, with special times for entertainment, religious programs, and international news. Virtual time allows flexibility to pick and choose in the order one wants, the time one wants, and the place one wants. One may arrange these previously fixed schedules to meet one's own needs. A major characteristic of virtual time is thus the possibility for manipulation and reorganization of real time according to one's agenda. Real-time schedules become frozen in time, to be reorganized as needed. Thus, with digitization, one may eventually become less dependent on scheduled television programs, since one has more freedom to access them through the Internet or via electronic storage devices whenever one wants.

To put it another way, in the digital city, we are moving more and more from a fixed-schedule (real-time) regime to a flexible-schedule regime. In a sense, what we are witnessing is not the meltdown of real time, as we measure it through our calendars and clocks, but a transformation of our relations to so-called "real" or "objective" time. Two variables are affected in the construction of virtual time: the role and status of the subject, and his or her relations to real time.

In the example above, the schedules of television programs are predetermined, and people must access the programs when they are made available in real time, in the order in which they are presented there. However, thanks to the virtual time, people are able to choose to watch them at different times, and also in a different linear order. Morning news or shows can be accessed in the evening, after the evening news. The subject disciplines the programs according to his or her own timeframe, not vice versa, and is not dependent on an imposed schedule. Virtual time thus dehomogenizes the viewing time of the audience. While the program continues to be homogeneous (the same for all in terms of content and organization), viewing time becomes heterogeneous.

In addition to transforming the status and role of the subject, virtual time also transforms the relation of the subject to real time. Because the people can view news programs out of their "real" or "objective" temporal order, for example, the relation of the viewer to the program is affected. It is one thing to see a morning news show in the morning, when one gains access to new information, but seeing this program in the evening after one has read about events in the newspapers or heard about them on the radio is likely to entice a different reaction. The disposition of the individual vis-à-vis the program is likely to change from one scenario to another.

Through virtual time, the industrial time regime is being restructured to meet the transformation of the office and individual needs. The discipline of the industrial time regime is based on the labor process and separates the time of work from the time of sleep, private time from public time. Industrial time is organized to bring about regularity, consistency, efficiency, rationality, and order.[22] The macrostructure equalizes time distribution, not the value of time for all, which temporally limits the individualization process. Virtual time returns control to the individual subject, with the freedom to manipulate and organize time according to his or her needs. Virtual time allows one not only the freedom of space (working where one wants), but also the freedom of time (working when one wants).

Synchronized and desynchronized connectivity

Virtual time makes possible the manipulation of real time in other ways, as well. Digital technology both desynchronizes and resynchronizes temporal connectivity that previously could occur only in local time and real time. Digitization allows a retarded connectivity because the message may not be recovered at the same time. The message is in a latent temporal phase before it becomes activated at the time when the receiver accepts and processes it. So the time of connectivity may be manipulated by the receiver. One may distinguish receiver connectivity from sender connectivity and intermediary connectivity from auxiliary or observer connectivity.

Digital technology also allows a mixing of time as the computer and the mobile telephone make it possible to interconnect at any time without paying attention to the time of the other. It does away with the strict formal segmentation of the week, with blocks of time when one is supposed to be available in the public sphere and blocks of time reserved for the domestic sphere. Through this technology, one sees a greater interpenetration of private time and public time. However, this form of desynchronization brings about a resynchronization, because one may connect with people in different time zones and engage in both workplace and home activities.

Digital technology thus has produced a new notion of time, new distributional mechanisms, new speed, new forms of receptivity, a new multiplicity of actors, and a new pattern of interactional relations.[23] Adam compares the old with the new mode of temporality when she notes that "where sequence, duration, rate and directional change dominate the technologies of previous centuries, simultaneity, plurality, networks and instantaneous feedback prevail in contemporary ones." She insists that "these contemporary developments have brought about a shift of emphasis from duration and succession to simultaneity and instantaneity," and she further concludes that "the computer's software entails pleistropic relations; its connections are not one: one but one: many, forming networks of non-linear event chains where a single change can have unpredictable effects throughout the system."[24]

In this new digital regime, the cyberweek is not based on any of the criteria of the other weekly cycles and their fixed peak days such as the day of rest (civil week), the day of worship (Jewish, Muslim, or Christian week), the market day (in preslavery Africa), or even the symbolic representations of the planetary week. The cyberweek is detached from these contingencies and displays the following characteristics constitutive of its virtual identity: It is based on the concept of a flexible, not necessarily bounded day; it is based on business or other activity cycles; it is not tied to the bounds of any civil or religious day; and it is a mechanism used to expand the civil or religious day.[25]

Conclusion

The effort to explain the identity and characteristics of virtual time in the digital city is not simply an intellectual exercise. Such an endeavor has a series of practical implications for society. As the electronic and telecommunications technology becomes more and more a mode through which social action is performed, there is a need to understand not only what it does to our everyday life, but also how we measure and enhance cyberspace productivity, evaluate work time and overtime, and compensate the new breed of cyberworkers.

Three aspects of virtual time need further analysis: the instantaneity of cybertime, its simultaneity, and its "malleability."[26] Instantaneity means that communication can be done through telepresence instead of physical presence. For courses taught on-line, for example, will telepresence count toward campus residency requirements, which always demand that one must be physically present on campus, or is the cyber-week, for the purpose of a completing a degree, equivalent to the civil time as measured in the civil calendar? Will the time requirements to complete an on-line degree be the same as those for classroom courses?

And if it is possible to be telepresent instantaneously and simultaneously in Paris, Madrid, Cairo, Jerusalem, and New York, then in New York, where blue laws still exist, will cyber-Sunday be a day off, or will the cyberweek totally undermine the ability of any states to enforce their Sunday legislation? Will new and improved legislation be needed to deal with cybertime and the cyberweek? We see similar problems with contractual agreements. Can cyber-Sunday be assumed as a working day in cyberspace, or should it be eliminated from all contracts as a non-working day? Likewise, how do we evaluate overtime for work done in cyberspace, when the normal load is within the sequential confines of the civil week? Should these two weeks—civil and cyber—use the same units of temporal measurement for the purpose of compensating workers?

Cybertime also is not exclusively linear, as time is understood in Newtonian physics. It can be linear at times and nonlinear at other moments. Because cybertime is fundamentally flexible and malleable, people can combine different time sequences, mixing past time with present time to produce new combinations, or mixing diverse localized times as a way of producing new temporal domains. Corcoran argues, for example, that "the digital culture of time is transforming our sense of the aesthetic."[27] Our notion of generation has also been altered and signifies a shorter span of time that is less than thirty years; for example, one speaks of the fifth generation of a given line of computers.[28] And what will a millennium be in cybertime? These sorts of questions, for which, at this time, there are no prefabricated or conventional answers, provide us with some general direction in our effort to conceptualize the parameters of virtual time and the processuality of cybertime.

7
Conclusion: The Digital City as the Virtual Embodiment of the Global City

The digital city is an important component of the global city. Global digital practices and communications have become part of the daily routine of digital city residents. In the digital city, the local is not a mere given that is then shaped by the global. Instead, the global and the local manifest themselves in and through each other.

The total identity of the digital city has three components, the *formal*, *informal*, and *virtual* aspects of its makeup. The vast majority of urban studies focus on the formal city because of the strategic importance in understanding its operation. A few studies have focused on the informal city in an effort to understand the multiple ways in which informal practices affect the daily routine of urban life.[1] This chapter focuses on the virtual aspect of the digital city and the way in which the global implodes into the local and the local explodes into the global.[2] It examines the diversity of global digital practices in the city, analyzes how diverse global flows have fragmented the identity of the local digital space, and shows that the global city must be seen as a processual node in a globally connected network of digital nodes such as the digital city. It concludes that digitization provides the city with a new global identity.

In the digital city, three processes affect the local shape of the global digital city and the global shape of the local digital city. They manifest themselves in different, but complementary ways. The global and the local are related through *implosion, explosion* and *circulation*. Implosion designates the ways in which global factors come to play a role locally. This is done by *appropriation, imposition*, and *intrusion*. When appropriation is the mode of implosion, external sources enable local actors to enhance the local system. For example, Alberthal (1999: 39) writes, "the word 'global' implies that engineers and other professionals will incorporate best thinking, practices, and research from around the world into their product designs." Imposition occurs because of the influence of external forces of power and dominance in a hierarchized scheme. Intrusion occurs because local sites are porous to in-coming communications.

Explosion, by contrast, refers to the outbound flow that can influence other nodes and whereby the local system finds itself in a position to influence other sites. This happens when a local site initiates an on-line communication and establishes a global social environment. Finally, circulation refers to the mobility of processes made possible by connectivity with interoperability in a system of flows.[3] Digital globalization has a digital infrastructure. The wiring of the city and of the whole world provides the infrastructure for flows to circulate between the local and the global and the global and the local. Technology does not determine the direction and content of these flows, but provides the channels they traverse. Such an infrastructure is used creatively by individuals to engage in their own activities. We can see all these processes at work in the relations between the local and the global in the digital.

Global digital practices of the city

Not all the global practices of the city are digital, and similarly, not all the digital practices of the city are global. What emerges from the study of the American metropolis is the diversity of its global digital practices. These practices come about because of different interests of segments of the urban population. These segments range from multinational corporations to families and individuals. Multinational corporations link up to satellites worldwide as part of their daily operations, while nonprofit organizations also maintain routine transnational relations with selected sites, depending on their focus and the intensity of the problem they are attempting to resolve and the specific country involved. These ongoing and more or less continual relations must be contrasted with multinational family and individual relationships, which can be either continual or occasional and that may tend to lose their strength over time.

All these global digital practices of the various sorts of local actors are instruments of their integration into the digital city. They use them to advance their corporate interests or individual careers, to make money, and to compete locally. Many individuals spend more time engaging in these global practices because of the psychological relief they provide: The use of the Internet has allowed some to develop virtual communities, people with whom they maintain a virtual presence, with whom they communicate on-line, and who give symbolic meaning to their daily lives. These communities are made up of individuals whom one calls upon at different times for different reasons and in order to accomplish specific goals.[4] In these diverse virtual communities, the local city is thus globalized through the implosion from and explosion into the virtual world and the circulation it makes possible.

> The majority of my communications with my close family members, my parents who are right now in Iran, my cousins, my relatives, people that are close to me, are being done through the computer. I talk to my parents through MSN Messenger. All of my relatives I talk to ... are all linked through the Internet. It is like my world. It is my banking. It is all the information that runs my life. Everything I am doing I feel like, literally, I get synched with my laptop. (Male student in the San Francisco Bay Area)

The diversity of the global flows that circulate attests to the difference of spatial circuits. The same individual may connect to more than one extraterritorial site, or several individuals may connect to different sites. These various spatial circuits contribute to both the integration and segmentation of the local in ways that intrinsically define the digital identity of the city.

When globalization is seen from the standpoint of local actors, the local appears in its polar intensity. Via widespread linkages, locality is able to explode into different parts of the world, and flows from the rest of the world implode at specific locality. The local thus is reinforced not in its own right, but because of the circulation that occurs through its global linkages.

Thus, local identity is constantly being made by globality as an essential part of its makeup, and vice versa. The local is constantly exploding into the global. Some local practices are global because of their global connections. While the points of origin of these global practices may be traced to a locality, the connections are to a diversity of extraterritorial places.

Because human agency lies at the heart of these processes, as we have seen throughout, they are segmented generationally as a result of different relations with IT. The digital city refracts the local ethnic, class, and gender composition of the real city's population. In a sense, however, digitization has fractured the city in a way that is different from earlier forms of stratification because the differentiation is based on different criteria. Older people who have not grown up using computers may have difficulty adjusting to the digital world because some lack digital literacy. They must be contrasted with the generation that designs the machines and develops the blueprints for the technology that will reach future generations, and in turn, this generation must be contrasted with a younger generation that is being socialized at an early age in the use of the machine. For them, unlike previous generations, it is a way of life.

There is a fascination with it at this point, in this stage of development of technology. I think our generation is running with it. We are the ones that actually are the consumers of it. The generation above us went through traditional routes. They are not really connected to it. The only connection they have is that they have to work or they have to be involved in it. The generation below us is totally into it, but in a different way, at a younger stage. There are really tapping into its potentials. Our generation is the one that is running with it to design our future with it, which is a weird thing. (Male employee at Yahoo)

For many, the meshing of virtual and real, local and global, as they enhance the performance of reality, has become part of the daily routine. Virtual presence is used to make up, to a certain extent, for the difficulty of achieving physical presence. The movement back and forth from virtuality to reality is also made possible by the multitasks in which the computer allows one to engage.

Every once in awhile, I think people take most of this technology for granted, but every once in awhile, I think people stop and are amazed at what they have in front of them. When they had a college NCCA championship game, a lot of us were at work and this guy had headphones on, streaming music through his computer. He was working, and checking the score of the basketball game, and every few seconds a message would pop up, and he was talking to six of his friends. I was just thinking how interesting it is. (A male undergraduate student in San Francisco)

The outward explosion from the local to the global that is made possible by digitization implies the possibility of some forms of control by local actors in the global construction of the local, while the corresponding implosion implies that the local is at the receiving end of a larger process. Thus, the explosive and implosive movements in the construction and reproduction of the local and the global are not identical, do not occupy the same spatial corridors, and do not coincide.

Digital practices are either initiated locally for the purpose of reaching out or find in the locality the point of destination of the global. The incubation of these practices, the dynamics they bring to bear, the relationships they twist, and the contents they affect, all transform, shape, and structure both the local and the global. One may speak then of the production and reproduction of both the local and the global through these locally circumscribed global practices.

Although the Internet does not make up for physical copresence, it does alleviate the problem of distance by achieving virtual proximity. These long-distance relationships are nurtured in the domain of virtuality and are another way of mixing reality with virtuality.

> My girlfriend, for example, lives in a different state [Canada]. Long-distance relationships used to break couples apart. I spend more time communicating with her now than I did ever when we were together. We have a Web cam, we see each other live, talk real live, and it is free because it is through the Internet, through MSN Messenger. There is no doubt that it has taken over our lives and that without it, you feel sort of disconnected.

Because of the change that the IT revolution brought about in some quarters, for example in housing, the digitization of the city affects not only digital workers, but also older local residents and those who are not directly related to the computer industry. For example, during the heyday of the e-commerce boom, some areas in San Francisco—South of Market and the Mission District—became gentrified to make room for the dot-commers. These sites became places of work as well as residences for these newcomers, displacing earlier residents in the process. Likewise,

> People living in Silicon Valley who are not related to the computer industry in any way are also affected by the environment. For example, there were Chinese who immigrated to San Jose twenty years ago. They used to rent an apartment, which was only $500, but now they have to rent it for $2000. The digital world has changed their life. They have to work harder to pay rent, which was not expensive as before. (A female Chinese American employee at an e-business firm)

Some older residents worry about the maintenance of family property and the reproduction of the local ethnic community. The perception of some informants is that because the computer industry has been experiencing an exponential job growth in Silicon Valley, the well-being of their children will depend on their ability to find jobs in the valley. Inability to do so may make them unable to continue to live there or even to keep the property that the previous generation had purchased.

Another thing is that Asian parents in Silicon Valley push their kids to study computer science because there are so many job opportunities out there. I think that the kids want to do something else, but if they do, they might not be able to get a job in Silicon Valley. I think that there is another societal aspect of that, too. The kids should be encouraged to pursue their own interests. If you are not working in a computer company in Silicon Valley, you would not get paid well. You cannot afford to live in Silicon Valley if you are not working in the computer industry. There are a lot of societal aspects. (A female Chinese American employee at an e-business firm)

As we have seen in many ways throughout this book, digitization disrupts the local. Some complain that the IT revolution is the cause of a lack of fit between management and workers in some infotech firms. Management schooled in the manufacturing regime does not function well in such firms because of digitization and globalization.

There is a person who just joined the company that I work at who came from a mainframe environment. He has a lot of experience and was hired to bring the established management processes to this company that was running like a dog released from its chain so fast that the expectation was that he would implement a manufacturing type process. Before you make any change, you are going to think about it, document it, get approval from everyone, you are going to test it, and then put it in production. That takes a lot of time and money. This market does not allow us to give it appropriate time. We are still in the frame of mind of trying to run these Internet companies by manufacturing type of standards, whereas the marketplace has changed enormously. We don't have the time anymore. We are doing it in the Internet way. (Male employee working at Yahoo)

A singular characteristic of the computer firms in Silicon Valley before the downturn of the semiconductor industry was the migration of workers from one firm to another not as single individuals, but as cohorts. A high-placed or influential worker from a firm was likely to bring over to the new firm coworkers from the previous firm.

During 1994–95, I worked for a different company in Oakland that was a startup. I worked for this lady who I thought was really terrific. She left the company along with a bunch of other people who founded this next company they worked for. About six months later, she called me and asked me if I wanted to work for her. I said yes because she was really very good and I had a lot of respect for her. So I went and started working for her. All of the top people in this company were the managers in the previous company. One left, the founder, and the top crew was all the people from this company.

There was an instance not long ago where the manager left and three or four others left. When I asked where they went, they all went after him. (A female employee at a computer firm in Silicon Valley)

In addition, under the regime of globalization, the status of local sites is not the same. Hence, one witnesses the fragmentation of social cohesion at the local level. These differences are important to understand because they may weaken specific actors or niches and in the process influence the local dynamic. The shift in status position depends to a certain extent on global linkages that rearrange the local order. For example, some blame the globalization process for the lack of loyalty of workers to the firms that employ them. Their rationale is that globalization has fractured the workplace by accelerating the international migration of workers, placing immigrants of different ethnic backgrounds in the same firm, allowing digital workers to telecommute, and eroding social solidarity while encouraging revenue maximization.

I would have to agree that loyalty does not matter. This colleague that I worked with, a couple of weeks ago, he told me that he was participating in a high-level meeting where there was a Japanese manager present in the meeting, and the Japanese manager expressed a concern that a particular project would impact loyalty to the company. My colleague turned to me and said that this guy must be coming from the Middle Ages. No one has loyalty anymore to the company. It was such an explosion. I would have to agree that people don't have loyalty at all. If there is a better opportunity somewhere else, they would go. (A salesperson at a computer firm in Silicon Valley)

The global and virtual fragmentation of the city

Fragmentation comes about because of the various virtual circuits that inhabit or traverse the digital city. The digital city is made up of virtual circuits with global reach. Virtual undertakings by residents of the global city all form parts of the virtual city. Since these virtual activities are undertaken for diverse reasons and goals, the digital city is not harmonious, but rather cacophonic, with different global fragments, at different stages of development, various degrees of cohesion, diverse modes of connectivity, and diverse modalities of relationships.

These fragments can be seen in the diverse manifestations of virtuality. Sectors that are intensely virtualized are in disharmony with other sectors in which virtuality is not dominant, but manifests itself in the interstices. The digital city comprises private and public layers that further fragment the system. Other fragments occupy various regions of cyberspace and are temporized because they do not operate according to the same temporal rhythm.

The local fragmentation of the digitally globalized comes about because although the city is traversed by global currents, it is the initial or destination point of global communicational networks and provides a central and marginal anchor for global processes. Conversely, one may speak of the global fragmentation of the digital city and the reordering of the local space according to this new logic—not just the logic of networks, but the logic of locally circumscribed global processes. The logic of the network accounts only for a portion of the process—its intranetwork articulation—but does not account for internetwork frictions, tensions, and interactions.

Another way of looking at the fragmentation question is through an analysis of marginality.[5] A new type of marginality is emerging—*digital marginality*—caused by the advent of digital technology. As institutions operate some transactions in cyberspace, the unconnected are put in a disadvantageous position vis-à-vis the connected and therefore are placed in a position of marginality vis-à-vis the dominant system of society. Traditionally, marginality was a status allocated to poor people and to racial, linguistic, religious, or ideological minorities and was often translated into marginalized places of residence. Digital marginality, which occurs because of lack of access (unwired neighborhoods, unavailability of computers in public facilities, inability to purchase a computer or to subscribe to an Internet connection), lack of computer literacy and skills, or lack of motivations to be on-line, cuts across those identifiers and includes both individuals who belong to traditionally marginal groups and others who do not. All have become marginal because of digitization. The digital marginality that some middle-class and upper-class people acquire is not based on poverty or minority status and has nothing to do with the location of their residences. It is the result of the lack of access to the Internet on the part of those who have enclosed themselves in a nondigital ghetto.

The virtual embodiment of the global city

In the early years of the third millennium, the three fundamental aspects of the American metropolis as expressed through its formal, informal, and digital dimensions have become the main corridors through which social practices are performed. By focusing on the digital dimension as a salient factor, I have attempted to show that it has contributed to the social transformation of the city because of the virtual practices it engenders. The virtual is not an added feature that remains external to quotidian urban life, but has become an intrinsic characteristic of the functioning of the city because of the various ways it molds everyday practices. The virtual has transformed the modern American city profoundly by turning it into a digital city, thus enabling it to engage in new processes of globalization.

This social reengineering of the city brought about by digitization transforms both the spatial and temporal parameters of urbanites, introduces a flexible regime of practices, and virtually reterritorializes spheres of social action to include sites that have until recently been unreachable because of a lack of connectivity. Social networks and layered global interactions that link daily practices to extraterritorial sites have become operable and sustainable because of the pivotal medium of virtuality. Digitization has facilitated the emergence of new forms and the revitalization of older forms of globalization, and these are differently experienced by various sectors of the city. As a result of the intermingling of virtuality with reality in the deployment of everyday life, the digital city ends being nothing more and nothing less than the virtual embodiment of the global city.

Notes

Introduction

1. In the sociological literature, a "digital city" sometimes refers to a central Web site or network developed by a city administration to provide information and transact business (Patrice Riemens and Geert Lovink, Local Networks: Digital City Amsterdam, In *Global Networks: Linking Cities* edited by Saskia Sassen. New York: Routledge, 2002, pp. 327–345; Alessandro Aurigi and Stephen Graham, The "Crisis" in the Public Urban Realm, In *Cyberspace Divide* edited by Brian D. Loader. New York: Routledge, 1998, pp. 57–80). The concept is also used to refer to the mass of virtual communications and transactions that fulfill human needs that were once met exclusively by the traditional physical city. In this book, "digital city" has three meanings: first, it is the expansion, transformation, and reconfiguration of urban practices brought about by the interface of reality with virtuality; second, it refers to aspects of the social and global networks of interaction that urbanites develop because of Internet connectivity; and third, it refers to the social and physical infrastructure that sustains the deployment, operation and reproduction of urban virtual practices.
2. The ethnographic research methods used to carry out this project consist mostly of interviews of about one hundred key informants and some participant observation. These are employees who work for infotech firms and government agencies, employees who provide on-line services to computer-literate residents, and individuals who use these services. Informants with managerial positions and lower ranking employees were selected to represent a variety of types of digital work and working conditions. Data on types of digital work, niches where they are carried out, the conditions under which these tasks are executed, and the integration of these in the architecture of the digital labor process were gathered. Male and female informants interviewed represent a variety of ethnic groups.

1 IT as process and globalization as outcome

1. Michel S. Laguerre, *The Informal City*. Basingstoke: Macmillan Press, 1994.
2. Robin Mansell and W. Edward Steinmueller, *Mobilizing the Information Society: Strategies for Growth and Opportunity*. New York: Oxford University Press, 2000, p. 11.
3. Manuel Castells, *The Informational City: Information Technology, Economic Restructuring and the Urban-Regional Process*. Oxford: Blackwell, p. 2.
4. Ibid., p. 10.
5. Ibid., p. 217.
6. Manuel Castells, *The Rise of the Network Society*. Oxford: Blackwell, 1996.
7. Ibid., p. 386.
8. Ibid., p. 412.
9. Ibid., p. 371.

10. Tarik A. Fathy, *Telecity: Information Technology and its Impact on City Form*. New York: Praeger, 1991.
11. Ibid., p. 5.
12. Ibid.
13. M. Christine Boyer, *CyberCities: Visual Perception in the Age of Electronic Communication*. New York: Princeton Architectural Press, 1996, p. 18.
14. Ibid.
15. Ibid., p. 139.
16. Ibid., p. 229.
17. Stephen Graham, Towards Urban Cyberspace Planning: Grounding the Global Through Urban Telematics Policy and Planning. In *Technocities* edited by John Downey and Jim McGuigan. London: Sage, 1999, p. 21.
18. Jim McGuigan, Introduction. In *Technocities* edited by John Downey and Jim McGuigan. London: Sage, 1999, p. 1.
19. James Martin, *The Wired Society*. Englewood Cliffs: Prentice-Hall, 1978, p. 193.
20. Simon Bell, Technocities and Development: Images of Inferno and Utopia. In *Technocities* edited by John Downey and Jim McGuigan. London: Sage, 1999, p. 166.
21. M. Batty, The Computable City. In *Proceedings: Fourth International Conference on Computers in Urban Planning and Urban Management* edited by R. Wyatt and H. Hossein. University of Melbourne, Australia, 11–14 July 1995, pp. 1–18.
22. *New York Times* 21 February 1993, Section 3, "A Baby Bell Primed for the Big Fight," by Edmund L. Andrews.
23. Mitchell L. Moss, Telecommunications and the Economic Development of Cities. In *Wired Cities: Shaping the Future of Communications* edited by William Dutton, Jay Blumler and Kenneth Kraemer. Boston: G.K. Hall, 1987, p. 144.
24. James Martin, *The Wired Society*. Englewood Cliffs: Prentice-Hall, 1978, p. 193.
25. For an early discussion on the "wired cities" theme, see Gerhard J. Hanneman, "The New Communications Media: Their Impact and Potential." In *Communication and Behavior* edited by Gerhard J. Hanneman and William J. McEwen. Reading, Mass.: Addison-Wesley Publishing Company, 1975, pp. 304–330.
26. William H. Dutton, Jay G. Blumer and Kenneth L. Kraemer (eds), Continuity and Change in Conceptions of the Wired City. In *Wired Cities: Shaping the Future of Communications*. Boston: G.K. Hall, 1987, p. 4.
27. John Howkins, Putting Wires in their Social Place. In *Wired Cities* edited by William Dutton *et al*. Boston: G.K. Hall, 1987, p. 428.
28. Glenn E. Wiggins, Future Cities: Cities of the Information Society and Developing Countries, pp. 1–15. In *Documentation on The Virtual City. Selected from Presentations at the International Making Cities Livable Conferences*. Carmel, California: IMCL Council, 1996.
29. On technology as socially constructed, see William J. Drake (eds), The Turning Point. In *The New Information Infrastructure: Strategies for US Policy*. New York: The Twentieth Century Fund Press, 1995, p. 10.
30. Robert McDowell and William Simon, *Driving Digital: Microsoft and Its Customers Speak About Thriving in the E-Business Era*. New York: HarperBusiness, 2001, p. 44.
31. Susan J. Winter and S. Lynne Taylor, The Role of Information Technology in the Transformation of Work: A Comparison of Post-Industrial, Industrial, and

Proto-Industrial Organization. In *Information Technology and Organizational Transformation: History, Rhetoric, and Practice* edited by JoAnne Yates and John Maanen. Thousand Oaks: Sage Publications, 2001, p. 19.

32. Paul J. Jackson and Jos. M. van der Wielen (eds), Introduction: Actors, Approaches and Agendas; From Telecommuting to the Virtual Organization. In *Teleworking: International Perspectives; From Telecommuting to the Virtual Organization*. London: Routledge, 1998, p. 1–20.

33. JoAnne Yates and John Maanen (eds), *Information Technology and Organizational Transformation: History, Rhetoric, and Practice*. Thousand Oaks: Sage Publications, 2001, p. xiv.

34. Jeffrey James, *Globalization, Information Technology and Development*. Basingstoke: Macmillan Press, 1999, p. 1.

35. Ibid., p. 2.

36. On the enabling rather than determining role of technology, see also H. Ernest and C. Jaeger (eds), *Information Society and Spatial Structure*. New York: Belhaven Press, 1989, p. xi.

37. Jan Pronk, Globalization: A Developmental Approach. In *Global Futures: Shaping Globalization* edited by Jan Nederveen Pieterse. London: Zed Books, 2000, p. 41.

38. Y. Masuda, *East and West Dialogue and the Global Information Society*. School of Social and International Studies Working papers, no. 5. Sunderland, UK: University of Sunderland, 1996.

39. Ken Ducatel, Juliet Webster and Werner Hermann (eds), Information Infrastructures or Societies. In *The Information Society in Europe: Work and Life in an Age of Globalization*. Lanham: Rowman and Littlefield Publications, 2000, p. 9.

40. D. Morley and K. Robins, *Spaces of Identity: Global Media, Electronic Landscapes and Cultural Boundaries*. London: Routledge, 1995, p. 116.

41. Jan Nederveen Pieterse (ed.), Shaping Globalization. In *Global Futures: Shaping Globalization*. London: Zed Books, 2000, p. 9.

42. Ralph Lee Smith, *The Wired Nation: Cable TV; The Electronic Communications Highway*. New York: Harper Colophon Books, 1972.

43. James Martin, *The Wired Society*. Englewood Cliffs, New Jersey: Prentice-Hall, 1978.

44. Starr Roxanne Hiltz and Murray Turoff, *The Network Nation*. Cambridge: MIT Press, 1993.

45. Manuel Castells, *The Rise of the Network Society*. Oxford: Blackwell Publishers, 1996.

46. Geoff Simons, *Eco-Computer: The Impact of Global Intelligence*. Chichester: John Wiley & Sons, 1987, p. 124.

47. William Sims Bainbridge, Information Infrastructure Issues in the Social Sciences. *STI* (Science, Technology, Industry) 24, 1999, p. 124.

48. For an elaborate discussion of the electronic infrastructure of the American city, see Frederick Williams, *The New Telecommunications: Infrastructure for the Information Age*. New York: Free Press, 1991.

49. JoAnne Yates and John Maanen, Introduction. In *Information Technology and Organizational Transformation: History, Rhetoric, and Practice*. Thousand Oaks: Sage Publications, 2001, p. xii.

50. Dan Schiller, *Digital Capitalism: Networking the Global Market System*. Cambridge: MIT Press, 1999, p. 28.

51. William J. Mitchell, *E-topia: Urban Life, Jim—But not as We Know It.* Cambridge: MIT Press, 2000, p. 13.

52. Linda M. Harasim (ed.), Global Networks: An Introduction. In *Global Networks: Computers and International Communication.* Cambridge: MIT Press, 1993, p. 4.

53. Saskia Sassen, Electronic Space and Power. *Journal of Urban Technology* 4(1), 1997: 1–17.

54. D. Massey, "Power-Geometry and a Progressive Sense of Place." In *Mapping the Futures: Local Cultures, Global Change* edited by J. Bird, B. Curtis, T. Putnam, G. Robertson and L. Tickner. London: Routledge, 1993, p. 61.

55. Linda Garcia, The Globalization of Telecommunications and Information. In *The New Information Infrastructure: Strategies for US Policy* edited by William J. Drake. New York: The Twentieth Century Fund Press, 1995, pp. 75–92.

56. Stephen Graham, Towards Urban Cyberspace Planning: Grounding the Global Through Urban Telematics Policy and Planning. In *Technocities* edited by John Downey and Jim McGuigan. Thousand Oaks: Sage, 1999, p. 10.

57. Eli M. Noam, Information and Communications Policy Research. In *The Information Resources Policy Handbook: Research for the Information Age* edited by Benjamin M. Compaine and William H. Read. Cambridge: MIT Press, 1999, p. 428.

58. Martin Dodge and Rob Kitchin, *Mapping Cyberspace.* New York: Routledge, 2001, p. 2.

59. James W. Cortada, *21st Century Business: Managing and Working in the New Digital Economy.* London: Prentice-Hall, 2001, p. 31.

60. Cortada (2001: 31) sees a similar evolution in the development of markets.

2 Teleworkers and telemanagers: IT and telecommuting in the digital city

1. Studies focused on the microchip industry have shed some light on various aspects of the labor process in Silicon Valley, despite their heavy top-down approach. See Kenney, Martin, *Understanding Silicon Valley.* Stanford: Stanford University Press, 2000. David Angel, High Technology Agglomeration and the Labor Market: The Case of Silicon Valley. *Environment and Planning* A23, 1991: 1501–1516. Chong-Moon Lee *et al.* (eds), *The Silicon Valley Edge: A Habitat for Innovation and Entrepreneurship.* Stanford: Stanford Business Books, 2000. Recent research on the labor force in Silicon Valley has focused on immigrant integration at the managerial level of the electronic industry in references to South Asians, Mexican engineers, Taiwanese entrepreneurs and Chinese computers technicians. Saxenian, Annalee, *Silicon Valley's New Immigrants Entrepreneurs.* San Francisco: Public Policy Institute of California, 1999. A few studies have analyzed the gendered division of labor and explained how gender plays a significant role in the organization of work in the electronic industry. Hossfeld, Karen J. (1988), *Divisions of Labor, Divisions of Lives: Immigrant Women Workers in Silicon Valley.* PhD dissertation, University of California at Santa Cruz; and Glenna Matthews, *Silicon Valley Women and the California Dream.* Stanford: Stanford University Press, 2003. Studies that focus on lower income immigrant labor in Silicon Valley are few.

See Zlolniski, Christian, The Informal Economy: Mexican Immigrant Labor in Silicon Valley. *Yale Law Journal* 103, 1994: 2305–2335; Chris Benner, *Work in the New Economy: Flexible Labor Markets in Silicon Valley.* Malden: Blackwell, 2002.

2. Gillepsie, Andrew and Ronald Richardson, Teleworking and the City. In *Cities in the Telecommunications Age* edited by James O. Wheeler *et al.* New York: Routledge, 2000.

3. Three types of formal office have been used by Bay Area telecommuters. One may speak of the *central office* that has been since the dawn of the industrial revolution the location where industrial or bureaucratic work is carried out— the location where workers and management assemble to use the facilities of the firm. Corporate culture develops and is nurtured through this close inter-action among the various actors at the workplace. The *satellite office* is a duplicate of the central office that comes about for the purpose of special-ization, decentralization, and geographical dispersion that responds to specific needs of the firm. Such an office may be established to exploit local physical and human resources and falls within the firm's plan for expansion and growth. The *drop-in center* is developed to facilitate workers' movement and is not a site where they perform their everyday work. It is often used to access a central or satellite office or to use the facilities on a temporary and transient basis. In regard to all of these sites, there is a hierarchy of use of space by digital workers. For example, the worker may engage in more travel to the central office than the satellite office depending on the type of work that is carried out or whether the satellite office is the central place for one's work or simply a subaltern one.

Each site—the *central office*, the *satellite office*, and the *drop-in center*—is invoked for different types of telework and the relations between the teleworker and a site depend on the nature of work done at such a location. One must distinguish a satellite, which is a permanent place of work developed either because of decentralization goals or proximity to places of residence, from a *drop-in center* that simply allows workers to use a facility on a temporary basis for the purpose of achieving a specific end. While a satellite may be a smaller or more specialized outfit of a company—a small duplicate—the drop-in center is likely to be a cooperative venture, that is, a building that houses facilities that accommodate a few firms.

4. Lisa Shaw, *Telecommute! Go to Work Without Leaving Home.* New York: John Wiley & Sons, 1996, p. 6.

5. Qvortrup, Lars From Teleworking to Networking: Definitions and Trends. In *Teleworking: International Perspectives; From Telecommuting to the Virtual Organization* edited by Paul J. Jackson and Jos. M. van der Wielen. London: Routledge, 1998, p. 34.

6. Probert, B. and J. Wajcman, Technological Change and the Future of Work. *Journal of Industrial Relations* September 1988: 432–448.

7. Jack M. Nilles, *Making Telecommuting Happen.* New York: Van Nostrand Reinhold, 1994, p. 5.

8. Wolfgang J. Steinle, Telework: Opening Remarks on an Open Debate. In *Telework: Present Situation and Future Development of a New Form of Work Organization* edited by Werner B. Korte, Simon Robinson and Wolfgang Steinle. New York: Elsevier Science Publishing, 1988, p. 8.

9. A. de Beer and G. Blanc, *Le Travail a Distance: Enjeux et Perspective; Une Analyse Documentaire.* Paris: Association Internationale Futuribles, 1985, p. 81.

10. Andre Bussing, Teleworking and Quality of Life. In *Teleworking: International Perspectives; From Telecommuting to the Virtual Organisation* edited by Paul J. Jackson and Jos. M. van der Wielen. New York: Routledge, 1998, p. 145.
11. Kugelmass, Joel, *Telecommuting: A Manager's Guide to Flexible Work Arrangements.* Lexington Press, 1995, p. 20.
12. Olson, Margrethe H., Changing Work Patterns in Space and Time. *Communications of the ACM* 26(3), 1983: 182 refers to telecommuting as any organizational work carried out "outside of the normal organizational confines of space and time." Osman E. Eldib and Daniel Minoli. *Telecommuting.* Boston: Artech House Inc., 1995, p. 2 accents more the mobility of the worker as he or she may work at the office, in a remote center, or on the road. Because of that flexibility, no location has preeminence over the activity of the teleworker. By focusing on the mobility factor, they provide a view of telework based on human agency and play down issues of information technology and organizational apparatus.
13. J. Stanworth and C. Stanworth, *Telework: The Human Resource Implications.* London: Institute of Personnel Management, 1991.
14. Kevin Daniels, David Lamond, and Peter Standen (eds), *Managing Telework: Perspectives from Human Resource Management and Work Psychology.* London: Business Press Thomson Learning, 2000, p. 2.
15. Jack M. Nilles, *Making Telecommuting Happen.* New York: Van Nostrand Reinhold, 1994, p. 6.
16. Korte, W.B. and R. Wynne, *Telework: Penetration, Potential and Practice in Europe.* Amsterdam: IOS Press, 1996, pp. 3–4.
17. Di Martino, Vittorio and Linda Wirth, Telework: A New Way of Working and Living. *International Labour Review*, 125(5), 1990: 529–554.
18. Ursula Huws, *Teleworking: Guidelines for Good Practice.* IES Report 329, 1997.
19. Kugelmass, Joel, *Telecommuting: A Manager's Guide to Flexible Work Arrangements.* Lexington Press, 1995.
20. Olson, Margrethe H, Telework: Effects of Changing Work Patterns in Space and Time. In *Information Society and Spatial Structure* edited by H. Ernest and C. Jaeger. New York: Belhaven Press, 1989, p. 134.
21. Jack M. Nilles, *Managing Telework: Strategies for Managing the Virtual Workforce.* New York: John Wiley & Sons, 1998, p. 14.
22. Lisa Shaw, *Telecommute! Go to Work Without Leaving Home.* London: John Wiley & Sons, 1996, p. 8.
23. Ibid., p. 36.
24. John Seely Brown and Paul Duguid, *The Social Life of Information.* Boston: Harvard Business School Press, 2000, p. 69.
25. J.A. English-Lueck, *Cultures@Silicon Valley.* Stanford: Stanford University Press, 2002.
26. Mitchell L. Moss and John Carey, Telecommuting for Individuals and Organizations. *Journal of Urban Technology* 2(1), 1994: 17–29.
27. Adriana T. Bernardino, *Telecommuting: Modeling the Employer's and the Employee's Decision-Making Process.* New York: Garland Publishing, Inc., 1996.
28. Di Martino, Vittorio and Linda Wirth, Telework: A New Way of Working and Living. *International Labour Review* 129(5), 1990: 540.
29. Ibid. pp. 529–554.

30. Niebel, Michael, The Action Plan of the European Commission. In *The Social Shaping of Information Superhighways: European and American Roads to the Information Society* edited by Herbert Kubicek, William Dutton and Robin Williams. New York: St Martin's Press, 1997, p. 64.

31. Paul McGrath and Maeve Houlihan, Conceptualising Telework: Modern or Postmodern. In *Teleworking: International Perspectives; From Telecommuting to the Virtual Organisation* edited by Paul J. Jackson and Jos. M. van der Wielen. London: Routledge, 1998, p. 70.

32. Sheila Moorcroft and Valerie Bennett, *European Guide to Teleworking: A Framework for Action*. Shankill, Dublin: European Foundation for the Improvement of Living and Working Conditions, 1995.

33. Olson, Margrethe H., Work at Home for Computer Professionals: Current Attitudes and Future Prospects. *ACM Transactions on Office Information Systems* 7(4), 1989: 318.

34. James Rule and Paul Attewell, What Do Computers Do? In *Computerization and Controversy: Value Conflicts and Social Choices* edited by Charles Dunlop and Rob Kling. Boston: Academic Press, 1991, p. 141.

35. Di Martino, Vittorio and Linda Wirth, Telework: A New Way of Working and Living. *International Labour Review* 129(5), 1990: 529–554.

36. Barbara J. Risman and Donald Tomaskovic-Devey, The Social Construction of Technology: Microcomputers and the Organization of Work. *Business Horizons* May–June, 71–75, 1989, p. 73.

37. Lotte Bailyn, Toward the Perfect Workplace? *Communications of the ACM* 32(4), 1989: 460–471, 468.

38. The telecommuting issue is not confronted by all the workers. Engineers and technicians who must be at the office so as to use office equipment usually do not have to worry about such an issue.

   In the engineering realm, the methods of promotion are a little different. You usually start out as an engineer or as a programmer, and then as you take on more responsibility, say a few people, and before you know it, you are leading a team. In my team, I work on the infrastructure as opposed to the actual products that you would see like mail, or anything like that. Each programmer is a sort of an automation. Each programmer knows what he or she is doing and is proficient at it. The managing is very minimal. He basically has an overview of what's going on and makes sure that people just don't reinvent the wheel, or otherwise just does his own thing and lets other people do their own thing. That said, there is a difference in the type of promotion. (Male programmer at Yahoo)

39. Olson, Margrethe and Sophia B. Primps. Working at Home with Computers. In *Computers, Ethics and Society* edited by M. David Ermann, Mary B. Williams and Claudio Guiterrez. New York: Oxford University Press, 1990, p. 190.

3 The digital office

1. Bonnie A. Nardi and Vicki L. O'Day, *Information Ecologies: Using Technology with Heart*. Cambridge: MIT Press, 1999, p. 111.
2. Ibid., p. 112.

3. Vincent E. Guiliano, The Mechanization of Office Work. In *Computers, Ethics and Society* edited by M. David Ermann, Mary B. Williams and Claudio Guiterrez. New York: Oxford University Press, 1990, p. 186.

4. Charles Handy, *Beyond Certainty: The Changing Worlds of Organizations*. Boston: Harvard Business School Press, 1996, p. 212.

5. Manuel Castells, *The Rise of the Network Society*. Cambridge: Blackwell, 1996, p. 247.

6. Michael Gell and Peter Cochrane, Learning and Education in an Information Society. In *Information and Communication Technologies: Visions and Realities* edited by William H. Dutton. New York: Oxford University Press, 1996, p. 254.

7. Pamela Hinds and Sara Kiesler (eds), *Distributed Work*. Cambridge: MIT Press, 2002.

8. Alistair Campbell and Charles Grantham, Organisational Assessment in the Distributed Work Environment: Using Measures of Intellectual Capital in the Planning Process. In *Telworking: International Perspectives; From Telecommuting to the Virtual Organisation* edited by Paul J. Jackson and Jos. M. van der Wielen. New York: Routledge, 1998, p. 169.

9. Robin Mansell and W. Edward Steinmueller, *Mobilizing the Information Society: Strategies for Growth and Opportunity*. Oxford: Oxford University Press, 2000.

10. Les Alberthal, The Once and Future Craftsman Culture. In *The Future of the Electronic Marketplace* edited by Derek Leebaert. Cambridge: MIT Press, 1999, p. 56.

11. Derek Leebaert (ed.), Present at the Creation. In *The Future of the Electronic Marketplace*. Cambridge: MIT Press, 1999, p. 10.

12. Kathleen Knoll and Sirkka Jarvenpaa, Working Together in Global Virtual Teams. In *The Virtual Workplace* edited by Magid Igbaria and Margaret Tan. Hershey, USA: Idea Group Publishing, 1998, p. 3.

13. Don Tapscott, David Ticoll and Alex Lowy, *Digital Capital: Harnessing the Power of Business Webs*. London: Nichols Brealey Publishing, 2000, p. 191.

14. J. Baal-Schem and D. Shinar, The Telepresence Era: Global Village or "Media Slums"? *IEEE Technology and Society Magazine* Spring 1998: 28–35.

15. The virtual pole of the campus is the "electronic campus"; see, for example, Jennifer J. Laabs, Electronic Campus Captures Apple's Corporate Memory. *Personnel Journal* November 1993: 104–110.

4 Virtual city hall: The governance of local e-government

1. Genie N.L. Stowers, Becoming Cyberactive: State and Local Governments on the World Wide Web. *Government Information Quarterly* 16(2), 1999: 111–127; Roger W. Caves and Marco G. Walshok, Adopting Innovations in Information Technology: The California Municipal Experience. *Cities* 16(1), 1999: 3–12; Fernando Gutierrez and Enrique Daltabuit, Mexican Cities in Cyberspace. *Cities* 16(1), 1999: 19–31; and Jo Steyaert, Local Governments On-line and the Role of the Resident: Government Shop Versus Electronic Community. *Social Science Computer Review* 18(1), 2000: 3–16. These studies of city Web sites have produced some interesting observations. Two distinct types of city Web sites, the "grounded" and "non-grounded," have been identified and analyzed.

For Aurigi and Graham (1998: 66–67), "non-grounded Web cities use the familiar interface of a 'city' as a metaphor to group together wide ranges of Internet services located across the world," while "grounded virtual cities... are actually supposed to feed back positively... to the development of specific cities." Alessandro Aurigi and Stephen Graham, The Crisis in the Urban Public Realm. In *Cyberspace Divide: Equality, Agency, and Policy in the Information Society* edited by Brian D. Loader. New York: Routledge, 1998, pp. 66–67.

2. Richard Davis, *The Web of Politics: The Internet's Impact on the American Political System*. New York: Oxford University Press, 1999.

3. Robin Mansell and W. Edward Steinmueller, *Mobilizing the Information Society: Strategies for Growth and Opportunity*. Oxford: Oxford University Press, 2000, p. 426.

4. Juliet Musso, Christopher Weare and Matt Hale, Designing Web Technologies for Local Governance Reform: Good Management or Good Democracy? *Political Communication* 17, 2000: 1–19.

5. Brian D. Loader (ed.), *The Governance of Cyberspace: Politics, Technology and Global Restructuring*. New York: Routledge, 1997; Barry N. Hague and Brian D. Loader (eds), *Digital Democracy: Discourse and Decision Making in the Information Age*. New York: Routledge, 1999; D. Lyon, *The Electronic Eye: The Rise of the Surveillance Society*. Cambridge: Polity Press, 1994; Brian Kahin and Charles Nesson (eds), *Borders in Cyberspace: Information Policy and the Global Information Infrastructure*. Cambridge: MIT Press, 1999; Kevin Robins and Frank Webster, *Times of the Technoculture: From the Information Society to the Virtual Life*. London: Routledge, 1999.

6. Richard Davis, *The Web of Politics: The Internet's Impact on the American Political System*. New York: Oxford University Press, 1999.

7. William Dutton and James N. Danziger, Computer and Politics. In *Computer and Politics* edited by James N. Danziger, William H. Dutton, Rob Kling and Kenneth L. Kraemer. New York: Columbia University Press, 1982, pp. 3, 20.

8. Sharon S. Dawes, Theresa A. Pardo and Ann DiCaterino, Crossing the Threshold: Practical Foundations for Government Services on the World Wide Web. *Journal of the American Society for Information Science* 50(4), 1999: 346–353; Minoo Safai-Amini, Information Technologies: Challenges and Opportunities for Local Governments. *Journal of Government Information* 27, 2000: 471–479; Arun Mahizhnan, Smart Cities: The Singapore Case. *Cities* 16(1), 1999: 13–18.

9. Robin Mansell and W. Edward Steinmueller, *Mobilizing the Information Society: Strategies for Growth and Opportunity*. Oxford: Oxford University Press, 2000, p. 92.

10. Zenia Kotval, Telecommunications: A Realistic Strategy for the Revitalization of American Cities. *Cities* 16(1), 1999: 33–41; Grant Ledgerwood and Arlene Idol Broadhurst, Creating Technology-Based Enterprise Televillages: Postmodern Regional Development Theory. *Cities* 16(1), 1999: 43–50.

11. The Sunshine Ordinance can be accessed at http://www.sfgov.org/sunshine/ordinance.htm.

5 Virtual diasporas and cyberspace

1. On the issue of whether or not "space" means the same thing in both reality and virtuality, we lean toward the interpretation provided by Micha Bandini

when he remarks that "we use spatial terms as metaphors within the electronic world and that the status of these metaphors is to remind us of 'the real thing' to make our use of computer software easier. Thus, place-making-and-belonging is dependent, because of its uniqueness, upon a physical 'sense of place' based on both the social interactions and the cultural attributions we give to that place" (Micha Bandini, Urbanism and Dis-urbanism: The Impact of Information Technology on the Construction of Place. In *Documentation on the Virtual City. Selected from presentations at the International Making Cities Livable Conferences*. Carmel, California: IMCL Council, 1996, p. 17).

2. Jerry Everard, *Virtual States: The Internet and the Boundaries of the Nation-State*. New York: Routledge, 2000, p. 51.

3. Diane Coyle, *The Weightless World: Strategies for Managing the Digital Economy*. Cambridge: MIT Press, 1998, p. 163.

4. David R. Johnson and David G. Post, The Rise of Law on the Global Network. In *Borders in Cyberspace: Information Policy and the Global Information Infrastructure* edited by Brian Kahin and Charles Nesson. Cambridge: MIT Press, 1999, p. 3.

5. Ibid.

6. Ibid.

7. Roger Burrows, Virtual Culture, Urban Social Polarisation and Social Science Fiction. In *The Governance of Cyberspace: Politics, Technology and Global Restructuring* edited by Brian D. Loader. New York: Routledge, 1997, p. 43.

8. David S. Bennahum, United Nodes of Internet: Are We Forming a Digital Nation? In *Crypto Anarchy, Cyberstates, and Pirate Utopias* edited by Peter Ludlow. Cambridge: MIT Press, 2001, p. 43.

9. Michael Benedikt (ed.), Introduction. In *Cyberspace: First Steps*. Cambridge: MIT Press, 1994, p. 18.

10. Dan Schiller, *Digital Capitalism: Networking the Global Market System*. Cambridge: MIT Press, 1999, p. xiv.

11. Michael Benedikt (ed.), Cyberspace: Some Proposals. In *Cyberspace: First Steps*. Cambridge: MIT Press, 1994, p. 122.

12. David J. Elkins, "Globalization, Telecommunication, and Virtual Ethnic Communities." *International Political Science Review* 1997, p. 148.

13. Sorin Matei and Sandra J. Ball-Rokeach, Real and Virtual Social Ties: Connections in the Everyday Lives of Seven Ethnic Neighborhoods. *American Behavioral Scientist* 45(3), 2001: 550–564, 559.

14. Robin Cohen, *Global Diasporas*. Seattle: University of Washington Press.

15. Michel S. Laguerre, *The Global Ethnopolis: Chinatown, Japantown and Manilatown in American Society*. Basingstoke: Macmillan Press, 2000; Michel S. Laguerre, *Urban Multiculturalism and Globalization in New York City*. Basingstoke: Palgrave Macmillan Press, 2003.

16. Amit S. Rai, India On-line: Electronic Bulletin Boards and the Construction of a Diasporic Hindu Identity. *Diaspora* 4(1), 1995: 31–58, 42.

17. David J. Elkins, Globalization, Telecommunication, and Virtual Ethnic Communities. *International Political Science Review* 18(2), 1997: 139–152, 150.

18. Ibid., p. 142.

19. Ibid., p. 139.

20. There exists a robust political literature on ethnic politics and foreign policies that assesses the effect of diasporic groups on American domestic and foreign affairs (see Sheila L. Croucher and Patrick J. Haney, Marketing the Diasporic Creed. *Diaspora* 8(3), 1999: 309–330). This literature is divided into five competitive approaches that can be summarized as follows: the community approach, which focuses on the strength and contribution of ethnic political participation to the democratic process (see David J. Vidal, *Defining the National Interest: Minorities and US Foreign Policy in the 21st Century: A Conference report*, New York: Council on Foreign Relations, 1996); the ethnic interest group approach, which advocates the deserving needs of the ethnic community and homeland (see Mitchell G. Bard, The Role of Ethnic Interest Groups on American Middle East Policy. In *The Domestic Sources of American Foreign Policy* edited by Eugene R. Wittkopf. New York: St Martin's Press, 1994, pp. 79–94); the diasporic approach, which stresses the loyalty of ethnics to both the homeland and the country of residence, thereby expanding American democratic values abroad (see Yossi Shain, *Marketing the American Creed Abroad: Diasporas in the US and Their Homeland*. Cambridge: Cambridge University Press, 1999; Charles King and Neil J. Melvin, Diaspora Politics: Ethnic Linkages, Foreign Policy, and Security in Eurasia. *International Security* 24 [1999–2000]: 108–138); the ethnic-identity approach, which sees politics as undertaken for the purpose of reinforcing or preventing the collapse of ethnic identity (see Sheila Croucher, Constructing the Ethnic Spectacle: Identity Politics in a Postmodern World. In *The Ethnic Entanglement: Conflict and Intervention in World Politics* edited by John Stack and Lui Hebron. Westport, CT: Praeger, 1999, pp. 123–140; Sheila Croucher, *Imagining Miami: Ethnic Politics in a Postmodern World*. Charlottesville: University Press of Virginia, 1997); and the transnational approach, which sees the engagement of the diaspora in the homeland and the host land as part of a cross-border political field (see Michel S. Laguerre, State, Diaspora, and Transnational Politics. *Millennium: Journal of International Studies* 28(3), 1999: 633–651).

21. Dingxin Zhao, *The Power of Tiananmen: State–Society Relations and the 1989 Beijing Student Movement*. Chicago: University of Chicago Press, 2001, p. 197.

22. Yi Mu and Mark V. Thompson, *Crisis at Tiananmen: Reform and Reality in Modern China*. San Francisco: China Books, 1989, pp. 73–74.

23. James A.R. Miles, *The Legacy of Tiananmen: China in Disarray*. Ann Arbor: University of Michigan Press, 1996, p. 216.

24. Ibid., p. 217.

6 Virtual time: The processuality of the cyberweek

1. The sociologial literature on electronic temporality attempts to define the contents and parameters of virtual time, its distinguishing features in comparison to objective time and its transformational impact on society. Castells (1996, p. 642) characterizes virtual time as "timeless time" because of its eternal or ephemeral temporal features, while others are more interested in unveiling its meaning in society (Mihalache 2002). The impact of virtual time on individuals, organizations and societies has been the focus of several empirical investigations (Lee and Whitley 2002). In this line of enquiry, one can think,

for example, of recent research on time management (Nandhakumar 2002); on the polychronicity of work (Sawyer and Southwick 2002); on mobile temporality (Green 2002); and on virtual time, locality, and globalization (Hongladarom 2002). This chapter takes stock of these studies because of the insights they provide, but it also departs from them in an attempt to map the processuality of the cyberweek, to analyze the implosion of virtual time in everyday life and to discuss some public policy issues that the practice of virtual time raises.

2. Jodi B. Cohen, Time, Space, Form and the Internet. *Editor and Publisher* 129(19), 1996: 28–29.

3. According to Walker and Sheppard, "telepresence is the enabling of human interaction at a distance, creating a sense of being present at a remote location," p. 1. G.R. Walker and P.J. Sheppard (eds), Telepresence: The Future of Telephony. In *Telepresence*. Boston: Kluwer Academic Publishers, 1999, pp. 1–13. See also, J. Baal-Schem and D. Shinar, The Telepresence Era: Global Village or "Media Slums"? *IEEE Technology and Society Magazine* Spring 1998: 28–35.

4. Starr Roxanne Hiltz and Murray Turoff, *The Network Nation*. Cambridge: MIT Press, 1993, p. 37.

5. This is the way it has been used by Joe Childley to describe time spent by Canadian students interacting over the net with friends and family and thereby reducing their phone bills while keeping in contact with people in other cities and other countries. Joe Chidley, Cyber Time: Living by the Credo "Boot up, log on and connect," University Students are mounting a techno-revolution. *Maclean's* 109(48), 25 November 1996: 68–69. Likewise Sean Cubitt sees cybertime as "another dimension of web communication." Sean Cubitt, Multimedia. In *Unspun: Key Concepts for Understanding the World Wide Web* edited by Thomas Swiss. New York: New York University Press, 2000, p. 185.

"Internet time," measured by an "Internet clock," is supposed to provide to all on-line users the same time, whether they are in New York, Tokyo, or Paris. This universal virtual time would presumably do away with the time zones that require time translation from one zone to another. David Moschella, Why It's Time for a New Way to Handle Time on the Net. *Computerworld* 33(14), 5 April 1999: 31; Mark Gibbs, Internet Time: Old Vine, New Bottles. *Network World* 15(46), 16 November 1998: 94; Nikhil Hutheesing, Space Jam. *Forbes*, 163(10) 17 May 1999: 45; The *New York Times* quotes one of its informants as saying: "Our classical notion of time that we've inherited from the industrial age does not fit with the way we live now. . . . Time zones made a lot of sense when we stayed in one zone. Now I find I'm living on CNN time rather than my local time. I can call you back at the end of the hour, but I have no idea which hour it is." Amy Harmon, It's @786. Do You Know Where Your Computer Is? *New York Times*, Sunday, 7 March 1999, Section 4, Col. 5, p. 2. Struebing explains how the borders of time zones have collapsed in the new regime of Internet time. She notes that "the internet recognizes no boundaries, including time." Laura Struebing, Internet-Based Research Breaks through Barriers of Language and Time. *Quality Progress* 30(6), 1997: 17.

Internet time has also been used in a more restricted fashion in the computer industry, where it means "something like dog years, denoting the ever-accelerating speeds of micro-processors, data transmission and startup companies going public." Some authors think of Internet time as "web time compression" to indicate the shorter time span of "web developer patience" for the development of a product and the longer time span of "web user patience" 5. Tom Thomas, Application Development in Web Time: Think of It Like Dog Years. *InfoWorld* 18(13), 1996: 63; see also, Claudia Graziano, There is no time like Web time. *Informationweek* 766, 20–27 December 1999: 102. For Douglis, Chapin, and Isaak, "the term 'internet time' has been used to refer to the speed with which companies bring new products and ideas to market. In internet time, new generations of products come out every few months rather than every few years." Fred Douglis, Steve Chapin and Jim Isaak, Internet Research on Internet Time. *Computer* 31(11), 1998: 76–78. Cusumano and Yoffie show how Internet time has called for different temporal rules in the management of the modern firm. They note that "the apparent compression of time is only one dimension of life in and around the Internet. For us, competing on Internet time is about moving rapidly to new products and markets; becoming flexible in strategy, structure, and operations; and exploiting all points of leverage for competitive advantage." Michael A. Cusumano and David B. Yoffie, *Competing on Internet Time: Lessons from Netscape and its Battle with Microsoft*. New York: Free Press, 1998, p. 6.

It is implied that Internet time has imploded the traditional structure of the week, on the one hand, and has contributed to the existence of the virtual week known as "the 'web weeks' business cycles," on the other hand. David Bollier (ed.), *The Networked Society: How Technologies Are Transforming Markets, Organizations, and Social Relationships*. Washington, DC: The Aspen Institute, 1997, p. 9. In fact, we are told that "Netscape (Navigator), Sun (Java), and Microsoft (Windows NT) have all exploited the web weeks cycle to establish their products as the ubiquitous, preferred standard software for the network." Ibid., p. 9. Clark argues that "many people are now managing their businesses in a new shorter time measure, 'internet years' " and proclaims that "we are living in Internet time." Graham Clark, Managing your Retail Business in Internet Time. *Chain Store Age* 72(10), 1996: 112. The concept of Internet years is not based on planetary motions, but is somewhat subjective because it is related to one's business cycle which is, speedwise, different from the operation of business in conventional and real time.

The very notion of Internet years is challenged by Goldberg, who notes that "you remember internet years. It was the new measurement of time that said all market dynamics happen 2–4 times faster on the web. As a result, companies rushed products to market as fast as they could. . . . Internet years were decidedly unnatural . . . the concept of Internet years is dead." Aaron Goldberg, A Stitch in Time: Internet Years are Dead. *MC Technology Marketing Intelligence* 18(7), 1998: 16.

Vigneault presents three noteworthy objections to the idea of Internet clock as proposed by Swatch:

> First, you can't convert your local time to internet time without using the GMT [Greenwich Mean Time]. Internet time is based on Central European Wintertime, as used in Biel, Switzerland (home of Swatch)—which is one time zone east of Greenwich, England—So where do the "no time zones" and "no geographical borders" jingles come from?

Notes   185

Second, internet time is based on 1000 "beats" per day, 000 to 999; each beat is 86.4 seconds. Internet time aligns exactly with regular time only once every 7 minutes and 12 seconds, and can differ by almost one and a half minutes. Third, claiming that internet time is "the same all over the world" is misleading. By raising the issue, it is implied that GMT isn't constant worldwide. In fact, GMT—the time of Greenwich—is equally independent of where you are standing. Internet time just moves the reference meridian from Greenwich to Biel.

Gregory S. Vigneault, Internet Time: Why Switch for Swatch. *Computing in Science and Engineering* 1(3), 1999: 5. Kilpatrick adds his own objection to Swatch Internet Time, "that the day of the week is not embodied in the time system itself." Alex Kilpatrick, Internet Time: Switch for Swatch. *Computing in Science and Engineering* 1(4), 1999: 5.

6. Stephen Graham and Simon Marvin, *Telecommunications and the City: Electronic Spaces, Urban Places*. New York: Routledge, 1996, p. 70.
7. M.L. Moss, Telecommunications, World Cities and Urban Policy. *Urban Studies* 24, 1987: 536.
8. N. Negroponte, *Being Digital*. London: Hodder and Stoughton, 1995, p. 193.
9. On the notion of "time transcended," see Barbara Adam, *Time and Social Theory*. Philadelphia: Temple University Press, 1990, p. 127.
10. Douglas Heller, If We Can Shop Online, We Can Vote Online. *San Francisco Chronicle* Thursday, 11 March 1999.
11. A. Giddens, *The Consequences of Modernity*. Oxford: Polity Press, 1990, p. 53.
12. Mark Hepworth, Information Technology and the Global Restructuring of Capital Markets. In *Collapsing Space and Time*, edited by Stanley D. Brunn and Thomas R. Leinbach. New York: HarperCollins Academic, 1991, p. 135.
13. A. Failla and S. Bagnara, Information Technology, Decision, Time. *Social Science Information* 31(4), 1992: 669–681.
14. Saxena, S. and P. Mokhtarian, The Impact of Telecommuting on the Activity Spaces of Participants. *Geographical Analysis* 29(2), 1997: 124–144.
15. Gabriela Paolucci, The Changing Dynamics of Working Time. *Time and Society* 5(2), 1996: 145–167; C. Hakim, Trends in Flexible Workforce. *Employment Gazette* 95, 1987: 549–560; P.P. Jovanis, Telecommunication and Alternative Work Schedules: Options for Managing Transit Travel Demand. *Urban Affairs Quarterly* 2, 1983: 167–189; F. Kinsman, *The Telecommuters*. Guilford: Biddles Ltd, 1987; S. McRae, *Flexible Working Time and Family Life*. Worcester: Billing and Sons Ltd, 1989.
16. Paul Adams, Bringing Globalization Home: A Homeowner in the Information Age. *Urban Geography* 20(4), 1999: 356–376.
17. Michael Shapiro and Deanne Neaubauer, Spatiality and Policy Discourse: Reading the Global City. In *Contending Sovereignties: Redefining Political Community* edited by R.B.J. Walker and Saul H. Mendlovitz. Boulder: Lynne Rienner Publishers, 1990, pp. 97–124.
18. Robert Reinhold, The Los Angeles Life on New York Time. *New York Times* 3 June 1988, Style, pp. 1–3.
19. Paul Virilio, *Pure War*. New York: Semiotex(e), 1983.
20. Eviatar Zerubavel, *Hidden Rhythms: Schedules and Calendars in Social Life*. Chicago: University of Chicago Press, 1981.

21. E.P. Thompson, Time, Work Discipline, and Industrial Capitalism. *Past and Present* 38, 1967, 56–97.
22. Lawrence Wright, *Clockwork Man*. London: Elek, 1968; George Woodcock, The Tyranny of the Clock. *Politics* 1, 1994, 265–266.
23. On the sociological ramifications of the relations between information technology and time, see Heejin Lee and Jonathan Liebenau, Time and the Internet at the Turn of the Millennium. *Time and Society* 9(1), 2000: 43–56; S.R. Barley, On Technology, Time and Social Order: Technologically Induced Change in the Temporal Organization of Radiological Work. In *Making Time: Ethnographies of High-Technology Organizations* edited by F.A. Dubinskas. Philadelphia: Temple University Press, 1988, pp. 123–169; and H. Lee, Time and Information Technology: Monochronicity, Polychronicity and Temporal Symmetry. *European Journal of Information Systems* 8(1), 1999: 16–26.
24. Barbara Adam, Modern Times: The Technology Connection and its Implications for Social Theory. *Time and Society* 1(2), 1992: 187.
25. Virtual time provides immigrant communities a novel way to activate the transnationality of their diasporic temporalities, to expand their temporal domains, to establish and participate in cross-border virtual communities, and to hybridize further their local temporalities. The cyberweek, however, poses for observant Jews an ethical dilemma for which the rabbinical literature has yet to propose guidelines. I am referring, for example, to the situation in which an observant Jew who, in a non-Sabbath day, engages in e-business transactions with a liberal Jewish partner who lives in a place where it is Sabbath day.
26. Manuel Castells, *The Rise of the Network Society*. Cambridge: Blackwell Publishers, 1996.
27. Marlena Corcoran, Digital Transformations of Time: The Aesthetics of the Internet. *Leonardo* 29(5), 1996: 375.
28. Arno Borst, *The Ordering of Time*. Chicago: University of Chicago Press, 1993, p. 128.

7 Conclusion: The digital city as the virtual embodiment of the global city

1. Michel S. Laguerre, *The Informal City*. Basingstoke: Macmillan Press, 1994.
2. Although it is possible to detach the virtual from the formal and informal in order to identify its identity, in everyday practice it is enmeshed in the two other realms. It is so because the agent who uses the virtual mode is also engaged as a member of society in formal and informal practices. The agent seamlessly moves back and forth from one to the other to accomplish stated goals to the extent that the boundaries between the virtual and formal or informal are sometimes blurred.
For example, in preparation for an office meeting, an employee may engage on-line with other employees to discuss matters of concern to the group and in the corridor may partake in a bit of gossip with a member of the clique before proceeding to the meeting room. Here is an individual who shuttles these three domains in order to better position himself to reap whatever benefits he can garner from attending the scheduled meeting.

The shape, content, and outcome of such a formal event cannot be understood without a reference to both the informal and virtual aspects that are constitutive elements of its structuration.

Despite the embeddedness factor, it may be useful to explain the relations of the virtual to both the formal and informal. The virtual is a pole of the formal as well as of the informal. It does not exist outside its relations to these other poles because it is a mechanism through which society operates, constitutes, and reproduces itself. It is called upon to deflect deficiencies of the formal and informal system. Not only can it enhance or undermine aspects of the functioning of the formal system of society, it can also relate units of the formal system to each other or to the informal system thereby playing an intermediary or broker role in the governance of society.

The digital provides an *in vitro* site for the incubation of issues and the resolution of problems thereby adding an extra layer to the formal system of society. It establishes and provides a global network for extraterritorial activities of the formal city. Such activities are no longer limited to the local site, but can also be undertaken by drawing people worldwide. It meshes with the formal system to the extent that one can be used to consolidate the other. Two main variables that distinguish the digital either from the formal or informal are its virtual mode of operation and the global network through which it operates. So electronic time and virtual space because they transcend local time and local space are two distinguishing aspects of its manifestation that set it apart from the two other components.

The analytical exercise that leads us to identify specific features of the digital mode should not confine us to the strictly speaking virtual domain. Since, as we have argued, the digital is enmeshed in the formal and informal, we must conceive of the digital city not as a separate reality, but rather as a transformational pole of the global city. Aspects of both the formal and informal are influenced and sometimes molded by digitization. The digital city is the virtual dimension that both implodes and globalizes formal and informal practices of society. One is thus justified to conclude that *digital globalization* is a specific operational mode of the global city.

3. For Johnson (1994: 156), "a network that provides connectivity without interoperability provides the 'plumbing' to communicate anything, anywhere, anytime, but not the intelligence to do so" (William R. Johnson, Jr, Anything, Anytime, Anywhere: The Future of Networking. In *Technology 2001: The Future of Computing and Communications* edited by Derek Leebaert. Cambridge: MIT Press, 1994, pp. 150–175.

4. Barry Wellman and Caroline Haythornthwaite (eds), *The Internet in Everyday Life*. Malden: Blackwell, 2002; Marc A. Smith and Peter Kollock (eds), *Communities in Cyberspace*. New York: Routledge, 1999; and Howard Rheingold, *The Virtual Community*. Reading, Mass.: Addison-Wesley Publishing Company, 1993.

5. Lisa J. Servon, *Bridging the Digital Divide*. Malden: Blackwell, 2002; Raneta Lawson Mack, *The Digital Divide: Standing at the Intersection of Race and Technology*. Durham: Carolina Academic Press, 2001; and Benjamin Compaine, *The Digital Divide: Facing a Crisis or Creating a Myth*. Cambridge: MIT Press, 2001.

Bibliography

Adam, Barbara. "Modern Times: The Technology Connection and Its Implications for Social Theory." *Time and Society* 1(2) (1992): 175–191.
——. *Time and Social Theory*. Philadelphia: Temple University Press, 1990.
Adams, Paul. "Bringing Globalization Home: A Homeowner in the Information Age." *Urban Geography* 20(4) (1999): 356–376.
Alberthal, Les. "The Once and Future Craftsman Culture." *The Future of the Electronic Marketplace*, ed. Derek Leebaert. Cambridge: MIT Press, 1999. 37–62.
Andrews, Edmund L. "A Baby Bell Primed for the Big Fight." *New York Times* 21 February 1993: section 3.
Angel, David. "High Technology Agglomeration and the Labor Market: The Case of Silicon Valley." *Environment and Planning* A23 (1991): 1501–1516.
Aurigi, Alessandro and Stephen Graham. "The Crisis in the Urban Public Realm." *Cyberspace Divide: Equality, Agency, and Policy in the Information Society*, ed. Brian D. Loader. New York: Routledge, 1998. 57–80.
Baal-Schem, J. and D. Shinar. "The Telepresence Era: Global Village or 'Media Slums'?" *IEEE Technology and Society Magazine* Spring (1998): 28–35.
Bailyn, Lotte. "Toward the Perfect Workplace?" *Communications of the ACM* 32(4) (1989): 460–471.
Bainbridge, William Sims. "Information Infrastructure Issues in the Social Sciences." *STI* (Science, Technology, Industry) 24 (1999).
Bandini, Micha. "Urbanism and Dis-urbanism: The Impact of Information Technology on the Construction of Place." *Documentation on the Virtual City: Selected from Presentations at the International Making Cities Livable Conferences*. Carmel, California: IMCL Council, 1996.
Bard, Mitchell G. "The Role of Ethnic Interest Groups on American Middle East Policy." *The Domestic Sources of American Foreign Policy*, ed. Eugene R. Wittkopf. New York: St Martin's Press, 1994. 79–94.
Barley, S.R. "On Technology, Time and Social Order: Technologically Induced Change in the Temporal Organization of Radiological Work." *Making Time: Ethnographies of High-Technology Organizations*, ed. F.A. Dubinskas. Philadelphia: Temple University Press, 1988. 123–169.
Batty, M. "The Computable City." *Proceedings: Fourth International Conference on Computers in Urban Planning and Urban Management*, eds R. Wyatt and H. Hossein. Australia: University of Melbourne, 1995. 1–18.
Beer, A. de and G. Blanc. *Le Travail a Distance: Enjeux et Perspective: Une Analyse Documentaire*. Paris: Association Internationale Futuribles, 1985.
Bell, Simon. "Technocities and Development: Images of Inferno and Utopia." *Technocities*, eds John Downey and Jim McGuigan. London: Sage Publications, 1999.
Benedikt, Michael, ed. "Introduction" and "Cyberspace: Some Proposals." *Cyberspace: First Steps*. Cambridge: MIT Press, 1994. 1–25, 119–224.
Bennahum, David S. "United Nodes of Internet: Are We Forming a Digital Nation?" *Crypto Anarchy, Cyberstates, and Pirate Utopias*, ed. Peter Ludlow. Cambridge: MIT Press, 2001. 39–45.

Benner, Chris. *Work in the New Economy: Flexible Labor Markets in Silicon Valley.* Malden: Blackwell, 2002.

Bernardino, Adriana T. *Telecommuting: Modeling the Employer's and the Employee's Decision-Making Process.* New York & London: Garland Publishing, Inc., 1996.

Bollier, David, ed. *The Networked Society: How Technologies Are Transforming Markets, Organizations, and Social Relationships.* Washington, DC: Aspen Institute, 1997.

Borst, Arno. *The Ordering of Time.* Chicago: University of Chicago Press, 1993.

Boyer, M. Christine. *CyberCities: Visual Perception in the Age of Electronic Communication.* New York: Princeton Architectural Press, 1996.

Brown, John Seely and Paul Duguid. *The Social Life of Information.* Boston: Harvard Business School Press, 2000.

Burrows, Roger. "Virtual Culture, Urban Social Polarisation and Social Science Fiction." *The Governance of Cyberspace: Politics, Technology and Global Restructuring,* ed. Brian D. Loader. New York: Routledge, 1997. 38–45.

Bussing, Andre. "Teleworking and Quality of Life." *Teleworking: International Perspectives; From Telecommuting to the Virtual Organisation,* eds Paul J. Jackson and Jos. M. van der Wielen. New York: Routledge, 1998. 144–165.

Campbell, Alistair and Charles Grantham. "Organisational Assessment in the Distributed Work Environment: Using Measures of Intellectual Capital in the Planning Process." *Teleworking: International Perspectives; From Telecommuting to the Virtual Organisation,* eds Paul J. Jackson and Jos. M. van der Wielen. New York: Routledge, 1998. 169–184.

Castells, Manuel. *The Rise of the Network Society.* Cambridge: Blackwell Publishers, 1996.

——. *The Informational City: Information Technology, Economic Restructuring and the Urban-Regional Process.* Oxford: Blackwell, 1991.

Caves, Roger W. and Marco G. Walshok. "Adopting Innovations in Information Technology: The California Municipal Experience." *Cities* 16(1) (1999): 3–12.

Chidley, Joe. "Cyber Time: Living by the Credo 'Boot up, log on and connect', University Students are Mounting a Techno-revolution." *Maclean's* 109(48) (1996): 68–69.

Clark, Graham. "Managing your Retail Business in Internet Time." *Chain Store Age* 72(10) (1996): 112.

Cohen, Jodi B. "Time, Space, Form and the Internet." *Editor and Publisher* 129(19) (1996): 28–29.

Cohen, Robin. *Global Diasporas.* Seattle: University of Washington Press, 1997.

Compaine, Benjamin. *The Digital Divide: Facing a Crisis or Creating a Myth.* Cambridge: MIT Press, 2001.

Corcoran, Marlena. "Digital Transformations of Time: The Aesthetics of the Internet." *Leonardo* 29(5) (1996): 375–378.

Cortada, James W. *21st Century Business: Managing and Working in the New Digital Economy.* London: Prentice-Hall, 2001.

Coyle, Diane. *The Weightless World: Strategies for Managing the Digital Economy.* Cambridge: MIT Press, 1998.

Croucher, Sheila L. "Constructing the Ethnic Spectacle: Identity Politics in a Postmodern World." *The Ethnic Entanglement: Conflict and Intervention in World Politics,* eds John Stack and Lui Hebron. Westport: Praeger, 1999. 123–140.

——. *Imagining Miami: Ethnic Politics in a Postmodern World.* Charlottesville: University Press of Virginia, 1997.

Croucher, Sheila L. and Patrick J. Haney. "Marketing the Diasporic Creed." *Diaspora* 8(3) (1999): 309–330.

Cubitt, Sean. "Multimedia." *Unspun: Key Concepts for Understanding the World Wide Web*, ed. Thomas Swiss. New York: New York University Press, 2000. 162–186.

Cusumano, Michael A. and David B. Yoffie. *Competing on Internet Time: Lessons from Netscape and its Battle with Microsoft.* New York: Free Press, 1998.

Daniels, Kevin, David Lamond and Peter Standen, eds. "Managing Telework: Perspectives." *Human Resource Management and Work Psychology*, London: Business Press Thomson Learning, 2000. 1–8.

Davis, Richard. *The Web of Politics: The Internet's Impact on the American Political System.* New York: Oxford University Press, 1999.

Dawes, Sharon S., Theresa A. Pardo and Ann DiCaterino. "Crossing the Threshold: Practical Foundations for Government Services on the World Wide Web." *Journal of the American Society for Information Science* 50(4) (1999): 346–353.

Denny, Rita F. and Patricia L. Sunderland. *Are We Becoming Our Computers?* Paper presented at 99th Annual Meeting of the American Anthropological Association, 17 November 2000, San Francisco, CA.

Di Martino, Vittorio and Linda Wirth. "Telework: A New Way of Working and Living." *International Labour Review* 125(5) (1990): 529–554.

Dodge, Martin and Rob Kitchin. *Mapping Cyberspace.* New York: Routledge, 2001.

Douglis, Fred, Steve Chapin and Jim Isaak. "Internet Research on Internet Time." *Computer* 31(11) (1998): 76–78.

Drake, William J. "The Turning Point." *The New Information Infrastructure: Strategies for US Policy*, ed. William J. Drake. New York: The Twentieth Century Fund Press, 1995. 1–27.

Ducatel, Ken, Juliet Webster and Werner Hermann, eds. "Information Infrastructures or Societies." *The Information Society in Europe: Work and Life in an Age of Globalization.* Lanham: Rowman and Littlefield Publications, 2000. 9.

Dutton, William and James N. Danziger. "Computer and Politics." *Computer and Politics*, eds James N. Danziger, William H. Dutton, Rob Kling and Kenneth L. Kraemer. New York: Columbia University Press, 1982. 1–21.

Dutton, William H., Jay G. Blumer and Kenneth L. Kraemer, eds. "Continuity and Change in Conceptions of the Wired City." *Wired Cities: Shaping the Future of Communications.* Boston: G.K. Hall, 1987.

Eldib, Osman E. and Daniel Minoli. *Telecommuting.* Boston: Artech House Inc., 1995.

Elkins, David J. "Globalization, Telecommunication, and Virtual Ethnic Communities." *International Political Science Review* 18(2) (1997): 139–152.

English-Lueck, J.A. *Cultures@Silicon Valley.* Stanford: Stanford University Press, 2002.

Ernest, H. and C. Jaeger, eds. *Information Society and Spatial Structure.* New York: Belhaven Press, 1989.

Everard, Jerry. *Virtual States: The Internet and the Boundaries of the Nation-State.* New York: Routledge, 2000.

Failla, A. and S. Bagnara. "Information Technology, Decision, Time." *Social Science Information* 31(4) (1992): 669–681.

Fathy, Tarik A. *Telecity: Information Technology and its Impact on City Form.* New York: Praeger, 1991.

Garcia, Linda. "The Globalization of Telecommunications and Information." *The New Information Infrastructure: Strategies for US Policy*, ed. William J. Drake. New York: The Twentieth Century Fund Press, 1995. 75–92.

Gell, Michael and Peter Cochrane. "Learning and Education in an Information Society." *Information and Communication Technologies: Visions and Realities*, ed. William H. Dutton. New York: Oxford University Press, 1996. 254.

Gibbs, Mark. "Internet Time: Old Vine, New Bottles." *Network World* 16 November 1998: 94.

Giddens, A. *The Consequences of Modernity*. Oxford: Polity Press, 1990.

Gillepsie, Andrew and Ronald Richardson. "Teleworking and the City." *Cities in the Telecommunications Age*, eds James O. Wheeler *et al*. New York: Routledge, 2000.

Goldberg, Aaron. "A Stitch in Time: Internet Years are Dead." *MC Technology Marketing Intelligence* 18(7) (1998): 16.

Graham, Stephen "Towards Urban Cyberspace Planning: Grounding the Global Through Urban Telematics Policy and Planning." *Technocities*, eds John Downey and Jim McGuigan. Thousand Oaks: Sage, 1999.

Graham, Stephen and Simon Marvin. *Telecommunications and the City: Electronic Spaces, Urban Places*. New York: Routledge, 1996.

Graziano, Claudia. "There is No Time Like Web Time." *Informationweek* 20 December 1999: 102.

Green, N. "On the Move: Technology, Mobility, and the Mediation of Social Time and Space." *The Information Society* 18 (2002): 281–292.

Guiliano, Vincent E. "The Mechanization of Office Work." *Computers, Ethics and Society*, eds M. David Ermann, Mary B. Williams and Claudio Guiterrez. New York: Oxford University Press, 1990. 186.

Gutierrez, Fernando and Enrique Daltabuit. "Mexican Cities in Cyberspace." *Cities* 16(1) (1999): 19–31.

Hague, Barry N. and Brian, D. Loader, eds. *Digital Democracy: Discourse and Decision Making in the Information Age*. New York: Routledge, 1999.

Hakim, C. "Trends in Flexible Workforce." *Employment Gazette* 95 (1987): 549–560.

Hammer, S. and R. Williams. *City of San Jose: Telecommuting Project Report*. Clearinghouse Report #42164. March 1997.

Handy, Charles. *Beyond Certainty: The Changing Worlds of Organizations*. Boston: Harvard Business School Press, 1996. 212.

Hanneman, Gerhard J. "The New Communications Media: Their Impact and Potential." *Communication and Behavior*, eds Gerhard J. Hanneman and William J. McEwen. Reading, Mass.: Addison-Wesley Publishing Company, 1975. 304–330.

Harasim, Linda M., ed. "Global Networks: An Introduction." *Global Networks: Computers and International Communication*. Cambridge: MIT Press, 1993. 4.

Harmon, Amy. "It's @786. Do You Know Where Your Computer Is?" *New York Times* 7 March 1999: 2.

Heller, Douglas. "If We Can Shop Online, We Can Vote Online." *San Francisco Chronicle* 11 March 1999.

Hepworth, Mark. "Information Technology and the Global Restructuring of Capital Markets." *Collapsing Space and Time*, eds Stanley D. Brunn and Thomas R. Leinbach. New York: HarperCollins Academic, 1991.

Hiltz, Starr Roxanne and Murray Turoff. *The Network Nation*. Cambridge: MIT Press, 1993.

Hinds, Pamela and Sara Kiesler, eds. *Distributed Work*. Cambridge: MIT Press, 2002.

Hongladarom, S. "The Web of Time and the Dilemma of Globalization." *The Information Society* 18 (2002): 241–249.

Hossfeld, Karen J. *Divisions of Labor, Divisions of Lives: Immigrant Women Workers in Silicon Valley.* PhD dissertation, University of California at Santa Cruz, 1988.

Howkins, John. "Putting Wires in their Social Place." *Wired Cities,* eds William Dutton *et al.* Boston: G.K. Hall, 1987.

Hutheesing, Nikhil. "Space Jam." *Forbes* 17 May 1999: 45.

Huws, Ursula. *Teleworking: Guidelines for Good Practice.* IES Report 329, 1997.

Jackson, Paul J. and Jos. M. van der Wielen, eds. "Introduction: Actors, Approaches and Agendas; From Telecommuting to the Virtual Organization." *Teleworking: International Perspectives; From Telecommuting to the Virtual Organization.* London: Routledge, 1998. 1–20.

James, Jeffrey. *Globalization, Information Technology and Development.* Basingstoke: Macmillan Press, 1999.

Johnson, Jr, William R. "Anything, Anytime, Anywhere: The Future of Networking." *Technology 2001: The Future of Computing and Communications,* ed. Derek Leebaert. Cambridge: MIT Press, 1994. 150–175.

Johnson, David R. and David G. Post. "The Rise of Law on the Global Network." *Borders in Cyberspace: Information Policy and the Global Information Infrastructure,* eds Brian Kahin and Charles Nesson. Cambridge: MIT Press, 1999. 3.

Jovanis, P.P. "Telecommunication and Alternative Work Schedules: Options for Managing Transit Travel Demand." *Urban Affairs Quarterly* 2 (1983): 167–189.

Kahin, Brian and Charles Nesson, eds. *Borders in Cyberspace: Information Policy and the Global Information Infrastructure.* Cambridge: MIT Press, 1999.

Kenney, Martin, ed. *Understanding Silicon Valley.* Stanford: Stanford University Press, 2000.

Kilpatrick, Alex. "Internet Time: Switch for Swatch." *Computing in Science and Engineering* 1(4) (1999): 5.

King, Charles and Neil J. Melvin. "Diaspora Politics: Ethnic Linkages, Foreign Policy, and Security in Eurasia." *International Security* 24 (1999–2000): 108–138.

Kinsman, F. *The Telecommuters.* Guilford: Biddles Ltd, 1987.

Knoll, Kathleen and Sirkka Jarvenpaa. "Working Together in Global Virtual Teams." *The Virtual Workplace,* eds Magid Igbaria and Margaret Tan. Hershey, USA: Idea Group Publishing, 1998. 2–23.

Korte, W.B. and R. Wynne. *Telework: Penetration, Potential and Practice in Europe.* Amsterdam: IOS Press, 1996.

Kotval, Zenia. "Telecommunications: A Realistic Strategy for the Revitalization of American Cities." *Cities* 16(1) (1999): 33–41.

Kraut, Robert. "Telecommuting: The Trade-Offs of Home Work." *The Information Gap: How Computers and other New Communication Technologies Affect the Social Distribution of Power,* eds Marsha Siefert, George Gerbner and Janice Fisher. New York: Oxford University Press, 1989.

Kugelmass, Joel. *Telecommuting: A Manager's Guide to Flexible Work Arrangements.* Lexington Press, 1995.

Laabs, Jennifer J. "Electronic Campus Captures Apple's Corporate Memory." *Personnel Journal* November 1993: 104–110.

Laguerre, Michel S. *The Informal City.* Basingstoke: Macmillan Press, 1994.

——. "State, Diaspora and Transnational Politics." *Millennium: Journal of International Studies* 28(3) (1999): 633–651.

——. *The Global Ethnopolis: Chinatown, Japantown and Manilatown in American Society*. Basingstoke: Macmillan Press, 2000.

——. *Urban Multiculturalism and Globalization in New York City*. Basingstoke: Palgrave Macmillan Press, 2003.

Ledgerwood, Grant and Arlene Idol Broadhurst. "Creating Technology-Based Enterprise Televillages: Post-modern Regional Development Theory." *Cities* 16(1) (1999): 43–50.

Lee, H. "Time and Information Technology: Monochronicity, Polychronicity and Temporal Symmetry." *European Journal of Information Systems* 8(1) (1999): 16–26.

Lee, Heejin and Jonathan Liebenau. "Time and the Internet at the Turn of the Millennium." *Time and Society* 9(1) (2000): 43–56.

Lee, H. and E.A. Whitley. "Time and Information Technology: Temporal Impacts on Individuals, Organizations, and Society." *The Information Society* 18 (2002): 235–240.

Leebaert, Derek, ed. "Present at the Creation." *The Future of the Electronic Marketplace*. Cambridge: MIT Press, 1999. 1–33.

Loader, Brian D., ed. *The Governance of Cyberspace: Politics, Technology and Global Restructuring*. New York: Routledge, 1997.

Lyon, D. *The Electronic Eye: The Rise of the Surveillance Society*. Cambridge: Polity Press, 1994.

Mack, Raneta Lawson. *The Digital Divide: Standing at the Intersection of Race and Technology*. Durham: Carolina Academic Press, 2001.

Mahizhnan, Arun. "Smart Cities: The Singapore Case." *Cities* 16(1) (1999): 13–18.

Mansell, Robin and W. Edward Steinmueller. *Mobilizing the Information Society: Strategies for Growth and Opportunity*. Oxford: Oxford University Press, 2000.

Martin, James. *The Wired Society*. Englewood Cliffs: Prentice-Hall, 1978.

Massey, D. "Power-Geometry and a Progressive Sense of Place." *Mapping the Futures: Local Cultures, Global Change*, eds J. Bird, B. Curtis, T. Putnam, G. Robertson and L. Tickner. London: Routledge, 1993. 61.

Masuda, Y. "East and West Dialogue and the Global Information Society." *School of Social and International Studies Working Papers, no. 5*. Sunderland, UK: University of Sunderland, 1996.

Matei, Sorin and Sandra J. Ball-Rokeach. "Real and Virtual Social Ties: Connections in the Everyday Lives of Seven Ethnic Neighborhoods." *American Behavioral Scientist* 45(3) (2001): 550–564.

McDowell, Robert and William Simon. *Driving Digital: Microsoft and Its Customers Speak About Thriving in the E-Business Era*. New York: HarperBusiness, 2001.

McGrath, Paul and Maeve Houlihan. "Conceptualising Telework: Modern or Postmodern." *Teleworking: International Perspectives; From Telecommuting to the Virtual Organisation*, eds Paul J. Jackson and Jos. M. van der Wielen. London: Routledge, 1998. 56–73.

McGuigan, Jim. "Introduction." *Technocities*, eds John Downey and Jim McGuigan. London: Sage, 1999.

McRae, S. *Flexible Working Time and Family Life*. Worcester: Billing and Sons Ltd, 1989.

Milahache, A. "The Cyber Space-Time Continuum: Meaning and Metaphor." *The Information Society* 18 (2002): 293–301.

Miles, James A.R. *The Legacy of Tiananmen: China in Disarray*. Ann Arbor: University of Michigan Press, 1996.

Mitchell, William J. *E-topia: Urban Life, Jim—But not as We Know It.* Cambridge: MIT Press, 2000.

Moorcroft, Sheila and Valerie Bennett. *European Guide to Teleworking: A Framework for Action.* Shankill, Dublin: European Foundation for the Improvement of Living and Working Conditions, 1995.

Morley, D. and K. Robins. *Spaces of Identity: Global Media, Electronic Landscapes and Cultural Boundaries.* London: Routledge, 1995.

Moschella, David. "Why It's Time for a New Way to Handle Time on the Net." *Computerworld* 5 April 1999: 31.

Moss, M.L. "Telecommunications, World Cities and Urban Policy." *Urban Studies* 24 (1987): 536.

Moss, Mitchell L. "Telecommunications and the Economic Development of Cities." *Wired Cities: Shaping the Future of Communications,* eds William Dutton, Jay Blumler and Kenneth Kraemer. Boston: G.K. Hall, 1987.

Moss, Mitchell L. and John Carey. "Telecommuting for Individuals and Organizations." *Journal of Urban Technology* 2(1) (1994): 17–29.

Mu, Yi and Mark V. Thompson. *Crisis at Tiananmen: Reform and Reality in Modern China.* San Francisco: China Books, 1989.

Musso, Juliet, Christopher Weare and Matt Hale. "Designing Web Technologies for Local Governance Reform: Good Management or Good Democracy?" *Political Communication* 17 (2000): 1–19.

Nandhakumar, J. "Managing Time in a Software Factory: Temporal and Spatial Organization of IS Development Activities." *The Information Society* 18 (2002): 251–262.

Nardi, Bonnie A. and Vicki L. O'Day. *Information Ecologies: Using Technology with Heart.* Cambridge: MIT Press, 1999.

Negroponte, N. *Being Digital.* London: Hodder and Stoughton, 1995.

Niebel, Michael. "The Action Plan of the European Commission." *The Social Shaping of Information Superhighways: European and American Roads to the Information Society,* eds Herbert Kubicek, William Dutton and Robin Williams. New York: St Martin's Press, 1997. 64.

Nilles, Jack M. *Making Telecommuting Happen.* New York: Van Nostrand Reinhold, 1994.

——. *Managing Telework: Strategies for Managing the Virtual Workforce.* New York: John Wiley & Sons, 1998.

Noam, Eli M. "Information and Communications Policy Research." *The Information Resources Policy Handbook: Research for the Information Age,* eds Benjamin M. Compaine and William H. Read. Cambridge: MIT Press, 1999. 428.

Olson, Margrethe H. "Changing Work Patterns in Space and Time." *Communications of the ACM* 26(3) (1983): 182.

——. "Telework: Effects of Changing Work Patterns in Space and Time." *Information Society and Spatial Structure,* eds H. Ernest and C. Jaeger. New York: Belhaven Press, 1989. 129–133.

——. "Work at Home for Computer Professionals: Current Attitudes and Future Prospects." *ACM Transactions on Office Information Systems* 7(4) (1989): 318.

Olson, Margrethe and Sophia B. Primps. "Working at Home with Computers." *Computers, Ethics and Society,* eds M. David Ermann, Mary B. Williams and Claudio Guiterrez. New York: Oxford University Press, 1990. 190.

Paolucci, Gabriela. "The Changing Dynamics of Working Time." *Time and Society* 5(2) (1996): 145–167.

Pieterse, Jan Nederveen, ed. "Shaping Globalization." *Global Futures: Shaping Globalization.* London: Zed Books, 2000.

Probert, B. and J. Wajcman. "Technological Change and the Future of Work." *Journal of Industrial Relations* September 1988: 432–448.

Pronk, Jan. "Globalization: A Developmental Approach." *Global Futures: Shaping Globalization,* ed. Jan Nederveen Pieterse. London: Zed Books, 2000.

Qvortrup, Lars. "From Teleworking to Networking: Definitions and Trends." *Teleworking: International Perspectives; From Telecommuting to the Virtual Organization,* eds Paul J. Jackson and Jos. M. van der Wielen. London: Routledge, 1998. 21–39.

Rai, Amit S. "India On-line: Electronic Bulletin Boards and the Construction of a Diasporic Hindu Identity." *Diaspora* 4(1) (1995): 31–58.

Reinhold, Robert. "The Los Angeles Life on New York Time." *New York Times* 3 June, Style, 1988: 1–3.

Rheingold, Howard. *The Virtual Community.* Reading, Mass.: Addison-Wesley Publishing Company, 1993.

Risman, Barbara J. and Donald Tomaskovic-Devey. "The Social Construction of Technology: Microcomputers and the Organization of Work." *Business Horizons* May–June 1989: 71–75.

Robins, Kevin and Frank Webster. *Times of the Technoculture: From the Information Society to the Virtual Life.* London: Routledge, 1999.

Rule, James and Paul Attewell. "What Do Computers Do?" *Computerization and Controversy: Value Conflicts and Social Choices,* eds Charles Dunlop and Rob Kling. Boston: Academic Press, 1991. 131–149.

Safai-Amini, Minoo. "Information Technologies: Challenges and Opportunities for Local Governments." *Journal of Government Information* 27 (2000): 471–479.

Sassen, Saskia. "Electronic Space and Power." *Journal of Urban Technology* 4 (1997): 1–17.

Sawyer, S. and R. Southwick. "Temporal Issues in Information and Communication Technology-enabled Organizational Change: Evidence from an Enterprise Systems Implementation." *The Information Society* 18 (2002): 263–280.

Saxena, S. and P. Mokhtarian. "The Impact of Telecommuting on the Activity Spaces of Participants." *Geographical Analysis* 29(2) (1997): 124–144.

Saxenian, Annalee. *Silicon Valley's New Immigrants Entrepreneurs.* San Francisco: Public Policy Institute of California, 1999.

Schiller, Dan. *Digital Capitalism: Networking the Global Market System.* Cambridge: MIT Press, 1999.

Servon, Lisa J. *Bridging the Digital Divide.* Malden: Blackwell, 2002.

Shain, Yossi. *Marketing the American Creed Abroad: Diasporas in the US and Their Homeland.* Cambridge: Cambridge University Press, 1999.

Shapiro Michael and Deanne Neaubauer. "Spatiality and Policy Discourse: Reading the Global City." *Contending Sovereignties: Redefining Political Community,* eds R.B.J. Walker and Saul H. Mendlovitz. Boulder: Lynne Rienner Publishers, 1990. 97–124.

Shaw, Lisa. *Telecommute! Go to Work Without Leaving Home.* New York: John Wiley & Sons, 1996.

Simons, Geoff. *Eco-Computer: The Impact of Global Intelligence.* Chichester: John Wiley & Sons, 1987.

Smith, Marc A. and Peter Kollock, eds. *Communities in Cyberspace*. New York: Routledge, 1999.

Smith, Ralph Lee. *The Wired Nation: Cable TV; The Electronic Communications Highway*. New York: Harper Colophon Books, 1972.

Stanworth, J. and C. Stanworth. *Telework: The Human Resource Implications*. London: Institute of Personnel Management, 1991.

Steinle, Wolfgang J. "Telework: Opening Remarks on an Open Debate." *Telework: Present Situation and Future Development of a New Form of Work Organization*, eds Werner B. Korte, Simon Robinson and Wolfgang Steinle. New York: Elsevier Science Publishing, 1988. 7–19.

Steyaert, Jo. "Local Governments Online and the Role of the Resident: Government Shop Versus Electronic Community." *Social Science Computer Review* 18(1) (2000): 3–16.

Stowers, Genie N.L. "Becoming Cyberactive: State and Local Governments on the World Wide Web." *Government Information Quarterly* 16(2) (1999): 111–127.

Struebing, Laura. "Internet-Based Research Breaks through Barriers of Language and Time." *Quality Progress* 30(6) (1997): 17.

Tapscott, Don, David Ticoll and Alex Lowy. *Digital Capital: Harnessing the Power of Business Webs*. London: Nichols Brealey Publishing, 2000.

Thomas, Tom. "Application Development in Web Time: Think of It Like Dog Years." *InfoWorld* 18(13) (1996): 63.

Thompson, E.P. "Time, Work Discipline, and Industrial Capitalism." *Past and Present* 38 (1967): 56–97.

Vidal, David J. *Defining the National Interest: Minorities and US Foreign Policy in the 21st Century; A Conference Report*. New York: Council on Foreign Relations, 1996.

Vigneault, Gregory S. "Internet Time: Why Switch for Swatch." *Computing in Science and Engineering* 1(3) (1999): 5.

Virilio, Paul. *Pure War*. New York: Semiotex(e), 1983.

Walker, G.R. and P.J. Sheppard. "Telepresence: The Future of Telephony." In *Telepresence*. Boston: Kluwer Academic Publishers, 1999. 1–13.

Wellman, Barry and Caroline Haythornthwaite, eds. *The Internet in Everyday Life*. Malden: Blackwell, 2002.

Wiggins, Glenn E. "Future Cities: Cities of the Information Society and Developing Countries." *Documentation on The Virtual City: Selected From Presentations at the International Making Cities Livable Conferences*. Carmel, California: IMCL Council, 1996. 1–15.

Williams, Frederick. *The New Telecommunications: Infrastructure for the Information Age*. New York: Free Press, 1991.

Winter, Susan J. and S. Lynne Taylor. "The Role of Information Technology in the Transformation of Work: A Comparison of Post-Industrial, Industrial, and Proto-Industrial Organization." *Information Technology and Organizational Transformation: History, Rhetoric, and Practice*, eds JoAnne Yates and John Maanen. Thousand Oaks: Sage Publications, 2001. 19.

Woodcock, George. "The Tyranny of the Clock." *Politics* 1 (1994): 265–266.

Wright, Lawrence. *Clockwork Man*. London: Elek, 1968.

Yates, JoAnne and John Maanen, eds. "Introduction." *Information Technology and Organizational Transformation: History, Rhetoric, and Practice*. Thousand Oaks: Sage Publications, 2001. xii.

Zerubavel, Eviatar. *Hidden Rhythms: Schedules and Calendars in Social Life.* Chicago: University of Chicago Press, 1981.
Zhao, Dingxin. *The Power of Tiananmen: State-Society Relations and the 1989 Beijing Student Movement.* Chicago: University of Chicago Press, 2001.
Zlolniski, Christian. "The Informal Economy: Mexican Immigrant Labor in Silicon Valley." *Yale Law Journal* 103 (1994): 2305–2335.

Index